THE SECOND BATTLE OF PRESTON, 1715

The Last Battle on English Soil

Jonathan D. Oates

'This is the Century of the Soldier', Fulvio Testi, Poet, 1641

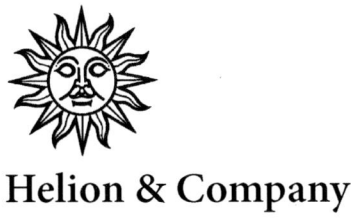

Helion & Company

Helion & Company Limited
Unit 8 Amherst Business Centre
Budbrooke Road
Warwick
CV34 5WE
England
Tel. 01926 499 619
Email: info@helion.co.uk
Website: www.helion.co.uk
Twitter: @helionbooks
Visit our blog http://blog.helion.co.uk/

Published by Helion & Company 2022
Designed and typeset by Serena Jones
Cover designed by Paul Hewitt, Battlefield Design (www.battlefield-design.co.uk)

Text © Jonathan D. Oates 2022
Illustrations © as individually credited
Front cover artwork by Patrice Courcelle © Helion & Company 2022
Maps drawn by George Anderson © Helion & Company 2022

Every reasonable effort has been made to trace copyright holders and to obtain their permission for the use of copyright material. The author and publisher apologise for any errors or omissions in this work, and would be grateful if notified of any corrections that should be incorporated in future reprints or editions of this book.

ISBN 978-1-915070-31-9

British Library Cataloguing-in-Publication Data.
A catalogue record for this book is available from the British Library.

All rights reserved. No part of this publication may be reproduced, stored in a retrieval system, or transmitted, in any form, or by any means, electronic, mechanical, photocopying, recording or otherwise, without the express written consent of Helion & Company Limited.

For details of other military history titles published by Helion & Company Limited, contact the above address, or visit our website: http://www.helion.co.uk

We always welcome receiving book proposals from prospective authors.

Contents

Acknowledgements	iv
Introduction	v
1. The Origins of the Battle, 1688–1715	13
2. The Campaign begins, 6–31 October 1715	34
3. Descent to Preston, 1–11 November 1715	63
4. The Armies	91
5. The Battle, 12–14 November 1715	126
6. The Consequences, 1715–1717	171
Conclusion	200
Appendix I: The Jacobite Army	203
Appendix II: The British Army	255
Bibliography	269

Acknowledgements

Many people have helped with the production of this book. Permission to refer to a document in the Royal Archives was given by Her Majesty Queen Elizabeth II. Dr Bill Shannon kindly allowed the author the use of some of his material as well as taking the author around the battlefield and sharing his topographical knowledge of the town, which was especially useful for chapter five. Dr Andrew Cormack highlighted details of soldiers who were wounded in the battle and later were awarded pensions. The National Portrait Gallery, the National Museum of Scotland and the Drambuie Collection have helped in the provision of some of the pictures used here, some of which have never previously been published. The work could not have been undertaken without the aid of the staff at the many libraries and record offices listed in the bibliography.

This book is dedicated to Dr Bill Shannon.

Introduction

Ask anyone to name the last battle on English soil, and you are likely to receive a number of possible answers. 'Something in the civil war?' Or Sedgemoor, which is often described as the last battle on English soil, occurring in 1685 when Monmouth's bid for the throne was defeated. Signage near the Somerset battlefield certainly heralds it as such. Or perhaps Culloden, dating as it does to 1746? To the latter the reply should be that this was the last battle on British soil, as it was fought in the Highlands of Scotland and so was hardly fought in England. Or the answer might be given as Clifton, fought on 18 December 1745, near Penrith. Yet this latter was, in this author's mind, more of a skirmish between a Jacobite rear guard and the vanguard of the pursuing British army.

Surely the second battle of Preston (one of four places in Britain where there have been two battles; the first battle being in 1648 as part of the second civil war where the Scots were defeated by Cromwell), fought in 1715, must be deemed the last battle, though to some internet sites it is a siege. It was not: there were no fortifications, besieging artillery, initial call to surrender, but a battle fought between two armies in a built up area (as with the first battle of St Alban's, in 1455), which led to bloody fighting and a very decisive result with one army surrendering without terms to the other. The battle of Dunkeld, fought in that town in 1689, is never termed a siege.

The battle has been largely neglected. There is no battlefield marker or plaque, no monument in the town itself (in stark contrast to the aforesaid Sedgemoor and Culloden). The battle has been covered in that small number of books about the little known Jacobite campaign of 1715, though is overshadowed by the Scottish campaign and the larger (though tactically indecisive) battle of Sheriffmuir. These books vary in their coverage of the battle. There were four books covering the 'Fifteen' in the eighteenth century; and the one which principally featured Preston was by an eyewitness, the Rev. Robert Patten.[1] Much of this account was soon repeated along with useful material about the campaign in the Lowlands in a book by the Rev. Peter Rae.[2] The nineteenth century saw the publication of Samuel Hibbert-Ware's collection of numerous primary sources (including extracts from Patten's book and the journal of a Lowlander, the anonymous Merse Trooper) about

---

1   Robert Patten, *History of the Late Rebellion* (London: J. Clark, 1745).
2   Peter Rae, *History of the Rebellion* (Dumfries: Publisher Unknown, 1746).

THE HISTORY Of the Late REBELLION.

With Original *Papers*, and *Characters* Of the Principal Noblemen *and* Gentlemen Concern'd in it.

By the Reverend Mr. ROBERT PATTEN.

LONDON:
Printed for J. BAKER and T. WARNER at the *Black-Boy* in *Pater-noster-row*.
1717.

INTRODUCTION

the Jacobite campaign in England in 1715, knitted together as a chronological account.[3] There was also a novel which was based on parts of this work, by an author known for his romantic historical fiction.[4] Here was a great deal of imagined dialogue and an invented character, a Mrs Scarisbrick, who forms an attachment with the Jacobite general, Thomas Forster, whilst at Preston, and leads him into overlooking elementary military precautions.

The twentieth century saw but two histories purely devoted to the episode, one with only a chapter covering the entire English campaign, but the current century has seen a relative renaissance in interest in it with six books to date. There has also been substantial work on the period in other studies. These cover a wider time span, notably in Leo Gooch's *Desperate Faction* about the Jacobite movement in north east England from 1689–1746 and in the present author's doctoral thesis, about actions against the Jacobites in north east England in 1715 and 1745, as well as several relevant journal articles.[5]

The coverage of the battle has been patchy. For instance, Reid's book, which despite its name is actually an attempt at a history of the entire campaign of the 'Fifteen', covers the battle in 12 pages and is mostly based on Patten's account, added to which are regimental histories and an article by this author.[6] Baynes' earlier account was also a campaign history and made much use of Patten's *History*, too, and is as lengthy as Reid's was to be.[7] Arnold used rather more sources and was a history of both the Earl of Derwentwater and the English campaign in 1715.[8] Tayler's account of the battle is very brief within a short chapter about the English dimension of the campaign and its leading Scottish personalities, as was Gooch's.[9] Szechi's account was concise, at four pages, but is the best sourced, using Patten, the Merse Trooper and a then hitherto unknown account by an anonymous Jacobite.[10] Generally speaking the battle and campaign are usually dismissed in a sentence or two and the battle's outcome is usually stated as being an inevitable defeat for the Jacobites.

To date there has only been one book solely on the subject, which is in part a study of the north western counties of England before, during and after the period of conflict. This book also gave coverage to the armies who fought in that battle, the campaign leading up to it, as well as the battle itself

Facing page: Title page, Robert Patten's *The History of the Late Rebellion* (1717). This is the first history of the campaign by an eyewitness; later editions gave fuller information. (Author's collection)

---

3 Samuel Hibbert-Ware (ed.), 'Lancashire Memorials of 1715', *Chetham Society*, V (1845).
4 William Harrison Ainsworth, *Preston Fight or the insurrection of 1715. A Tale* (London: Tinsley Brothers, 1875).
5 Leo P. Gooch, *The Desperate Faction: The Jacobites of North East England, 1689–1746* (Hull: Hull University Press, 1995); Jonathan Oates, *Responses to the Jacobite Rebellions of 1715 and 1745 in North East England*, Reading University PhD (2001), 'Popular Disturbances in the North of England, 1714–1719', *Northern History* (2004). 'Responses to the Jacobite Rebellion of 1715 in the north of England', *Northern History* (2006), 'The Aftermath of the Fifteen', *Northern History* (2008), 'The Armies operating in the North of England in 1715', *Journal of the Society for Army History Research* (2012).
6 Stuart Reid, *Sheriffmuir 1715* (Barnsley: Pen and Sword, 2014), pp.89–100.
7 John Baynes, *The Jacobite Rising of 1715* (London: Cassell, 1970).
8 Ralph Arnold, *Northern Lights: The Story of the Earl of Derwentwater* (London: Constable, 1959).
9 Alastair and Henrietta Tayler, *1715: The Story of the Rising* (London: Thomas Nelson and Sons, 1936).
10 Daniel Szechi, *1715: The Great Jacobite Rebellion* (Yale: Yale University Press, 2006), pp.177–180.

THE SECOND BATTLE OF PRESTON, 1715

THE HISTORY OF THE REBELLION,

Rais'd against His MAJESTY King *GEORGE* I.

By the FRIENDS of the POPISH PRETENDER.

CONTAINING

An Account of the Settlement of the Succession to the Crown of *Great-Britain*, in the Illustrious Family of *HANOVER*, and the *Tory Scheme* to defeat it, during the last four Years of the late Queen *Anne*.

Of His Majesty's Happy Accession, the Rebellious *Conspiracy* form'd by his Enemies, and the Execution thereof; both by the High-Church Mobs, on Pretence of the *Church's Danger* under His Majesty's Administration, and by the open *Rebellion*; which is here exposed in all its Parts, from its first Rise to its final Extinction.

By the Reverend Mr. PETER RAE.

THE SECOND EDITION.

To which is now added, A Collection of ORIGINAL LETTERS, and AUTHENTIC PAPERS, relating to that *Rebellion*.

LONDON:

Printed for A. MILLAR,

INTRODUCTION

and its aftermath. The battle chapter there is far longer and far better sourced than any of its predecessors, but even here, there is room for improvement.[11]

This new account will draw on contemporary sources found in England and Scotland, from the National Records of Scotland, the Royal Archives, the National Archives, diaries, letters, newspapers and other sources written as close to the time of the events as possible, and by those directly involved wherever possible. To cite an early historian of the era: 'The Facts here narrated are carefully collected from Acts and Votes of Parliament, Proclamations of Council, Private Letters, approved Authors, and good Informations from such as were Witnesses of the Matters informed of; or, at least, had sufficient Opportunities of knowing them.'[12]

There are a number of contemporary narratives of the battle, but most were written by those in the Jacobite ranks (denting the popular fallacy that it is the victors who write history). Best known and most quoted, for it was published three times between 1717 and 1745, is that by the aforesaid Patten. He was chaplain to Thomas Forster, the Jacobite general, who turned King's Evidence after the battle, but who wrote a very even handed account of the English (and Scottish) dimensions of the campaign in one of the first books to be written about the campaign. He was very supportive of his former master. Patten was present with the army from 20 October 1715 until its demise on 14 November, so was an eyewitness to much that happened and being Forster's chaplain doubtless had knowledge of the army's inner workings. He probably also learnt about the army's earlier activities during the later march.[13]

All other accounts are far shorter. There was Peter Clarke, a Kendal lawyer's clerk, who accompanied the Jacobite army in an unknown capacity, and who also wrote an account of its march through Westmorland and Lancashire, as well as briefly describing the battle itself and it is a shame that he wrote of the battle 'It may be expected that I should here give account … But for some reasons I shall omit it.'[14] He is at pains to stress how civilised and orderly the force was, in later contrast to that of its enemies. He writes only about what he saw, and his account covers 2–14 November. It was published in parts in 1845 and as a whole in 1894 and is perhaps the most accessible account after Patten's. The original manuscript is at Edinburgh University Library and adds a little to what is in the published version.

Then there are three or four Scottish accounts, written by men who were not among the army's elite, but were probably junior officers or NCOs. Best known is the one by a Lowlander who was a member of the Merse Troop of Lowland cavalry under James Hume who joined the Jacobite army in Northumberland on about 10 October 1715 and wrote a bitter invective about the aforesaid Forster (in stark contrast to Patten's account which is an

Facing page: Title page, Peter Rae's *The History of the Rebellion rais'd against His Majesty King George* (2nd edition, 1745). (Author's collection)

---

11 Jonathan Oates, *The Last Battle on English Soil: Preston, 1715* (Farnham: Ashgate, 2015), pp.123–158.
12 Rae, *History*, p.xi.
13 Patten, *History*.
14 Paton, Henry (ed.), 'Journal of several Occurrences from 2nd November 1715', *Scottish History Society Miscellany*, I, series 1, 15 (1894), p.520.

apologia for the aforesaid man). This was published anonymously as an eight page pamphlet and extracts were reproduced in 1845.[15]

Far less well known are two other Scottish accounts which may be by the same hand (much of the phrasing, content and bias is very similar), which condemns the army's generals, as did that of the Merse trooper above. This writer was a member of the Lowland horsemen under Viscount Kenmure and covers the campaign from 12 October–14 November. Neither have been published, but exist in three page manuscript form at Blair Castle and at the National Archives. There is also another brief, anonymous, account in a newspaper in 1716, by another Lowlander who joined the Jacobite army on 23 October, who adopted a very similar bias to these other Lowlanders.[16]

There are three other early-eighteenth-century accounts of the insurrection, two being published in book form in 1716 and the third and best known in 1718, reprinted in 1746. The latter was by the Rev. Peter Rae, a Lowland clergyman of Whig sympathies. The first two seem to cull their accounts from newspaper reports of the time, as does Rae, but he also uses other accounts, such as Patten's and other published works. All three are anti-Jacobite in tone, but as none is a first-hand account, they are less useful in describing the battle than those already mentioned.

Curiously there are only very sketchy notes on the battle by those in the British army and their allies. Lord Forrester and ensign Colville, both officers in Preston's Foot, and Major General Wills, all provide brief accounts; as does Lieutenant General Carpenter for the surrender negotiations. He uses his letter to criticise Wills' handling of the battle on its first day. The memoir of Captain Lieutenant Marcellus La Roone of Stanhope's dragoons which deals with the battle is also brief. There are also several contemporary newspapers, letters and diaries to provide some contemporary, though probably second-hand, information about the battle and its aftermath.

The campaign in Scotland is well documented by the British army as there is a long run of correspondence from its commander, the Duke of Argyle, written on an almost daily basis to his political masters in London. There is virtually none from the generals employed in England. The reason for this is surely that Argyle was mostly stationary in Stirling, on the strategic defensive, from September 1715 to January 1716 and being so made it easier to write and read correspondence. Wills and Carpenter were almost constantly on the move in the north of England, trying to pin down an often elusive and faster moving foe, in a far shorter and swifter moving campaign. This made it more difficult to produce paperwork as a commander needed to focus on the day to day needs of his troops; quartering, feeding and paying, rather than spending time in writing to his political masters, except on a very few occasions.

Naturally, many of these accounts conflict. Witnesses saw the battle from differing viewpoints. According to Patten, Forster could do no wrong and fellow Jacobite general, Brigadier Mackintosh, could do no right;

---

15 Anon., *A Letter of the Occurrences from and at Preston* (Edinburgh: Publisher Unknown, 1718).
16 Blair Atholl Castle, Box 45, 12/97, Atholl Papers, account of the Jacobite southern army to Preston; The National Archives (TNA): SP 54/9/107, Jacobite prisoner's experiences in the rebellion, Secretaries of State: State Papers Scotland, November 1715; *Weekly Journal*, 10 March 1716.

other contemporary Jacobite narratives argue that Forster was incapable of anything effective, and likewise the majority of the Jacobite high command. This book will provide the reader with differing accounts of the same event and offer solutions to these conflicts where possible. It inevitably focusses on the marches and activity of the Jacobite army because of the lack of material for their opponents.

There are a number of controversies that this book will deal with. Firstly, was Wills' attack on Preston precipitate and incautious, as alleged by Carpenter and by a modern historian? Secondly, could this have been a Jacobite victory, as claimed by some of the vanquished, or was it an inevitable defeat, as stated by another modern historian? And finally, for such a relatively small battle, how important was it?

This book will take the campaign in a chronological order. Chapter 1 deals with the origins of the campaign in England and Scotland. Why was there fighting and what was at stake? Chapter 2 explores the early stages of the campaign in October 1715 as the participants gathered in Northumberland and then marched along the borders. Chapter 3 sees the Jacobite army marching south through the north western counties of England, with very little opposition, whilst the British forces were gathering for a two pronged attack on them. On the eve of conflict, Chapter 4 explores the officers, men, arms and tactics of the Anglo-Scottish Jacobite army, their strengths and weaknesses. It also deals with their opponents in the British army and their allies, with the same foci as their enemies. Chapter 5 focuses on the three day battle and the surrender negotiations. The final chapter examines the consequences for both victor and vanquished and summarises the battle's importance in English and British history. There is also an appendix focussing on the officers and men of both armies.

It should be noted that this book is not a revised version of the author's previous book of seven years ago. It has been completely rewritten from scratch. Naturally much of the same source material has been utilised, but fresh information has been located, and the focus of it is less that of a regional political-military history of the north west of England in 1715. It is more about the men who fought in the battle and about the fighting itself. Considerably more attention is paid here to the armies which fought, especially the Jacobite army, and less to the activities of the county community and so it is more of a military history than the other. Concerning the battle itself, this book will show that there was a plan for the Jacobites to have fought outside Preston and that there was a cavalry action in the town itself as part of an attack on the churchyard. It also suggests that Jacobite numbers were higher than sometimes supposed and ditches the long held theory about the Jacobite barrier on Tithebarn lane.

1

The Origins of the Battle, 1688–1715

The long term origins of what was to lead men to fight and in some cases, die, at Preston in 1715, lay in the previous century. A major cause of the conflict was a disputed royal succession and that stemmed ultimately from the inability of Queen Catherine of Braganza to give birth. Other eighteenth century wars in Europe stemmed from similar causes: the death of the childless Carlos II of Spain led to the War of Spanish Succession (1701–1714) and Charles VI's lack of a male heir led to the War of Austrian Succession (1740–1748). Historians, though not contemporaries, referred to these struggles as the wars of the British Succession. Catherine was the Queen of Charles II (1630–1685) and the lack of any legitimate royal offspring meant that on Charles II's death the throne would naturally pass to his younger brother, James (1632–1701), Duke of York, who became James II. What made this politically contentious was that James had converted to Catholicism and made no secret of his new faith. During 1678–1681 there had been several attempts to push through legislation in Parliament to exclude him from the succession and a majority of MPs had backed these Exclusion Bills. All failed.

The faith of a ruler was no small matter in the sixteenth and seventeenth centuries. In England, religious controversy arose with the break with Rome, followed by the adoption by Henry VIII as head of the Church of England and when that Church became Protestant in his son's reign. Politics and religion thus fused. Catholics found themselves unable to legally worship in public as the saying of mass became a criminal offence and attendance at Anglican worship became compulsory. Clergy and people thus prayed for the monarch as head of the Church, not the Pope. This was far from being universally accepted, leading to a major revolt in northern England in 1569, headed by nobility and gentry who adhered to the old faith. Catholic powers such as Spain were not averse to assisting such rebellions. The memory of the burning of Protestants during Mary's reign, 1553–1558 and the Gunpowder plot of 1605, as well as persecution of Protestants in Catholic Europe also made anti-Catholicism seem a worthy cause among the majority in Britain (saving Ireland, with its Catholic majority). Catholicism was linked to absolutism, too, a political as well as a religious system of oppression. One factor in the great civil wars of 1642–1651 was the faith of Charles I's Queen and the suspicion that Charles I was sympathetic to Rome, with his advancing Laudian reforms in England and episcopacy in Scotland.

Despite the noise generated by the Exclusionists in 1678–1681, many remained loyal to the monarch and despite Charles II's notorious easy going nature he was rigid in his desire to see his brother succeed him as King. When Parliament opposed him he merely ruled without it. Since the country was at peace and he enjoyed a stable income he could do so. He had a small standing army and no one wished a return to civil war. When he died in February 1685, his brother became James II and much of the nation rejoiced.

This happy state of affairs did not last long. There were two rebellions against him and because they were crushed, they led the new King to believe that he could follow his conscience rather than political reality, as had his late brother. James II wished to make it possible for Catholicism to flourish in Britain. To do this he needed Parliament to abolish the penal laws banning Catholic worship and the more recent legislation that prevented Catholics from playing a full role in civic society (they were excluded from Parliament, the armed forces, the professions, local and national government by the Test and Corporation Acts) and for this he needed Parliament (in both England and Scotland) to agree with him. These parliaments in 1685 were mainly composed of supporters of his late brother, who were staunchly Royalist but also staunchly Protestant and they refused. James II then dismissed them and ruled without parliaments, hoping that subsequent parliaments would be more agreeable to his wishes, by remodelling the electorate. In the meantime he used his dispensatory powers as King to promote Catholics to positions of power, positions that legally they had no right to, for example as army officers in an expanded army, and in the civil state and at the universities. He tried to encourage support from the Protestant Dissenters, another religious minority denied the full fruits of the state and who were also unable to worship legally.

These measures alienated many of those, especially the Anglican Tories, who had supported Charles II and who had initially supported James. Yet there was little that they could do about it and in any case, James had no legitimate male heirs (his two daughters were staunch Protestants). Once he died, his policies would die with him, for his heirs were the resolutely Protestant William of Orange (1650–1702), Stadtholder of the Dutch Republic, and his wife, James II's eldest daughter, Princess Mary (1662–1694). However, at the end of 1687 it was known that Mary of Modena, James' Queen, was expectant. Once again biology played its part in history. This led to a number of noblemen making overtures to William to assist in the replacement of the King. William was happy to do so for he needed England as an ally in his struggle with Louis XIV's France.

On 10 June 1688 James Francis Stuart (1688–1766) was born, but rejoicings were muted. William was assembling an invasion force in the meantime, but weather conditions prevented him from arriving in the south west of England until 5 November. Despite having assembled superior forces against him, James did not trust his army and decided against putting the question to the test of battle. By the end of the year he had fled to France

THE ORIGINS OF THE BATTLE, 1688–1715

where he was granted asylum by Louis XIV (1638–1715) at the chateau of St Germain, near Paris.

Britain was briefly without a king. There was much discussion about how this state could be rectified, from inviting James back, with suitable restrictions on his powers, as had been suggested prior to his becoming King, to accepting William and Mary as joint monarchs. Many were unhappy about the deposition of a monarch to whom they had previously sworn allegiance to and was still alive. Some thought the Crown should be offered to Mary alone. Eventually in February 1689 it was offered to William and Mary who were crowned jointly as William III and Mary II.

This led to an end to the immediate hopes of any relief for Catholics and so solved one political problem that had existed in the past few years. Yet it unleashed new issues. Some in the Church of England were unable to swear allegiance to the new monarchs whilst the King they had already sworn allegiance to was still alive and so left the Church, forming congregations of the like-minded, known as the Non Jurors.

Perhaps of more immediate significance was the fact that James II was still alive and was determined to regain his thrones, especially as he had support from France, which was now at war with Britain as part of the European Nine Years' War. James arrived in Ireland with French troops and was soon able to raise sizeable forces of Catholic Irishmen who had benefitted from his reign. On a far smaller scale, there was armed support for him in Scotland, though the Scottish government had sided with William. However, in 1689 James' supporters were frustrated in both countries: in Ireland the Ulster Protestant strongholds held out and were eventually relieved. In Scotland, despite a stunning, yet costly victory at Killiecrankie, defeat followed at Dunkeld and the Jacobite forces were checked there, too.

The next year was full of further Jacobite frustrations. There were defeats at the Boyne in Ireland and at Cromdale in Scotland. The French naval victory off Beachy Head was not followed up. James fled back to France. Yet the Jacobite armies were still in existence, especially in Ireland. However, in 1691 they were defeated at Aughrim and made the peace of Limerick; in Scotland peace was made at Achallader. A British naval victory at La Hague in 1692 seemed to seal the success of the Williamites.

However, the potential challenge to the new regime had not been snuffed out. It was merely dormant. James was allowed to set up an alternative British court at the palace of St Germain. Louis XIV remained as sympathetic as ever. There remained disgruntled men in Britain who looked with hope to the exiled monarch. Yet William survived assassination attempts and plots and his alliance against France succeeded in stopping further French expansionism as testified to by the Treaty of Ryswick in 1697, ending the Nine Years' War. Louis even had to acknowledge William as King of Britain.

When James died in 1701, he was succeeded by his son, James Francis, now aged 13. He was recognised by Louis XIV as rightful King, despite testifying four years earlier to the contrary. This event helped push Europe into conflict once more, the War of the Spanish Succession. In Britain, William died in 1702 and was succeeded by his sister in law, Anne (1664–1714), Mary having predeceased him.

THE SECOND BATTLE OF PRESTON, 1715

Statue of Queen Anne, Leeds Art Gallery. (Author's photo, 2017)

Biology again played a crucial part in history. William and Mary had been childless. Despite many pregnancies, none of Anne's children had survived childhood; the last, the Duke of Gloucester, died in 1700.

The next in line was therefore, her half brother, James Stuart, James III and VIII to his supporters, or the Pretender to his enemies. As a Catholic his faith was abhorrent to most in Britain. The quest for a new and Protestant heir resulted in the discovery that a descendant of James I and VI (1566–1625) was Sophia Dorothea, James's granddaughter, and her son was George (1660–1727) Elector of Hanover, a small Protestant north German state. The Act of Settlement of 1701 named him as Anne's heir. The English Parliament was happy with this arrangement but there was no certainty that the Scottish Parliament would be so compliant and that was why the Act of Union had to come about, uniting the two kingdoms with one Parliament in 1707, to the anger of many, but by no means all, Scots.

With the war on the Continent going badly for France, an invasion force was put together to take James and 5,000 French troops to Scotland. There was bad weather, less than enthusiastic French commanders, and a British naval squadron snapping at their tails, so that although the country was poorly defended, the expedition failed. James never stepped foot on Scottish soil in 1708 and so an opportunity to change history was lost.

The war ended for Britain and France in 1713 with the Peace of Utrecht. France had to acknowledge the Protestant succession and expel James and his court (they went to the nearby Lorraine, a small client state of France). With peace breaking out, conflict was looming in Britain. Anne's health was visibly deteriorating and she would not have long to live. Politically there were divisions, not only between the governing Tories and the opposition Whigs, but within the Tories themselves.

The Tories were divided over whether to accept George as the new monarch on Anne's death or whether overtures be made to James who was king by hereditary right. The difficulty in accepting James was that he was a Catholic and would not change his faith, though he had the better hereditary claim. The Tories had angered George, though, in the recent war, by unilaterally breaking off hostilities with France so as to make a separate peace (Hanover had fought with the allies against France). Yet upon Anne's death on 1 August 1714 the Tory government had George proclaimed king and sent emissaries to invite him to come to England. The Whigs had been strong advocates of both the war and the Hanoverian succession and happily acceded.

George arrived into a politically divided nation and as monarch and thus head of the government could not remain neutral. Despite being welcomed by the Tories he chose the Whigs to form his government, whilst not entirely neglecting their enemies. Few of the latter, though, chose to respond to his overtures. The two principal secretaries of state, William Bromley and Viscount Bolingbroke (1678–1751), were replaced by James Stanhope (1673–1721) and Viscount Townshend (1674–1738). The Captain General, the Duke of Ormonde (1665–1745), was replaced by the Duke of Marlborough (1650–1722). The Duke of Montrose replaced the Earl of Mar (1675–1732) as secretary of state for Scotland. The Duke of Argyle (1680–1743) became commander in chief in Scotland and Robert Walpole (1676–1745) became paymaster of the forces. Many other senior political posts changed hands. In placing allies in these key positions, a dispossessed constituency of disappointed and desperate Tories were created, but at first all seemed peaceful and the succession took place in an air of apparent political calm. Bolingbroke was exaggerating when he wrote, 'If milder measures had been pursued, certain it is that the Tories had never universally embraced Jacobitism. The violence of the Whigs forced them into the arms of the Pretender', but neither was he wholly wrong.[1]

George I After Sir Godfrey Kneller, Bt. Oil on copper, based on a work c. 1714. (NP 488. Courtesy of the National Portrait Gallery)

There were, however, a number of public demonstrations in England against the new King, his government and allies. This was first noticeable on coronation day, on 20 October. These occurred 'in a tumultuous and furious manner to knock down his majesty's loyal subjects in the midst of their solemnity, break the windows that were illuminated in Honour of the occasion, pull down their bonfires and threaten the lives of those loyal Protestants, for no other cause than their loyalty to King George'. The cries of the crowds were primarily antagonistic towards the King and government, not chiefly celebratory of James Stuart. They took place mostly in the south west, but also in Reading, Norwich and Birmingham.[2]

Despite the fact that George's accession should have been foreseen, given that Anne's health was poor in the months preceding her death, and this was no secret, the Jacobites seem to have made no preparations to act when

---

1 Bolingbroke, *Works, I* (London: Publisher Unknown, 1844), p.129.
2 Rae, *History*, p.108.

THE SECOND BATTLE OF PRESTON, 1715

James Francis Stuart, titular James III and VIII, the (Old) Pretender to his enemies. (Public Domain)

she died. It was only at the end of October that James Stuart penned a formal protest against George's accession:

> James the 8th by the Grace of God of Scotland, England, France and Ireland, King, Defender of the faith, to all our loving subjects of what degree or quality whatsoever, Greeting. As we are firmly resolved never to lose an opportunity of asserting our undoubted Title to the Imperial Throne of these Realms, and of endeavouring to get the possession of the Right which is devolved on us by the Laws of God and Man; so we must in justice to the Sentiments of our own Hearts, declare, That nothing in the World can give us so great Satisfaction as to owe to the happy settlement, which can alone deliver the Church and Nation from the Calamities which they at present lye under and this future Miseries which may be of the Consequences of the present Usurpation.[3]

He stressed the foreign nature of George I and his family, of being very much Germans in contrast to himself, born in England and of an English father. He noted that the new government was made up of Whigs, replacing the Tories and that they would use their new power for their own self interest, as opposed for the good of all. He appealed to both the politically disenfranchised of the elite and to the xenophobic instincts of the mass of the people and urged that his declaration be published throughout the country.[4]

The manifesto had no discernible effect in Britain, but as James Fitzjames (1670–1734), the Duke of Berwick, a marshal of France and an illegitimate son of James II, noted, in November 1714, his half brother, James was by no means downhearted; it was just a question of time:

> The King [ie James Stuart] is firmly resolved to goe himself in person to them as soon as he possibly can, and to carry me along with him [as commander in chief] … a little time must be allowed for getting together what is necessary, especially for raising of money, and for taking measures with friends in England, without which little good can be expected.[5]

The Stuarts had been the beneficiaries of two great slices of luck in the seventeenth century: James VI becoming James I of England in 1603 and

---

3 Tayler, *The Story*, p.311.
4 Tayler, *The Story*, pp.312–315.
5 *Calendar of the Stuart Papers belonging to His majesty in Windsor Castle*, 1 (London: HMSO, 1902), pp.336–337.

then Charles II regaining his throne in 1660. The question remained, would they be so fortunate in the next century?

The death of a monarch signified the requirement for a general election. There had been one in the previous year, when the Tories, building on their electoral victory in 1711, again secured a handsome majority. They had had the patronage of the Crown on their side and the fact that they had secured peace in that year was also beneficial. They also had the backing of the Anglican church as they were passing laws hostile to the Protestant Dissenters, who, following the limited Toleration Act of 1689 were making strides in society. In 1715, however, circumstances were changed. George I put the Crown's influence behind the Whigs. Whilst the Anglican cry of 'the Church in danger' was still strong and even more so given that George I also favoured toleration for Dissenters, there was a rival allegation that the Tories favoured James Stuart and thus the equally hated Catholicism. The election was bitterly fought but resulted in a Whig triumph and they then rewarded their supporters. Their enemies would be thrown into the political wilderness.

The ripple of political protest on 20 October 1714 became a far larger wave in 1715, now there were disaffected Tories, on three days which were full of symbolic political importance. The first was 28 May, the day of George I's birthday; 29 May, the anniversary of Charles II's restoration day of 1660; and 10 June, the birthday of James Stuart. On all these occasions, many people took to the streets of towns and cities throughout England to display their political creed and to attack, either verbally or otherwise, their opponents. Given that there was no police force and the army was small and scattered, official interference was limited in the first instance.

These demonstrations were particularly noted in London, Oxford, the south west of England, Lancashire and the Midlands. Given that the military campaigning depicted in this book took place in the north of England, it is pertinent to examine the riots there, as these were taken as a gauge of political public opinion, especially among the lower orders. Warrington and Manchester in Lancashire seem to have been particular flashpoints of conflict. On 5 May, at Warrington, Jacobites gathered in a crowd in disguise and had proclaimed James as King three times that day. This was merely an overture, for on 28 May their enemies celebrated the new King's birthday, usually by having churches' bells rung, having bonfires, fireworks and lighted windows. They went further, however, and provoked others. Some of these Whigs were also Dissenters and 'inadvertently, made some Reflections upon the Church [of England]. Which were soon aggravated to that height, that the two Parties came to blows'. The Jacobites won, smashing illuminated windows and destroying the bonfire. There was similar, but undescribed, conflict in Manchester on the same day.[6]

It was in Manchester that the worst of the rioting occurred in the north of England. Townshend wrote of it in strong terms:

---

6   *Flying Post*, 3660, 18–21 June 1715; Anon., *History of all the Mobs from the Conquest to the Present Time* (London: Publisher Unknown, 1715), pp.56–57.

> The King has receiv'd several accounts of the tumultuousness and Disorderly proceedings at Manchester have not only continued there for many days without any check to the great terror and Damage of many of his Loyal and Dutifull Subjects, but have also grown more daring and dangerous by spreading further into the Neighbourhood.[7]

The focus of anger was the Dissenting chapel at Cross Street, the first built in the town, and since 1689 such were entirely legal, as long as they were registered with the county justices of the peace (JPs). Dissenters strongly identified with the Whigs and George I, and no surprise, because the Tories had passed legislation against this religious minority in Anne's last Parliament, and the Whigs favoured a degree of toleration.

Initially the damage to the chapel was limited to some pews being removed on 1 June, before being burnt in the street. No steps were taken against this affront, so the attackers became bolder. Windows were then broken, on 5–6 June. On 9 June a crowd of between 300 and 400 people appeared before the chapel, behaving in an orderly manner, but with drums beating. They entered the building and destroyed the moveable furniture within. Next day, the slates from the roof were taken down and the walls were attacked, 'they are resolved to continue until they level the whole within the ground'. Gravestones were not immune from damage. Finally, on 12 June, there was a further attack, where pillars were knocked down and the chapel was in danger of collapse. That was the end of the Jacobites' attention for fear it would fall on their heads.[8]

It was not just the chapel that attracted the attention of the crowd. Dissenters were verbally harassed in the street, especially if they did not show their approval of James Stuart. Their homes were also threatened. Some left the town but others armed themselves in order to defend their homes. Guns were even fired and there was physical violence.[9]

The Jacobite crowd did not restrict their attentions to Manchester. They attacked other Dissenting chapels in the county. These included those in Blakeley, Green Acres, Monton, Stand and Plat later in the month. That at Monton was destroyed, with the others suffering lesser damage. Similar attacks took place in Cheshire, too, and there were fears that they might spread elsewhere, perhaps into the west riding of Yorkshire.[10]

The sympathies of the crowds were made clear by their shouts. They would shout 'Down with the Rump' and 'God damn King George', both of which were obvious proof of anger against the King and his government. They would drink the health of James Stuart and proclaim him as the true King.[11]

---

7   TNA: SP44/116, pp.306–307, Secretaries of State, State Papers, Entry Books, 1714–1715, Townshend–Aston, 19 June 1715.
8   *Flying Post*, 3660, 18–21 June 1715; TNA: PL 28/1, 230, Palatinate of Lancaster (PL), Minute Book, 1715.
9   *The Flying Post*, 3660, 18–21 June 1715; 3667, 5–7 July 1715.
10 *The Flying Post*, 3670, 12–14 July 1715.
11 *The Flying Post*, 3660, 18–21 June 1715.

One question to explore is who made up these Jacobite crowds; particularly how socially diverse they were? Certainly, the bulk of the rioters which came before the JPs were craftsmen and workmen; weavers and other textile workers (predictably enough in a town where this was the predominant trade), a blacksmith, shoemakers, husbandmen, bricklayers and labourers.[12] They were led by the said blacksmith, a middle aged Manchester family man, Thomas Sydall, described by his foes as 'Colonel of the Mob at Manchester … a notorious offender & of great esteem amongst the disaffected'.[13] Apparently he told his fellows, 'he did not doubt ere long to wear a Gold Chain or a Halter'.[14]

However, although they may have not been physically present during the assaults on Dissenters and their property, there was encouragement given to the crowd by some of their social superiors. Apparently, a group of gentlemen had gathered at the King's Head pub in Manchester prior to the rioting and drank healths supportive of the Jacobite cause. They also supplied the crowds with free drink, thus encouraging them in their subsequent behaviour. Some individuals were noted as having abetted the violence, with the rioters alleging 'Let's consult J. Va-l-n before we proceed further'.[15]

Generally, those of the elite were more discreet, as they had more to lose and were able to congregate in a less public, but perhaps even more serious manner. Apart from informal gatherings at each other's country houses, there were clubs for the like-minded to meet. These were the 'mock corporations' and three existed in Lancashire at this time, at Walton le Dale, founded in 1701, at Rochdale, founded in 1712 and at Ardwick, founded in 1714. Each club had a number of annually appointed officers which a real corporation would have, such as mayor and recorder, as well as a number of seemingly apolitical office holders such as Slut Kisser and Custard Eater. It is not known what was discussed at these meetings, but quite possibly politics, religion and matters of contemporary importance. However, a mayor of the Walton Mock Corporation was James Radcliffe (1689–1716), the third Earl of Derwentwater, and of him, more anon. According to Robert Walpole, 'yet to my knowledge, he had been tampering with people, to persuade them to rise in favour of the Pretender, six months before he appeared in arms'.[16]

It is worth noting that these public demonstrations of Jacobitism were far from universal. None were recorded as occurring in Northumberland, Durham, Cumberland or Westmorland in 1715. Only two were noted in Yorkshire, in Sheffield and Leeds, when in the latter case church bells were rung and a bonfire was lit in the town on 10 June. Even in Lancashire, no disturbance was noted as occurring in the more northerly towns such as Lancaster and Preston or in the western port of Liverpool.[17]

---

12 Lancashire Record Office (LRO): QJ1/2/10, pp.522–523; TNA: PL28/1, pp.234–238.
13 British Library (BL), Stowe Ms. 750, f.157r; Original Letters addressed to Lord Parker, 1704–1739, Boothe-Parker, 29 January 1716; TNA: PL28/1.
14 *Flying Post*, 3730, 28 November–1 December 1715.
15 *Flying Post*, 3670, 12–14 July 1715.
16 Peter Lole, 'A Digest of the Jacobite Clubs', *Royal Stuart Society Paper* (2002); William Coxe (ed.), *Memoirs of an Administration: Walpole, I* (London: T. Cadell, 1798), p.72.
17 *Flying Post*, 12–14 July 1715.

George Byng, *Universal Magazine*, 1756. (Author's collection)

In any case, the rioting was short lived. Troops were sent to the worst affected districts, such as Manchester, where Major John Wyvill led two troops of Cobham's dragoons to restore order, after the event. He may have been disconcerted to discover Jacobite sympathies among his own men, with cornet Sadler and one of the troopers displaying such on a verbal level.[18] However, the county's JPs took action in having some of the rioters arrested and sentenced. By the end of the summer such public Jacobite displays were over, at least for now.

How important were these demonstrations as a barometer of public opinion and as a gauge as to depth of commitment to the Jacobite cause is another question. Certainly some among the Jacobite councils and their enemies believed they were significant. One Daniel Dearing wrote on 9 August, 'The Tories by their rebellious riots and their disrespects to the King had encouraged the Pretender to think of invading us.'[19] Scottish Jacobites took heart (there had not been any Jacobite riots in Scotland), 'the mobs and broiles in England had rowzed the Scots Tories'.[20] Abroad the Stuart court, which was optimistic of mass support, as Bolingbroke observed, 'Every meeting house which the populace demolished and every little drunken riot seemed to confirm them in these sanguine expectations'.[21]

It was on 20 July that it became public news that there was a serious Jacobite attempt on the throne. The exact nature of this is unknown, but the correspondence among the leading members of the Jacobite court showed clear discussion about the practical steps needed to bring this about.

The government, led by Townshend and Stanhope, took a number of decisions to thwart the Jacobite plans. They ordered that eight new battalions of infantry (3,450 men) and 13 regiments of dragoons (2,574 men) be raised to supplement the small peacetime army at the cost of £265,754 7s 6d for one year's service. Admiral George Byng (1663–1733) was ordered to take his fleet to the Downs to patrol the Channel and the garrison at Portsmouth was reinforced by two battalions.

---

18 TNA: SP44/116, p.346, Townshend to Pulteney, 30 July 1715 ; *Flying Post*, 18–20 June 1715.
19 BL, Additional Manuscripts: 47028, f.56r, Egmont Papers, 1st Lord Egmont, Letters CVIII, 1697–1731, Dearing–Egmont, 9 August 1715.
20 Walter Scott (ed.), *Memoirs of the Insurrection in Scotland of 1715* (Edinburgh: Abbotsford Club, 1845), p.66.
21 Bolingbroke, *Works*, I, p.137.

Three battalions of foot guards and troops of horse guards formed a camp in Hyde Park under Lieutenant General William Cadogan (1672–1726). Troops from the Dutch Republic were requested. The lords lieutenant of the counties were instructed to implement the anti-Catholic legislation. This entailed seizing arms and horses (if valued over £5) from Catholics who it was thought, would naturally assist a Catholic claimant to the throne. Catholics and other suspects could be imprisoned if they did not swear allegiance to the King. Finally, there were orders that the county militia be raised to assist in any necessary security measures; this was seen of particular note in London.[22]

Jacobite plotting can be discerned at the high level by an examination of the papers of the exiled Stuart court. Principally the major personalities were James Stuart himself, his secretary of state, Viscount Bolingbroke, the Duke of Ormonde and James' half brother, the Duke of Berwick. Bolingbroke had been a leading Tory politician in Anne's reign but had fled England in March 1715 for fear of being impeached for high treason. Another key figure was Ormonde, a fellow Tory peer, who had left England in the summer to avoid arrest. They aimed to use military means to bring about a change in regime.

Initially great consideration was made to the insurrection being centred on Northumberland: easy for ships from abroad to bring men and arms to and at this stage, the Jacobites had hopes of assistance from Sweden and France. William of Orange had also considered arriving in the county in 1688. John Erskine, the sixth Earl of Mar and a Scot, another disenfranchised politician who desired a return to the wealth and power that high political office would bring him, wrote an extensive memorandum on 6 July to this effect:

> Holy island is looked upon as the most proper place, provided the King's passage through the Channel be thought not too dangerous. It is of good access, has a little fort, and is pretty safe from attempts by land. It is near Newcastle, which is well affected, and would probably declare for the King. A body of Foot might be provided out of the colliers there, and the town would serve as a place of arms. About 1,000 horse might be expected from the neighbouring country to join the King soon after his landing.
>
> The possession of Newcastle would be of great advantage in many ways, particularly in respect to the obstruction that might be given by that means to the coal trade, which would either induce London to declare or at least distress the government.
>
> From Holy Island, Berwick (where there is a magazine of arms and ammunition) might be surprised or forced, having but a small garrison in it, and there the King's friends from Scotland might the most easily join him.
>
> Early notice should be given of his landing (in Holy Island) to his friends in Scotland that they may march with all the expedition towards him; to those in Ireland that they may make what diversion they can, in order to oblige the government to leave part of the troops there, and to those in Cornwall, Devonshire,

---

22 Rae, *History*, pp.169–171; *Political State of Great Britain* X (1715), p.109.

Wales and Lancashire, that they may immediately rise and act as they shall see best in his service.[23]

It was not Mar alone who thought that Northumberland should be where the restoration attempt should take place, but Berwick wrote: 'Newcastle was the fittest place for an army to repair unto, for it will be there in the neighbourhood of James, who by that time will be with his friends the Scotch, as also of an English country seat, where there is plenty all that he can want, especially of horse'.[24]

However, the strategy was questioned later in the month. Bolingbroke wrote on 15 August that instructions were:

> … immediately to be given to such of the King's friends as are the most powerful in those parts to be ready to join these forces, to guide and assist them in any operations on that side, or in their march towards the Scots army. If these troops are to land at Newcastle, it seems necessary that their first attempt should not be left to hazard, but even how as far as possible determined.[25]

In fact, the south west of England became increasingly to be seen as the place where an overseas attempt should be made. This could have been because of the widespread rioting that there had been in 1714–1715 (compared to none in Northumberland in 1715) and because Ormonde had more interest in those counties. Furthermore, no help from would-be ally Sweden was now expected (France and now Spain were still being courted and so the south west was more convenient for them). Northumberland was not forgotten, but it was no longer the exclusive county where action was being planned. Plymouth, Bristol and Portsmouth were seen as the places to take, and from which a march on London could be best affected, echoing the thoughts of Monmouth in 1685 and William of Orange in 1688. This change was not confirmed until 1 September.[26]

The importance of having regular forces was paramount and for these France and Spain were lobbied (albeit eventually unsuccessfully). As Mar noted:

> … there is no hope of succeeding in it without the assistance of a regular force, or without a general rising of the people, in all parts of England, immediately upon the King's landing, and that the latter of these depends very much on the former. For though the generality of the people are extremely averse to the Court and Ministry (whom they hate and despise) and well inclined to the restoration; yet it is not to be expected that they should declare themselves all at once, unless they see the King attended with such a force as will give some reputation to his undertaking, and encourage the country to come in to him.

---

23 *HMC, Stuart Papers*, 1, p.521.
24 *HMC Stuart Papers*, I, p.525.
25 *HMC Stuart Papers*, I, p.527.
26 *HMC Stuart Papers* 1, pp.532–535.

Without such a support even the well affected in these parts of the kingdom, which are distant from the places where the King shall land, will not venture to make any attempt in his favour, the lieutenancy and shrievalty of the several counties being now lodged in confiding hands, will be a good check on the inclinations of the people everywhere, these, who are only enemies to the set of men now in power and not thoroughly engaged for the King (which is the case of many in the Tory Party) will either stand and gaze, and expect the event, or join with the present government, as thinking that way out of danger, whichever side prevails.[27]

By early October the plan for the main Jacobite thrust had been altered from the north east to the south west as noted in the minutes of a meeting between Bolingbroke and James Stuart:

… to inform the King's friends in the west that the Duke of Ormonde sets out almost as soon as they, and may be every moment expected on the coast, so that they are to look out on the coast for him and to lose no time in being ready to join him.

That the Duke of Ormonde make the best of his way to the coast of England, as near Plymouth as possible, and put himself at the head of such as shall be ready to rise; that he make the best disposition he can for the King's landing, and in general take all such measures as shall appear to be necessary for his majesty's service and for annoying the enemy … No person whatever to stir, till such time as the King is sailed'.[28]

All well and good, but there were two flaws in this scheme. Firstly, there is no evidence that the Jacobites in the north east were told of this switch in planning, and even if there was an intent to do so, communication would have been slow and difficult, with messages and messengers liable to be intercepted. Secondly, there was no thought that counter measures might be taken by their opponents to nip the Jacobite plans in the bud. However, in any event, the Jacobites abroad had scant resources with which to support a domestic insurrection, whether in the north east or the south west. But since the government focused on the south west it did allow those Jacobites in the north east a brief respite and a small window of opportunity.

In order to tap this latent support, James would need to land in Britain with about 3,000–4,000 regular troops, as Ormonde also acknowledged. Therefore, Berwick thought that a restoration attempt would be doomed, 'without the assistance of 4000 men at least, and a quantity of arms, and of a considerable sum of money, it would be rash and even impossible to commence an Insurrection'. An unarmed mob or even a semi-disciplined and variously armed force as Monmouth's rebels had been in 1685, risked defeat by regular troops.[29] The Jacobites were certain, however, that they had

---

27 *HMC Stuart Papers*, I, p.520.
28 *HMC, Stuart Papers*, I, pp.532–533.
29 James, Duke of Berwick, *Memoirs of the Marshal Berwick* (London: T. Cadell, 1779), pp.197, 200, 202.

the support of the bulk of the nation, including the nobility, the gentry, the clergy and the army.

Ormonde had been briefly captain general of the army from 1712–1714 before he had been dismissed at George's accession. He was a leading member of the Tory party and a strong advocate of James as King. He was known about, but before he could be arrested, he had fled to France on 21 July and joined Bolingbroke at the Jacobite court. It is possible that he could have led an insurrection in the west of England, but many fellow Jacobites doubted his mettle and one later wrote that he was 'a very brave officer, tho's he had never that [reputation] of a very able one … irresolute and timorous … apt to lose good opportunities'.[30]

Yet the government became aware of this focus and sent troops to the West Country. Two battalions of infantry and part of a cavalry regiment were stationed in Bristol. Three more units were sent to Bath under Major General George Wade (1673–1748). Horses, arms and men were seized. Oxford was garrisoned by troops after a number of Jacobites were captured there.[31] By the beginning of October, matters were looking bleak for the Jacobite cause in south west England.

Plotting on the ground in England is more difficult to uncover. Clearly unsuccessful conspirators will hardly leave papers implicating themselves in such actions. In the summer of 1715 the north east of England was seen as the initial theatre of operations. When Mar sailed northwards from London on 1 August he stopped off at Newcastle and presumably met fellow Jacobites to discuss the rising in the north east. Patten later wrote, 'There had been Measures concerted in London, by the Pretender's Friends, some time before'. Their agents were John Shaftoe and John Hunter, both former army officers and Northumberland gentlemen, and were joined by Robert Talbot, a Catholic Irishman and fellow military veteran. All three were to become junior officers in the Jacobite army.[32]

This trio arrived at Newcastle, quite possibly following Mar's visit there, and the 'Resolutions taken at London were first communicated to their friends in the North of England, and means us'd to persuade and prepare the Gentlemen they had embark'd with them, to be ready to rise upon warning given'.[33] The groundwork had already been prepared, as Patten noted, with 'long Debates, frequent correspondences, carrying and receiving of Letters, Orders &c., and abundance of People employed to concert Measures, and ripen things up to the Height they afterwards were brought to'. The paper trail was not entrusted to the general mail, which could be opened, but to trusted messengers and in Northumberland these were Henry Oxburgh, Nicholas and Charles Wogan, the aforesaid Talbot: all Irish Catholics. They rode about the county in the pretence of being tourists but in reality 'carrying intelligence, discoursing with persons, and settling and appointing

---

30 James Keith, *Fragment of a Memoir of Field Marshal James Keith, 171–1734* (Edinburgh: Spalding Club, 1843), p.3.
31 Rae, *History*, pp.215–216.
32 Patten, *History*, p.16.
33 Patten, *History*, p.16.

THE ORIGINS OF THE BATTLE, 1688–1715

James Radcliffe, 3rd Earl of Derwentwater. (Author's collection)

their Business'. Others employed as a second tier were Messrs Beaumont and Clifton, Nottinghamshire gentlemen, with Mr Buxton, a Derbyshire clergyman. They rode through the country with their servants, armed with swords and pistols, 'always moving, and travelled from Place to place'.[34]

However, no steps had been made to stockpile the arms and ammunition that would be needed should any fighting be required or even enough to present a show of strength. Perhaps the Jacobites in the north east believed that the restoration of James Stuart would be as bloodless as it had been for Charles II in 1660 or that significant numbers of foreign troops would arrive as in 1688 and that they had no need of any actual fighting.

The groundwork, such as it was, for the insurrection was being finalised in September. Lord William Widdrington (1678–1743), a Northumbrian Catholic, visited his brother-in-law, Richard Towneley (1687–1735) in Lancashire. The latter, a Catholic gentleman, assured him that there would be an enthusiastic welcome for the Jacobites in Lancashire and an addition of 20,000 men.[35] That there should be a Jacobite movement in Northumberland in 1715 should come as no surprise as there had been gatherings of men in the county in the 1690s

---

34 Patten, *History*, pp.16–17.
35 Hibbert-Ware, 'Memorials', p.27.

Derwentwater Memorial, Acton Park. This once stood in the grounds of a private house nearby, though Derwentwater never went to Acton, Middlesex, alive or dead. (Author's photo, 2021)

in favour of James II (as there had been in Cumberland and Lancashire), led by Derwentwater's and Widdrington's fathers. Derwentwater was a grandson of Charles II and so nephew of James II and was cousin of James Stuart who he had played with as a boy in France.[36]

Later in the year, the principal Jacobites in Northumberland were questioned about the insurrection's origins. Thomas Forster, MP, seems to have been the mainspring. The man himself claimed 'he had promis'd the Duke of Ormond to rise whenever he should land, but was precipitated into it sooner by the order to seize him, that he came out of town when the Duke made his escape'.[37] Others claimed 'they had promised Mr Forster, whenever he called upon them they would rise and that they were so simple as to do it, and to believe him when he told them, that all England would do the same'.[38] Some apparently acted out of peer pressure, with Widdrington alleging 'he had no other encouragement to take arms, but that he thought he would make a bad figure with his religion and his opinion to sit still in this cause when his neighbours and so many others had'.[39] Widdrington and Derwentwater claimed not to know anything about the conspiracy in advance and Forster said 'He does not own any concert with other people'. Forster made the assumption that there would be a mass rising, 'in general he look'd on the whole body of the Torys to be in it'.[40] After the campaign was over, Derwentwater bitterly noted, that the active Jacobites had 'given Credit to our Neighbour Tories … such Rogues in Disguise, that promised to join us, and animated us to rise with them'.[41] The conspirators believed that this campaign would be entered into by both aggrieved parties: Catholics and Anglican Tories, with the latter being in the majority.

The government, too, believed that a number of disgruntled Tory MPs throughout the country were to act as leaders. Henry Liddell (1673–1717), a Whig gentleman, outlined what this was: 'Harvey was to have seiz'd St. James, Wyndham Bristol, Packington was to have rais'd his men at Worcester and joined Kynaston in Shropshire, your neighbour [Forster] was to have

---

36   Monod, *Jacobitism*, p.309.
37   *Manuscripts of the Marquess Townshend* (London: HMSO, 1887) p.171.
38   *HMC Townshend*, p.169.
39   *HMC Townshend*, p.169.
40   *HMC Townshend*, p.171.
41   Patten, *History*, p.105.

secured the town [Newcastle] and Tinmouth castle. Some others were to have attempted the Tower and the Bank.'[42]

On 14 September Stanhope informed the Commons that 'His Majesty having just cause to suspect, that Sir William Wyndham … Forster and others … are engaged in a Design to support the intended invasion of the kingdom, hath given orders for apprehending them'.[43] A few days later there were orders to take up another prominent Northumbrian, 'Warrt. To, Richard Shereman, John Hutchin and John Turner for apprehending the Rt. Honble. The earl of Derwentwater for suspicion of treason Dated 22 Septr. 1715'.[44] On 30 September, William Cotesworth (c. 1668–1725), a Gateshead coal merchant, was informed that Valentine Rowland, a King's Messenger, had arrived in Newcastle with Colonel Follick of the Guards. They had been ordered to arrest Sir William Blackett (1690–1728), a Tory MP for Newcastle, and hoped Cotesworth could assist them in finding him.[45]

The taking of these suspects did not always go to plan, but was to have far reaching consequences. Derwentwater learnt, at the end of September, that there was a warrant made out for his arrest and those men who had come to execute it had arrived at Durham. Derwentwater went to the house of a neighbouring gentleman who was also a magistrate. This man did not arrest him nor did he persuade him to surrender himself. The peer then went to Richard Lambert's house, where he thought he would be safer.[46]

Forster was also forewarned about his imminent arrest. To escape he travelled from place to place but found nowhere in which he felt himself safe. Eventually he reached Fenwick of Bywell's house. His pursuer was within a half mile of the said house, but delayed reaching there in order to find a constable to assist with the arrest. Possibly Forster had notice of who was coming for him, but in any case he managed to escape the net.[47] John Hall, JP, a Northumbrian Jacobite, suggested to Forster that the county magistrates be seized, but Forster demurred and so no action was taken. This was a minor piece of inaction in itself, but suggestive of Forster's lack of appetite for daring action.[48]

The result of these botched attempts to take Derwentwater and Forster was that they and others met together and concluded that 'since there was no safety any longer in shifting from place to place; that in a few days they would all be secur'd', imprisoned and questioned, that 'they would immediately appear in arms'. Previously, Derwentwater's horses had been in the custody of a justice of the peace, one Coatsforth, but he had these returned by the peer giving a great deal of money to the man.[49] Yet apart from these two, all

---

42 Joan Ellis (ed.), 'Liddell–Cotesworth letters', *Surtees Society* 118 (1987), p.180.
43 Rae, *History*, p.212–213.
44 TNA: SP44/79a, p.29, Secretaries of State, State Papers, Criminal Correspondence and Warrants, 1713–1721, Stanhope to Messengers, 22 September 1715.
45 Tyne and Wear Archives (TWAS): CM2/331, Carr-Ellison Manuscripts, Letter of ? to William Cotesworth, 30 September 1715.
46 Patten, *History*, pp.17–18.
47 Patten, *History*, p.18.
48 Patten, *History*, p.112.
49 Patten, *History*, pp.18–19.

the other suspect MPs were arrested, and apparently the government was 'out of all apprehensions from any attack in England'.[50]

Meanwhile, one of the main players in the Jacobite campaign, the Earl of Mar, was very active. Up to 1714 he had been secretary of state for Scotland. A cultured and artistic man, and a great improver of his own estates at Alloa, near Stirling, he needed money which went with political office. On losing his post, he turned to the Jacobite cause. At the beginning of August, he left London, perhaps concerned he might be taken into custody. Travelling by small boat he stopped at Newcastle, perhaps significantly to discuss the Stuart restoration with fellow Jacobites. When in Scotland he called together numbers of nobility and gentry to support a bid to restore James. In the early days and weeks of September, groups of armed Jacobites were gathering together in the Highlands.

They made two major moves, one successful, the other not. On 14 September, they took Perth from the loyalists, despite local volunteers being present there. The provost had called for no violence and so the Jacobites had a bloodless victory. They took over the city and made it their base for the next few months. It was an important place, as a great regional commercial centre. However, an attempt to take Edinburgh castle by a coup de main, after bribing three of the garrison, was an utter failure. Elsewhere, in the light of no resistance, defenceless towns and cities in the Highlands (Aberdeen, Dundee and Inverness) were taken by the Jacobites, simply by walking into them with armed men. Most of the Highlands were thus in Jacobite control.

The government's strength in Scotland was restricted to four battalions of infantry and a regiment of dragoons. These were concentrated at Stirling in order to block any Jacobite march southwards, and were led by Major General Joseph Wightman. Loyalist militia were formed at Glasgow and Edinburgh, and a more senior officer, who was also the most powerful peer in Scotland, John Campbell, the Duke of Argyle, was sent northwards to command, but outnumbered as he was, could not take the offensive until he received the promised reinforcements from Ireland and from the Dutch Republic, Britain's sole European ally. The Jacobites had secured themselves in Scotland and awaited a build up of clans from the west and other Highlanders from the north. Yet the Jacobite high command were insistent that it would be in England that the campaign would be decided, despite Scotland being the centre of their support.[51]

The insurrection in Scotland was felt in England and the government was particularly concerned that it might spill over into northern England, which was generally bereft of troops, except small packets in castle garrisons. On 16 September the privy council had letters sent out to the Lords lieutenant, to acquaint them of the 'open and unnaturall rebellion … in that part of His Majesties Dominions in Scotland' and the pressing need to implement civil defence. They had two orders. Firstly, 'to cause the Militia, both Horse and

---

50 *HMC Townshend*, p.27.
51 Rae, *History*, pp.218–219.

Foot, to be put into such a posture as to be in readiness to meet upon the first order'. The first duty of the militia was to 'Seize, with the assistance of the Constable, the Persons and Arms of all Papists, Non Jurors or other Persons that you have manner to suspect to be Disaffected'. All Lords lieutenant were instructed, on 19 September, to return to their county.[52]

Charles Howard, third Earl of Carlisle (1669–1738), Lord lieutenant of Cumberland and Westmorland, ignored the precept that he should leave his seat in Yorkshire, but he wrote to his deputy Lords lieutenant on 22 September, passing on the privy council's instructions thus, 'I must recommend to your care and vigilance a strict and Due Execution of them', urging that any Catholics arrested should be taken to Carlisle castle as 'the properest place to send the persons you take into Custody to'.[53]

Three days after this letter was written, one of Carlisle's deputies, Henry Lowther (1694–1751), Viscount Lonsdale, assumed the role of Carlisle's representative, despite his age. He urged on his fellows the importance of executing the privy council's instructions, 'I believe it will be advisable to proceed as soon as possible upon this order'. He also wanted to hold a meeting of the deputy lieutenants and this was held on 4 October at the house of one Henry Hayton at Penrith. Fourteen attended, including William Nicholson (1650–1728), Bishop of Carlisle and Brigadier Thomas Stanwix, lieutenant governor of Carlisle castle. The aim was to raise the county militia, though they found that some on the roll of militia officers were dead or infirm. Enough men were appointed to raise seven companies of foot militia and one troop of horse militia. Each captain should send instructions to the high constable of each ward within the counties, to order 'every [petty] constable within the ward to return and Summon three persons between the ages of twenty and fifty, to appear before such captains at such time and place as he shall appoint it for and in respect of every one person so deceased or superannuated'. Constables had to provide weapons and three men from each parish to serve in the militia and for the whole force to be ready by 17 October.[54]

The other northern county to react thus was Northumberland. The Earl of Scarborough, the county's Lord lieutenant, returned to the county but did not give such an order to raise the militia until 1 October with the intention that they should be in arms on 14 October. In this he was a little more prompt that his western colleagues, but came under criticism for the perceived delay. Cotesworth wrote, 'He is very hearty in his duties, but for want of health and vigour things are not done with the despatch that is necessary for affairs of this nature'.[55]

What the government needed was intelligence of their enemies' movements. On 22 September, Henry Liddell in London, told his business associate, Cotesworth in Gateshead 'if he could recommend any notable

---

52　Rupert Jarvis, *The Jacobite Risings of 1715 and 1745* (Carlisle: Cumberland County Council, 1954), pp.149–150; TNA: SP44/118, p.29, Secretaries of State, State Papers, Entry Books, 1715–1716, Townshend to Derby, 14 September 1715.
53　Jarvis, *The Jacobite Risings*, pp.152–153.
54　Jarvis, *The Jacobite Risings*, pp.153–155.
55　Hertfordshire Record Office, D/EP F95, Cotesworth to Liddell, 11 October 1715.

person in your parts who could be trusted and on whose intelligence one might depend'. Liddell told his contact that 'I knew none so capable in every respect as your self'. Cotesworth was assured of secrecy and of a reward for his services, and was asked for any news from Scotland, too.[56]

Cotesworth was quick to act. Four days after Liddell had written, he contacted the Lord Provost of Edinburgh, Sir George Warrender:

> I need not tell you the restless Condition we are come into by the Restless Malice of our enemies. We think all Honest men ought at this juncture to exert themselves in the support of our present happy Government: we are a Club of us who have sent messengers throughout these Counties to enquire of our friends what appearance the enimie makes.

He asked Warrender about the strength of the Jacobites and how strong the city residents were to oppose them. He had also been in contact with Anthony Compton, Mayor of Berwick, on the same topic and the latter was also in correspondence with Warrender. Compton referred to Cotesworth as 'a Gentleman of very great Worth and very zealous to this Government'. Cotesworth was primarily concerned with the state of the Jacobites in Northumberland and the extent that they posed a danger to Newcastle 'where they are often imposed upon by such Reports as the Jacobites spread amongst them'.[57]

Scarborough was Lord Lieutenant of Durham as well as Northumberland (the lieutenant of the former was usually the Prince Bishop but the present incumbent, Nathaniel Crewe, had been sympathetic towards James II and so had lost his civil jurisdiction) and his arrival in the county was expected by the end of September. Cotesworth wrote 'Our Lord lieutenant will be here in 3 or 4 dayes when we hope there will be a meeting of Gentlemen that will strike Terrour into the enimies of the Government that are among us'.[58]

Argyle was also concerned about a potential Jacobite insurrection in England, writing on 1 October to Townshend, 'I am glad to hear of the Discovery that is made in England, and have received informations that confirm your of the rebels intending an insurrection in the northern parts of England, which terrifies to the greatest degree our well affected people'.[59] The government's strategy was to give priority to the security of England. Once it was secure, Scotland could then be given priority, but that meant vanquishing any Jacobite threat in England first. To lose England was to lose Scotland but vice versa was not true. England was the richer and more populous of the two countries, the seat of administrative and commercial power. Thus the greater part of the army was stationed there.

---

56 Ellis, 'Liddell–Cotesworth Letters', p.179.
57 William Kirk Dickson (ed.), 'Warrender Letters: Correspondence of Sir George Warrender, Bt., Lord Provost of Edinburgh, and Member of Parliament for the City, with Relative Papers, 1715', *Scottish History Society*, 3rd series, 21 (1935), pp.98–99.
58 Dickson, 'Warrender Letters', p.99.
59 TNA: SP54/9, 2A, Secretaries of State, State Papers Scotland, October 1715, Argyle to Townshend, 2 October 1715.

Plot and counterplot were both truly well advanced and the culmination of both were about to show fruit. The initiative lay with the Jacobites and their activity was to burst into the open, though initially with a damp squib rather than a bang. However, this mole hill was, as time went by, to develop into something rather more dangerous and it is unwise to adopt the benefit of hindsight as some historians have done merely because they are aware, as contemporaries were not, of its final outcome.

The Jacobites were embarking on a very dangerous course of action. Regime change by violent means had not been successful in England since the civil wars. In 1660 the Cromwellian regime had collapsed from within and in 1688 foreign assistance was crucial to overthrow James II. This would not necessarily happen again.

2

The Campaign begins, 6–31 October 1715

In October 1715 three Jacobite forces came together on the Scottish border. We need to examine these as well as noting the opposition that they faced in order to see how the military campaign in England began, and how it progressed in its first few weeks.

We shall take the English Jacobites first, following the steps taken against them in the previous weeks. On the morning of Wednesday 6 October at Green-rig, to the north of Newcastle, Forster and 20 men met together. They did not stay there, concerned that it was an inconvenient meeting place, so rode to a hill, Waterfalls, 'from whence they might discover any that came either to join them, or to oppose them'. They had not long to wait until Derwentwater, with some friends and servants, arrived, having ridden from his seat, Dilston, near Corbridge, earlier that day. As they rode through Corbridge they drew their swords. Others joined them as they progressed to the meeting place. Once there the gathering numbered almost 60 horsemen, mostly gentlemen with their servants.[1]

There was a short council of war and they concluded they would ride towards the river Coquet in order to reach Plainfield. They were joined by others there and after a short stay at Plainfield they then left, riding to the north east to reach Rothbury, a small market town, and stayed the night there.[2] It was a long journey of about 24 miles. That same day, Forster wrote a letter to Mar, the latter later writing 'telling me of their actually being in Arms there, and next day they would be seven hundred Horse, and very soon a great many more'.[3] Forster was extremely confident that there would be much more support, especially among the Tories. As an enemy of his wrote at this time:

> What these Rebels hoped for was that the High Church would have joined them, and no doubt there was too good a Disposition in some People to it. They talk

---
1   Patten, *History*, p.19.
2   Patten, *History*, p.19.
3   Rae, *History*, p.439.

now of a great Number of Horse and Foot they expect will join them from the South of Scotland.[4]

Next day, with others joining them, they marched to another market town, the coastal Warkworth, riding about 10 miles eastwards. According to Patten, during their stay here, 'nothing material happened'. However, on Sunday 10 October, Forster, now styling himself as 'general', sent one Buxton, a clergyman, to see the parish's minister, the Rev. Henry Ion, with orders to pray for James Stuart as King and to omit the names of the Hanoverian royal family during the morning's church service. Ion refused and fled south to Newcastle to give information about the insurrection that he was witnessing.[5]

Ion arrived at Newcastle and told what he had seen to John Johnson, the county sheriff. He told Johnson that the Jacobite plan was 'for seizing the Militia at Killingworth Moor on Tuesday next [12 October], and take from them their Horses and Arms'. The Jacobites had also sent one Robert Lisle to Newcastle, presumably to gather intelligence and seek support there, but he had been arrested on entering Pandon Gate on 8 October on orders of Johnson and Alderman White and thrown into Newgate.[6]

Loyalists in Edinburgh were just as soon aware of the Jacobite insurrection as their English counterparts. Adam Cockburn (1656–1735), Lord Justice Clerk, wrote early on 7 October that he had news from Berwick about it and feared that correspondence between loyalists in Scotland and northern England might be threatened by the Jacobite forces lying between them. There was also concern that 'all the disaffected persons on this side of the Forth and in the south of Scotland one way or other joyn those in the north of England'.[7] Cockburn was extremely worried about the potential for a mass uprising, with numerous Jacobite bodies, including Mar's, coalescing. Later that day he wrote:

> … the alarme this morning of ane Insurrection in Northumberland damps all, it agrees too well with the informations I had notice off, and if they draw so such a body as is given out, to be some thousands of horse, earl Mar's march into England will be too easy, what the consequences will be seen as easy to guess.[8]

As already noted, there had been steps taken to defend Newcastle and the county against any Jacobite threat. Some of these were now deemed too leisurely, especially Scarborough's summoning of the militia. Johnson acted promptly. He had ten keel boats sent to North Shields fort to take the cannon that were there in case they were seized by the Jacobites and used against Newcastle's town walls. The trained bands were already in arms, thanks to Johnson and Cotesworth. On 9 October, Johnson, in his capacity as county sheriff, raised the posse comitatus 'to prevent the Rebels further strolling into this Country,

---

4   S. Cowper (ed.), *The Diary of Mary, Countess Cowper* (London: John Murray, 1865), p.187.
5   Patten, *History*, pp.19–20.
6   Cowper, *Diary*, p.185.
7   TNA, SP54/9, 18a, Cockburn–Townshend, 7 October 1715.
8   TNA, SP54/9, 26a, Cockburn–Townshend, 7 October 1715.

THE SECOND BATTLE OF PRESTON, 1715

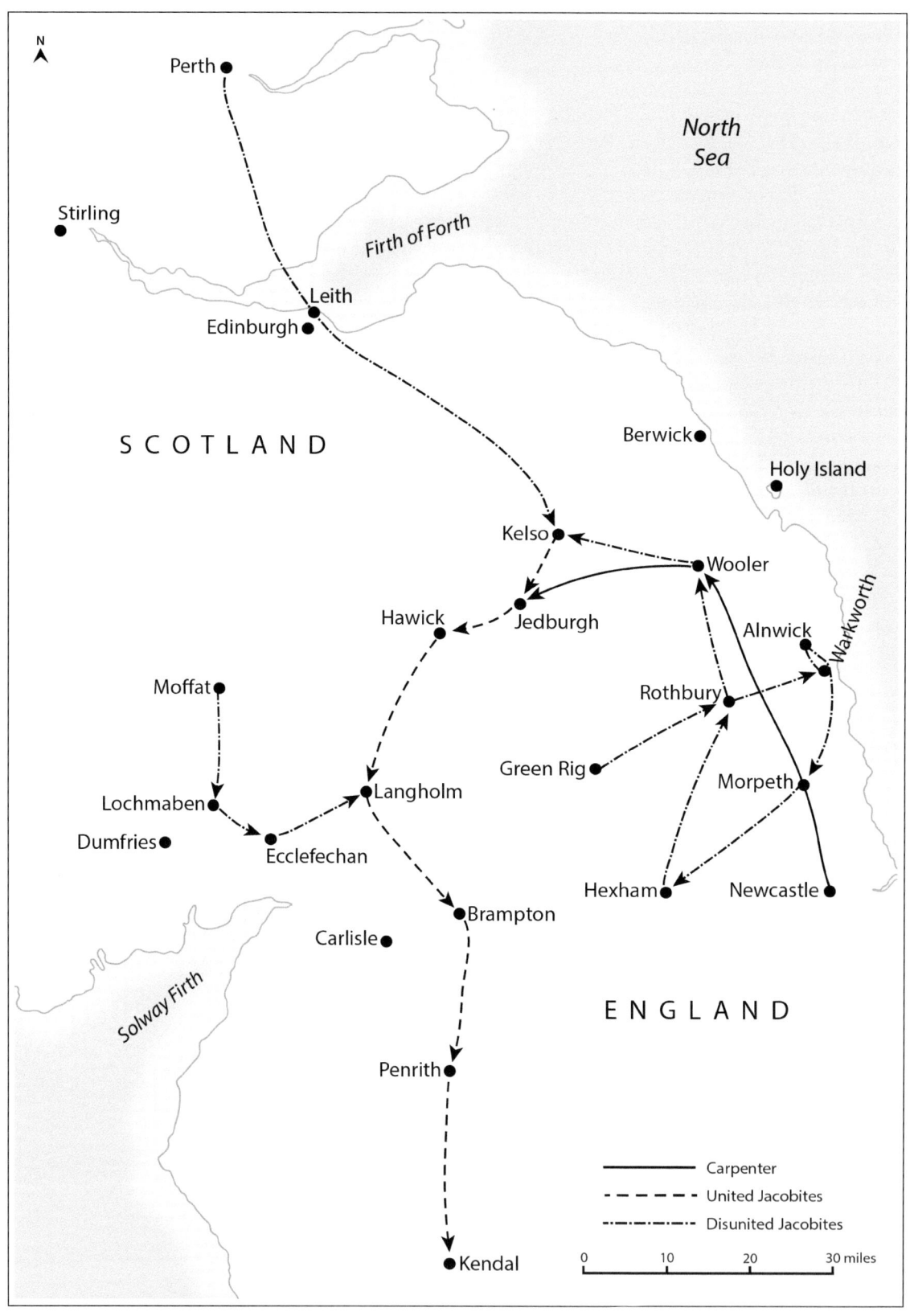

and am in expectation thereby entirely to secure this Town, which they so much aim at'. He was also expecting regular troops from Sir Charles Hotham's battalion of Foot, who were on their way to Berwick, and hoped that the three companies expected on 12 October could be kept at Newcastle 'through the Insinuations of Lord Scarborough'. In all, working with Cotesworth and Alderman White, who were all 'zealous and hearty, I don't question but we shall keep them out here till such Times as we shall get further assistance, most people in Town being better inclined than thought of'.[9]

In the autumn of 1715, the British army's forces in Scotland were concentrated in Stirling, and those in England in the south west and London. There was no regular presence in the north of England except in small garrisons in Berwick, Carlisle and Chester. Troops were being readied, however, with William Pulteney (1684–1764), Secretary at War, having ordered the cavalry regiments on 29 September to have their horses taken off grass feeding and on 1 October the dragoon regiments 'were in a readiness to take the field'.[10] There had also been lobbying in London for the despatch of troops to the north east. Lady Cowper, wife of the Lord Chancellor and of a Northumbrian family, noted in her diary: 'I was mightily solicited from my Friends at Newcastle to procure them from some Assistance, which I effectually did my Baron Bernstorff, to the great vexation of Lord Townshend and Mr Walpole, who at that time were for palliating Everything, and beating down the Report of the Rebellion.'[11]

It seems that her efforts were successful. On 13 October, Liddell told Cotesworth:

> You will have 3 or 4 regiments off dragoons and a battalion of Foot with all expedition. I doe assure you a good Kensington lady has sollicited for speedy succour and press'd harder than any whatever for the relief off our own country, but this to yourself. She will not leave them until she has effected and succeeded very well in her sollicitations.[12]

At eleven o'clock on 11 October, three dragoon colonels, Charles Churchill, Richard Molesworth and Richard Baron Cobham, met their political master, Pulteney, in London. The two former were given plans for the routes their regiments would take towards Newcastle, via Derby, Leeds, Northallerton and Durham and told 'there being no excuse for want of necessarys and accoutrements your regiment being to be completely armed and mounted'. Cobham was told, as were they, 'make such marches as will best suit the present occasion' and that speed was essential.[13] The regiments of dragoons left London on the following day, 12 October. On 13 October, Townshend

Facing page: North-east England and the borders, October 1715.

---

9   Cowper, *Diary*, pp.185–186.
10 TNA: WO4/17, pp. 205, 209, War Office, Secretary at War Out Letters, 1715–1716, Pulteney–colonels, 29 September and 1 October 1715.
11 Cowper, *Diary*, p.49.
12 Ellis, 'Liddell–Cotesworth Letters', pp.184–185.
13 TNA: WO4/117, pp.227–228, 235, Pulteney to Churchill, Molesworth and Cobham, 10 and 11 October 1715; War Office, Secretary at War, Marching and Militia Orders, 1714–1716, WO5/20, p.130, Pulteney to Churchill, 10 October 1715.

wrote to Pulteney to 'forthwith despatch another express to the regiments that are marching towards Newcastle with repeated orders to hasten their march with the utmost expedition'.[14]

An overall commander for these regiments was needed. Lieutenant General George Carpenter (1657–1732) was chosen and was given his instructions on 14 October:

> You are without loss of time to repair to those parts (Northumberland/Lothian), & to take upon you the command of the said regiments (Cobham's, Churchill's and Molesworth's), as also of our regiment of Foot of Hotham.
>
> As soon as you arrive there, you are with your utmost application, to inform yourself of any insurrections in those parts, and according to the intelligence you receive, you are to march with these our forces, or such part of them as you shall judge sufficient & attack the rebels wherever you can find them.

He was also to keep the government informed and to arrest all suspected persons. It was a relatively small force to command, perhaps just under 1,000 men but more than enough to deal with the several hundred English Jacobites with ease.[15]

Meanwhile, with Warkworth dominated by the little Jacobite force, Buxton read prayers at the church and preached there. He 'gave mighty Encouragement to his Hearers, being full of Exhortations, flourishing Arguments and Cunning Insinuations to be hearty and zealous in the Cause'. Outside the church, later in the day, James was proclaimed as King. Apparently, Forster did so in disguise, with a trumpeter gathering attention.[16]

The Earl of Widdrington joined the Jacobites on about the 8 October, bringing with him 20 horsemen. Other Jacobites that were gathered at Warkworth by this time were Charles Radcliffe, Derwentwater's brother, Phillip Hodgson, John Talbot, the Shaftoes and others. This was known about by Newcastle's defenders, but their list also included men who did not join the Jacobite army.[17]

We now move to the second Jacobite force in the vicinity. At the same time, the Honourable James Hume raised 70 Scottish horsemen. They marched to Coldstream, proclaimed James Stuart as King and placed his proclamation at the market place there. They did likewise at Wooler and on 10 October had the parson mentioning the king without stating who this was. That day they heard that the garrison at Berwick was planning to attack them there. The troop marched to Warkworth.[18]

On the next day a number of East Lothian men joined them at Felton, numbering 60 horsemen. There was news on about 12 October that Hotham's

---

14 TNA: SP44/118, p.61, Townshend to Pulteney, 13 October 1715.
15 TNA: SP54/10, 30, 63, Secretaries of State, State Papers, Scotland, October 1715, Pulteney–Carpenter, 14 October 1715.
16 Patten, *History*, p.20.
17 Cowper, *Diary*, p.186.
18 Anon., *A Letter of the Occurrences from and at Preston* (Edinburgh: Publisher Unknown, 1718), p.1.

battalion of infantry was about to march north to surprise the few men at Felton (some had in fact just arrived at Newcastle). A Merse trooper was sent to Warkworth to tell Forster about this. He went to Forster's lodgings, passing through the men 'without being challeng'd'. He was unable to find Forster's manservant and so knocked on Forster's door. He was then told he had to find the servant who had the keys to the door. This was an urgent matter 'That being an Express about matters of Consequence, I had no time to go a hunting Grooms'. He thrust open the door, 'where finding the Lord Widdrington and Forrester in Bed'.[19]

Thomas Forster, MP. Courtesy of John Nicholls, MBE.

He told them his news and begged that reinforcements be sent to Felton. Forster gave the following answer, 'That it was not possible for any Forces could came from Newcastle without his Knowledge, for he had a settled Intelligence Forty Miles round'. The trooper replied, 'That a Gentleman of known Integrity had rode Twenty miles to give us Notice of our Danger; so that we being but a Handful, might easily be cut off'. Widdrington recognised the danger and 'pressed an immediate Reinforcement'. They sent John Hunter's troop of cavalry to Felton where it was discovered that this was another false alarm.[20] Yet this was not the only time that Forster would ignore news of potential or real danger.

Forster wrote another optimistic letter to Mar, informing him that they were 300 strong 'and was to be joined next day by all the Border, and to go straight to Newcastle, which they were sure of, and getting good Numbers of the best Foot in the North of England to join them'. He also advised Mar to attack Argyle before the latter were reinforced.[21] Meanwhile, had they but known it, matters for the Jacobite cause were looking less than good. On 11 October three companies of Hotham's infantry arrived in Newcastle. On the previous day Colonel George Liddell mustered over 1,200 of the county militia on Gateshead Fell. On the next day the militia horsemen and the posse horsemen were stationed on Shield Field. The militia cavalry of Durham was expected in Gateshead on the evening of 11 October. Cotesworth was in discussions with Sir William Williamson, the county sheriff of Durham, about these forces continuing at Newcastle.[22]

---

19 Anon., *A Letter*, pp.1–2.
20 Anon., *A Letter*, p.2.
21 Rae, *History*, p.441.
22 Cowper, *Diary*, p.187.

Cotesworth was not only confident about the defence of Newcastle, writing 'We got the Town of Newcastle put into a state of holding out against 2,000 Men, if they come without a Train [of artillery]', but was eager for an offensive. He was in discussion with Lord Scarborough about the plan 'that the Militia Horse of both Counties, as soon as my Lord Cobham's Dragoons come up, shall join them, and as many other armed Horse as we can get, and go out and drive the Rebels into the sea … I have promised my lord, that if but 20 Gentlemen in our County will go upon this Expedition, I shall make one. This, I am sure, is the way to strike Terror into all the Enemies of our happy Constitution and Government'.[23]

On the following day the Jacobites marched to Felton and then to Morpeth, 12 miles to the north of Newcastle. At Morpeth there was fresh news of immediate danger. The men were camped on Morpeth Common, when that night there came news that the enemy would be on them. The Merse troop was sent to 'enquire into the Truth of the Enemy's marching towards us'. Again, they found it to be false. The force then rode into the town.[24]

At Morpeth the force was counted and numbered about 300, 'all Horse, for they would entertain no Foot, else their number would have been very large, but as they neither had nor could provide Arms for those they had mounted, they gave the common People good words, and told them that they would soon be furnished with Arms and Ammunition'. George Home of Whitfield wrote to Mar about this in 1717, 'it was the want of these [arms and money] which occasion'd our not employing them and put us under a woeful necessity to send home who had travelled several miles after us on our march'. The intention was to surprise Newcastle and then take the arms and give these to their would be followers.[25]

It was when they were at Morpeth that Forster heard that Lancelot and Mark Errington had taken the little castle at Holy Island on 10 October. Lancelot had arrived there and was allowed inside by Samuel Phillipson, the master gunner, who was also a barber. Once shaved, the Jacobite left and later returned, claiming he had left his watch key behind. Once inside again, he clapped a pistol to Phillipson's head and forced him and the other member of the garrison out of the fort. When they returned with five other soldiers, Errington declared 'What I have done I stand by whilst I have a breath of life in my body'. However, Colonel Laton, governor of Berwick, soon learnt what had happened. Next day he sent 30 soldiers and they and 50 volunteers marched over the sands at low tide, before the Erringtons could be reinforced with men and supplies. The fort was attacked 'sword in hand' and Lancelot Errington fled, but was hit by a musket ball and captured.[26]

The importance of the fort was that it could have been a magnet for overseas aid. Patten claimed that it was 'to give Signals to any ships that seem'd to make to the Coast to land soldiers, for by the Assurances they had

---

23 Cowper, *Diary*, pp.186–187.
24 Anon., *A Letter*, p.2.
25 Patten, *History*, pp.20–21; *HMC Stuart Papers*, V, p.214.
26 James Raine, *History and Antiquities of North Durham* (London: John Bowyer Nichols and Son, 1852), pp.166n–167n.

from Friends beyond Sea, they expected them to land on that Coast with supplies of Arms and Officers'. The ships never arrived until the month's end, when two ships sailed by, but finding no answering signals, sailed on.[27]

Newcastle was the main goal for the Jacobite force. At Morpeth a few more joined them and a few more would have done, but were refused, as before. Yet one account claims that it was here that they recruited a company of infantry, 60 men strong, for the first time.[28] The Jacobites were optimistic, 'promising themselves great things at Newcastle'. Before they did, Buxton, acting as herald, again proclaimed James as King. A number of Jacobites took the mail at Felton Bridge and seized Thomas Gibson, a Newcastle blacksmith, who was believed to be a spy sent from Alderman White, 'a zealous Gentleman for the government'.[29]

It was at Newcastle that 'they receiv'd their first Disappointment'. The Jacobites expected that the town's gates would be opened to them. This did not happen, but they convinced themselves that this was only a delay, and all they needed was a little patience and that in a few days' time they would be in possession of Newcastle. So they marched south westwards to Hexham, 14 miles from Morpeth. They were joined by more Scottish horsemen and rode to Dilston moor, three miles away, and halted there. As at Morpeth, they hoped to take Newcastle by surprise, though they had expected this to have happened sooner.[30]

There was certainly support within Newcastle and its environs for the Jacobite cause. In October 1714 there had been street fighting in the town between allies of George I and the Jacobites. Alderman White had his house windows broken. A year later there was verbal support for the Jacobite cause from some individuals within the walls, mouthing such phrases as 'God damn King George' and another shouting his support for the Earl of Mar.[31]

Cotesworth was concerned about three specific individuals. The Recorder of Newcastle was a friend of Derwentwater's. Dr Sacheverell's brother was a customs officer on the Durham coast, 'which is a dangerous Thing, in my Opinion'. Dr Sacheverell was a leading Jacobite clergyman who, in London in 1709, had garnered national attention from friends and foes through a sermon that was strongly supportive of James Stuart and though he was briefly imprisoned he gained 'martyr' status among his supporters.[32] The third, and principal among them was Sir William Blackett (1690–1728), a Newcastle MP and a Tory. He was reputed to have Jacobite sympathies, too. Yet it was not known how far he was involved in the cause. Potentially he was very influential, for he was a major figure in the Newcastle coal trade, employing colliers, keelsmen and miners. These men had been provided with arms and had been told to take orders from Blackett's steward. Whether

---

27 Patten, *History*, pp.21-22.
28 Anon., *The Annals of King George the second Year* (London: A. Bell, 1717), II, p.76.
29 Patten, *History*, pp.22–23.
30 Patten, *History*, pp.22–23.
31 Edward Hughes (ed.), 'Some Clavering Correspondence', *Archaeologia Aeliana*, 3rd series, XXXIV (1956), p.21; TWAS: QS/NC/1/3, Newcastle Quarter Sessions Order Book, 1700–1719.
32 Cowper, *Diary*, p.187.

they were to support the government or the Jacobites remained an open question.[33] On 11 October, Cotesworth wrote, 'I have taken a good deal of Pains' to have him secured from joining the Jacobites. One Mr Wilkinson was shadowing Blackett who was now at Wallington, but there would be no immediate order for an arrest 'till we are in a more quiet or secure state'.[34]

Liddell was very anxious about the loyalties of the said keelsmen, who were the workers who took coal in their narrow boats from and to ships in the Tyne. There had been disputes and strikes between coal owners and these workers as recently as 1710. Liddell enquired twice, writing on 10 October, 'Pray how stand your keelmen affected?' and again on 27 October, 'Do you really think your keelmen right and tight and may be depended on occasion?'[35] At least one man whose support was expected was unhelpful, Liddell writing 'The High Sheriff wrote to me last post that Robert Lawson off Chirton refus'd to appear or so much as send a horse to the posse comitatus'.[36]

Given all this potential sympathy, the Jacobites sent a man into Newcastle to gauge the level of active support their force might receive on entry, following the capture of Lisle a week ago. On his return to Hexham they were told that the town was being securely held against them. It was certainly a very important town to hold, given its economic importance was of national as well as regional standing. Newcastle controlled much of the capital's coal supply. For the Jacobites to seize it, it would be the greatest town they held and would serve as a base for recruits and supplies. The supplies and money gained there would also fund their campaign.

Meanwhile Celia Fiennes described Hexham thus:

> … this is one of the best towns in Northumberland except Newcastle, which is one place the sessions are kept for the shire, its built of stone and looks very well, there are 2 gates to it many streetes some are pretty broad all well pitch'd with a spacious market crosse.[37]

The Jacobites remained there for three days. There was a suggestion that they should make it their base of operations and fortify it. It was a geographically important place, on the river Tyne and was on routes from both Scotland and Lancashire and they expected to be joined by many from both places.[38]

There was some support here, and another company of infantry was formed whilst at Hexham; remaining in one place allowed recruits to join them.[39] Active recruitment also occurred. Christopher Croft of Dilston, steward to Derwentwater, went to Caine Liddell's house in Hexham and asked him 'will ye not go to my Lord Derwentwater if you will go and fight

---

33 Patten, *History*, p.23.
34 Cowper, *Diary*, pp.187–188.
35 Ellis, 'Liddell-Cotesworth Letters', pp.183, 192.
36 Ellis, 'Liddell-Cotesworth Letters', p.189.
37 Christopher Morris (ed.), *The Journeys of Celia Fiennes* (New York: Chanticleer Press, 1949), p.208.
38 Anon., *Annals*, II, p.76.
39 Anon., *Annals*, II, p.76.

THE CAMPAIGN BEGINS, 6–31 OCTOBER 1715

for ye Church of England you shall have a horse and arms'. Liddell did so and was given a horse and a pistol. William Westby made a similar remark about the defence of the Church to a would be recruit. Errington gave another recruit a shilling and a horse.[40]

They also looked for weaponry and horses, searching the property of those loyal to the government. Between 14 and 23 October, 27 horses were taken; Matthew Robson of Bellingham recalled that they threatened to either 'stop or shoot him' and he chose the first.[41] However, not even their enemies claimed that there was any plundering. Naturally Buxton required the curate, the Rev. George Ritschell (1657–1717), to read out prayers and to mention James as King. He refused, but apparently had also promised to join the Jacobites, but never did. Buxton read the prayers. On their last night at Hexham, they drew up around the market cross. James was proclaimed there as King and a document announcing this was pinned to the cross and remained there for three days.[42]

In fact much of the hoped for support never materialised. Cotesworth's suspicions of Blackett were proved unfounded, whatever the latter's inner convictions. Liddell later admitted, 'As to Sir William Blackett I was over and above cautious I was pump'd by several to know my opinion how farr he was ingaged: my answer was that gentleman was in possession of too large a fortune'.[43] Likewise, as Patten stated, within the walls there was 'no more Churchman and Dissenter' but a common unity among Protestants. As to the keelsmen, the majority, who were Presbyterian Scots, were formed into an armed regiment of volunteers to defend the town.[44] In retrospect, Derwentwater said 'You see what we have brought ourselves to, by giving credit to our Neighbour Tories as Will Fenwick, Tate, Green and Allgood … such Rogues in Disguise, that promised to join us, and animated us to rise with them'. The arrest of Sir William Wyndham, a leading Tory MP, on 3 October may also have been decisive for some, 'it was a feeling cold blow to all the Party, especially to the Northumberland Rebels who found themselves very much lessened by this Gentleman's Confinement'.[45]

Yet even this reduced Jacobite force needed dealing with. Johnson was well aware of the Jacobites' movements. On 16 October he was looking forward to the arrival of Cobham's dragoons. There was no concern that Newcastle was in any danger, but rather that the Jacobites would evade a confrontation. Rather, they were 'afraid the rebels will march into Lancashire and quit this Country before we can give them Battle'.[46]

It was at Hexham that the English Jacobites learnt of the proximity of a friendly force of Lowland horsemen. They also heard that men from Mar's

---

40 TNA: KB8/66, ff.11r, 10r, 16r, Court of King's Bench, Crown Side, Baga de Secretis, 1715–1717.
41 TNA: FEC1/827, Forfeited Estates Commission: Northumberland depositions, 1716.
42 Patten, *History*, pp.26–27.
43 Ellis, 'Liddell–Cotesworth Letters', p.212.
44 Patten, *History*, pp.24–25.
45 Ibid, pp.105, 223.
46 Cowper, *Diary*, p.188.

army had arrived at Haddington and then that these Highlanders were at Seton House. We shall now turn to these groups.[47]

By early October, Mar was well established in Perth and was beginning to form an army from the groups of Lowlanders and Highlanders who were arriving there from the north of Scotland, both clan troops and forces raised by other Highland magnates, such as Earls Huntley and Seaforth. Time was now needed to organise, equip and arm this raw material. There had been success in the north with the bloodless seizure of Inverness by Mackintosh of Borlum. They could not advance into the Lowlands yet because of Argyle's forces being camped at Stirling.

So Mar decided to take the initiative. By 8 October, despite having no concrete knowledge of what was happening in Northumberland, he wrote: 'I have ordered 2000 Men to cross the water from Bruntisland to Leith, and most of them will be at Bruntisland tonight; so Tomorrow, I hope, they will get over without Opposition, there being no men of war in the road'.

The intention was to encourage others in the Lowlands and England to join the Jacobite cause, as he continued: 'Our Friends in the South are to be together both of Scots and English on Monday next, to a goodly Number, and, if it please GOD, to give this Detachment a fair Passage, we shall have our enemies in a hose-net'.

Furthermore, in order to prevent Argyle from interfering with this march, he would move the rest of the army towards Stirling as a distraction.[48]

William Mackintosh of Borlum, styled 'brigadier', who had recently arrived at Perth after taking Inverness, was appointed as commander. According to Patten, he was given command of six battalions of infantry, totalling 2,500 men, though the Master of Sinclair, who was on the spot, stated that it was 2,200 and as noted Mar claimed they were 2,000. Boats were gathered on the north side of the Forth in order to cross. The crossing was made on the evenings of 11 and 12 October. Some boats were forced back to the Fife side, in part by the naval vessels on patrol. Lord Strathmore and his lieutenant colonel did not reach the south, and one boat with 40 men was captured. In all, perhaps only 1,500 men or less got to the other side, landing at North Berwick and Aberlady. They quartered at Tranent and Haddington. It was an impressive feat, with Patten writing, 'This was a bold, and, to give them their due, a brave Attempt, for Men in open Boats to cross an Arm of the sea sixteen or seventeen Miles broad, in sight, and indeed in Defiance of three Men of War, whom they fell among, but received no Damage from them'.[49]

The orders given were vague and allowed considerable latitude. Sinclair, always hostile to Mar, certainly wrote that he had not given any instructions. He wrote that Mackintosh 'no more than those who sent him over having no positive orders, and hearing from those who he was told would joyn him, and instead of a body that would be of any use to him'. In fact, Sinclair insinuated that Mar's real agenda was completely different, 'it's plaine that Mar had no other aime, in sending the detachment over the Forth, than

---
47 Anon., *A Letter*, p.2.
48 Rae, *History*, p.435.
49 Scott, *Memoirs*, p.106; Patten, *History*, p.6.

ridding his hands of so many men for feare we had obliged him to marche, to passe Forth'.[50]

Once gathered together, on 13 October, Mackintosh's men marched westwards towards Edinburgh 'where they caused greater Fear than there was real danger'. They expected support from within the city, but the civil authorities had the place in order. They were reinforced by a portion of Argyle's army including the man himself. Lacking artillery or any encouragement, the Jacobites returned to Leith, where they fortified the old fort and took supplies from ships in the harbour. On 15 October, Argyle, with 400 infantry (taken from Shannon's and Forfar's battalions), 200 dragoons (taken from Portmore's, Stair's and Carpenter's dragoons), 400 militia and 120 of the Edinburgh Town Guard, marched to Leith. Yet without guns, Argyle could not hope to take the citadel, so retired to Edinburgh, with the intention to rectify this and return on the next day.[51]

The Jacobites left Leith that evening, marching to Seton House, which they reached on 16 October. En route there had been several false alarms, a man was shot and booty was taken. They were pursued by the Earl of Rothes with 300 gentlemen volunteers and 200 dragoons under Lord Torpichen. However, as with Argyle before Leith, they found it too strong a place, with a strong, high wall, to take without artillery, which as with Argyle, they did not possess (artillery tended to slow down faster moving troops, such as cavalry). This emboldened the Jacobites and some skirmishing ensued, without any casualties. On 18 October, a boat brought two emissaries from Forster, letting them know of the Northumbrian and Lowland Jacobites having risen. Therefore, they marched out on 19 October, reaching Longformachus, 17 miles away. On 20 October they were at Duns and two days later marched to Kelso.[52]

We now come to the Lowland Jacobites. On 26 August Mar had gathered a number of Scottish lords and gentlemen together at Braemar. They apparently included the Earl of Nithsdale, Viscount Kenmure, the Earl of Carnwath and others.[53] He prevailed upon them to gather their followers and be prepared to rise in favour of King James.

According to Patten, Kenmure was 'the only Noblemen in that part of Scotland capable of commanding forces on that Account'. Although initially

William Gordon, 6th Viscount Kenmure. By Robert Grave after unknown artist. Line engraving, published 1819. (NPG D27643. Courtesy of the National Portrait Gallery)

---

50 Scott, *Memoirs*, pp.129, 144.
51 Patten, *History*, pp.8–9.
52 Patten, *History*, pp.11–14.
53 Rae, *History*, pp.188–189.

reluctant, he was apparently persuaded by fellow Jacobites to do so. Kenmure, along with Winton, Carnwath and Nithsdale, were among those Scottish notables who had been ordered to turn themselves in at Edinburgh on the grounds that they were suspected Jacobites, but as with the majority, did not do so, and this attempt to take them may have pushed some towards open insurrection.[54] Rae wrote that Kenmure had a commission from Mar as general and that the plan was to rise at the same time as the Northumbrians. Different parties of Lowland Jacobites gathered at places known to be loyal to the cause, 'moving secretly from Place to place, in order to put Matters in a Readiness for the speedy Execution of their traiterous Designs'.[55]

The Lowland nobility and their followers met at Moffat in Allendale on 12 October, just a few days after the Northumbrians first began to gather. It may have been here that they first unfurled the Jacobite banner that they possessed. It was allegedly made by Lady Kenmure and 'was very handsome'. On one side it was blue, with the Scottish arms in gold, and on the reverse was depicted a thistle, under which were the words 'No Union' and then 'Nemo me impune lacessit'. There were also pendants of ribbon and on these were written 'For our wronged King and Oppressed Country' and on the other 'For our Lives and Liberties'.[56] Their first success was to seize 17 muskets intended for the Lowland loyalists, at John Henderson of Bradeholme's house near Lochmaben.[57]

On 13 October they marched south towards Dumfries. They had hoped to surprise the town, but the Marquis of Annandale, the lord lieutenant, whom they had followed on the previous day, had entered the town first and had organised a makeshift defence there. This was enough to deter Kenmure. As an anonymous follower of his later wrote, he had 'not the courage to attaque the town', where as another account stated that the town, 'from which we might have armed battalions with arms and ammunition'. Kenmure's decision was clearly controversial among his band, for Patten then stated 'many Disputes happened thereupon'.[58]

Apparently the Jacobites were not initially aware of how matters stood at Dumfries and so they rode straight there from Moffat. At two in the afternoon they were a mile and a half away, 'not doubting but in a short time they should be Masters of it'. However, James Robson, whose son was with the Jacobites, told them that the 'Town was full of People well arm'd, who were then in Readiness to give them a Warm Reception'. The Jacobites were 153 men strong and had to decide whether to attack or to wait for a better opportunity. Kenmure was reported as declaring 'He doubted not but there were as brave Gentlemen there as himself, and therefore, he would not go to Dumfries that day'.[59]

---

54 Patten, *History*, p.26.
55 Rae, *History*, p.246.
56 Patten, *History*, pp.26–27.
57 Rae, *History*, p.250.
58 TNA: SP54/9/107, Jacobite prisoner's experiences in the rebellion; BC: 45/12/77, account of the Jacobite southern army to Preston; Patten, *History*, p.27.
59 Rae, *History*. p. 252.

As soon as the Jacobites had been spotted, Annandale, with the agreement of the magistrates of Dumfries, caused barricades and entrenchments to be put in place to block up the main roads into the town. The men were readied to defend them. Some were even eager to march out to attack the Jacobites in the open, but their leaders blocked such a move.[60]

According to Rae, their intention to take Dumfries had been leaked a few days prior to this attempt. An 'honest Countryman' of Lockerbridge Hill, had informed John Gilchrist, one of the bailies of Dumfries of it, apparently planning to do so at the time of the Sunday service. On 8 October, Gilchrist had informed the town's provost and others. As early as 23 July, the town had already made steps to defend themselves against the Jacobites, forming seven companies of militia, led by the provost as colonel and 'carefully trained up in Military Exercises'.[61]

Initially the town merely doubled its guards, but on 10 October, there came further news of the Lowland Jacobites' designs and were offered the help of other loyalist Lowlanders. This was initially refused, but on the next day there came a letter from Adam Cockburn, written on 8 October, 'Having good Information that there is a Design, framed of rising in Rebellion in the Southern parts against His Majesty and the Government, I send you this Express to advise you thereof, that you may be upon your Guard'.[62]

This removed all doubt that Dumfries was in potential danger. The provost called a town meeting and they resolved to send for other loyalists from Kirkcudbright to help in the town's defence. Another 50 men from this place thus arrived at Dumfries that night. By the 12 October the town was bristling with militia and volunteers.[63] John Macky later noted 'This town hath been Famous for being firmly zealous towards the Protestant Interest ever since the Reformation and that firmness contributed very much towards the Lords Nithsdale, Carnwath and Kenmure's throwing themselves away at Preston in England: If they could have been Masters of Dumfries, they had played a securer Game'.[64]

Instead of an assault, the Jacobites stopped at Lochmaben, where on the 14 October they unveiled the Jacobite banner and proclaimed James as King. James Dalzell was appointed as the standard bearer. Later that day they were further south, at Ecclefechan. On their march there they reached a common and then divided the command, which was nearly 200 men (180 according to Rae), having been joined by Sir Patrick Maxwell of Springfield and 14 men, into two squadrons. Under Kenmure as colonel of the regiment, the Earls of Winton and Carnwath were made commander of each squadron. William Calderwood was appointed as quartermaster.[65]

On the 15 October they were at Langholm and then went further north eastwards to Hawick. Their numbers increased along the march. At Hawick,

---

60 Rae, *History*, p.254.
61 Rae, *History*, pp.182–183, 246–247.
62 Rae, *History*, p.247.
63 Rae, *History*, p.250.
64 John Macky, *A Journey through Scotland* (London: J. Pemberton, 1728), pp.9–10.
65 Patten, *History*, p.27; Rae, *History*, p.254.

on 16 October, they were alarmed and began to argue over what to do, whether to press on or to return. A march to the defenceless Teviotdale was suggested. The latter was decided on, and when they were two miles from Hawick a messenger arrived, Captain Robert Douglas. He was from Forster, with an invitation to meet him at Rothbury. So that night they marched to Jedburgh, where they heard that Mackintosh's force had crossed the Forth. They were concerned to hear that Argyle was planning to attack Mackintosh 'which put them in a mighty Pain how the Consequence would prove'. They were clearly suffering from apprehensions of being attacked, for on the way to Jedburgh the advance guard had been alarmed by a shout that Portmore's regiment of dragoons [who were in Stirling], had fallen on them 'and had cut the Quarter master and those with him into pieces'. Those around Kenmure told him this was impossible because Calderwood 'being better used to Military Affairs' would never have been caught napping, so they continued into Jedburgh.[66]

Next day they marched southwards into Rothbury, arriving on 18 October. It had been a difficult day's marching, 'being very mountainous, long, tedious and marshy', 'such a march as few People are acquainted with'. Once at Rothbury, Mr Burnett of Carlips was sent to Hexham to let Forster know of their proximity and to ask him whether he wanted them to ride towards Hexham or would Forster go to Rothbury. Forster replied that the latter was preferable. The two forces joined at Rothbury on the evening of 19 October, Forster being spurred on by fears that his force might be attacked by Carpenter.[67]

They then marched to Wooler on the next day and there rested on Friday 21 October. It was here that they were met by a small reinforcement of men. These were a number of keelsmen from Newcastle, accompanied by the Rev. Robert Patten and were 'kindly entertained by the Chiefs'. It was also here that one Errington brought news of Mackintosh's march south to join them and were last at Dunse. This led the army to march to Kelso.[68]

Meanwhile, turning to their opponents, Carpenter had arrived in Newcastle on 18 October after a three day ride north from London. There he found Hotham's battalion of infantry. It was perhaps nearly 400 men strong, for a newspaper referred to it as having '200 [men] … and 3 or 4 companies more'.[69] They were also less than wholly equipped, lacking uniforms and bayonets; Carpenter writing 'the men seem to be good but are not yet cloathed having only muskets and cartouche boxes'.[70] The remaining companies had marched from York and on 14 October, Pulteney wrote to their colonel, 'to continue with your regiment of Foot at Newcastle until further orders'.[71]

It is probable that five of the six squadrons of Cobham's dragoons arrived in the next few days. However, Molesworth's and Churchill's were slower in

---

66 Patten, *History*, pp.27–28.
67 Patten, *History*, p.28.
68 Patten, *History*, pp.28–29
69 *Daily Courant*, 4361, 16 October 1715.
70 TNA: SP54/9, 63a, Carpenter–? 21 October 1715.
71 TNA: WO4/17, p.233, Pulteney–Hotham, 14 October 1715.

arriving. By 20 October the former were at Boroughbridge, where they made a good impression on some of the populace, with a newspaper reporting that the men were 'so well cloathed, mounted and equipt, that it looked more like an old regiment, than one of the new levies'.[72] Yet Pulteney seemed less concerned than he might have done, about their progress, telling their colonel, that the King was 'extreamly well pleased in yo[ur] making such despatch in the march of ye regiment to Newcastle … your zeal … by having yo[ur] regiment in so forward a condition'.[73] Stanhope also seemed confident, writing on 20 October, 'Our rebels in Northumberland are rather decreased than otherwise, and are not 400 men, tho they have been up a fortnight. Carpenter with three regiments of dragoons will be up with them in two or three days at furtherest'.[74]

Local Whigs wanted action as soon as possible. Liddell wrote on 15 October that this was so because 'while they lye undisturbed in the open country, itt gives incourgaem [ent] to people to join them daily and is a precedent for other countreys to rise in hopes off like success'.[75] Carpenter wrote on 21 October to tell his superiors, 'I have constant spyes out'. He was certainly well aware that the Jacobites had moved from Northumberland, 'The rebells being marched to Scotland, so I am impatient to follow them … Had the troops of the Royal Regiment [Cobham's] been here two days sooner they might have confounded the Rebells of Hexam'.[76] Carpenter had considered marching to Stirling to join Argyle, but had to defer this.

Johnson was aware on 23 October that the Jacobites had left Wooler, crossed the Tweed at Coldstream and had met their Scottish allies. There, 'I am sorry to acquaint you', they were 'as strong as 1500'. He believed that their aim was to 'press the Duke of Argyle's camp on this side, whilst Lord Mar does the Like on the other'. Carpenter planned to march with his infantry and two regiments of dragoons on 24 October and his other regiment, not then arrived, would follow (expected in Newcastle on 26 October). They would reinforce Argyle's camp at Stirling. Johnson may have been a little uneasy at the prospect of the troops leaving as he wrote 'so that at the present we shall have the Guard of this Town to ourselves'. The soldiers' uniforms and bayonets had not arrived yet, and though a ship was thought to be at Tynemouth, when Johnson sent two keel boats to gather in the supplies, the ship had not arrived, 'so they'll be obliged to march without them'.[77]

Meanwhile the Jacobite forces were meeting at the border town of Kelso, described thus by Daniel Defoe:

> … a handsome market town upon the bank of the Tweed. Here is a very ancient church, being built in the place of an old monastery of friars, the ruins of which

---

72 *The Flying Post*, 3716, 27–29, October 1715.
73 TNA: WO4/17, p.242, Pulteney–Molesworth, 20 October 1715.
74 TNA: SP78/160, f.138v, Secretaries of State, State Papers Foreign, France, 1715, Stanhope–? 20 October 1715.
75 Ellis, 'Liddell–Cotesworth Letters', p.186.
76 TNA: SP54/9, p.63a, Carpenter –?, 21 October 1715.
77 Cowper, *Diary*, pp.189–190.

are yet to be seen. Kelso, as it stands on the Tweed, and so near the English border, is a considerable thorough-fare to England, one of the great roads from Edinburgh to Newcastle lying through this town, and a nearer way by far than the road through Berwick.[78]

On the march there, several horses and one Mr Selby were taken. Before entering the town they drew up on a moor outside it. The men formed into troops, each being over officered in order to please all the gentlemen there who deemed they should be such. Whilst organising themselves, some townsmen arrived with useful news. Sir William Bennett of Grubbet had been in Kelso, organising a defence of the place with militia and other civilians. Streets had been barricaded. The situation was similar to that at Dumfries, but because now the Jacobites were far more numerous, Bennett, taking only his servants, had decamped on the night of 21 October. Therefore the town could now be entered without opposition. Though the river Tweed was deep and rapid, it was crossed without difficulty.[79]

On what was probably the evening of 22 October the Jacobites in Kelso were joined by Mackintosh's force, marching into the north side of the town, 'their Bag-pipes playing, led by old Mackintosh; but they made a very indifferent Figure; for the rain and their Marches had extremely fatigued them, tho' their old Brigadier, who march'd at the Head of them appear'd very well'. The next day was Sunday, so Kenmure, who was the army's leader, ordered Patten to preach at the Great Kirk, and not at the episcopal meeting house. Kenmure also ordered all the army to attend the service. The place of worship was probably chosen because the building was so large, albeit in ruins, and the episcopal church may have been shunned, not just because of its size but also because it may have caused religious disquiet and that had to be avoided at all costs. Catholics as well as Protestants attended together. In the afternoon, there was a sermon by a Scottish preacher, William Irwine, who apparently preached to an earlier Jacobite army, prior to their costly triumph at Killiecrankie (27 July 1689).[80]

Buxton read the prayers and Patten gave the sermon, preaching on Deuteronomy XXI, 1, 'The Right of the First Born is his', which was of clear relevance as the force was fighting for a man who claimed the throne by hereditary right. Patten claimed that the services were very successful, full of exhortations to fight for what was right and the man who was God's anointed.[81]

There were further attempts to boost morale on the next day, Monday 24 October. The Scottish infantry were drawn together in the churchyard and then marched to the market place, colours flying, drums beating and bagpipes playing. They formed a circle, with the lords and gentlemen standing centrally. The inner circle was formed by the gentlemen volunteers from the Lowlands. Silence was followed by a trumpet being sounded and James was proclaimed by Seaton Barnes, claiming to himself the title of the

---

78 Pat Rogers (ed.), *Daniel Defoe: Tour of the Whole Island* (Harmondsworth: Penguin, 1971), p.620.
79 Patten, *History*, p.30.
80 Patten, *History*, pp.30–31.
81 Patten, *History*, pp.30–31.

Earl of Dunfermline. He began as follows: 'Whereas by the Decease of the late King James the VIIth, the Imperial Crowns of these Realms did lineally descend to his lawful Heir and Son our Sovereign James the VIIIth: We the Lords, &c. do declare him our lawful King over Scotland, England, &c.'

Next was read the manifesto written by Mar, which stressed James' right to the thrones and their duty to support him in that claim. He talked about the iniquity of the Act of Union, 'the late unhappy Union, which has brought about by the mistaken Notions of some [including, ironically enough, Mar himself], and the ruinous and selfish Designs of others, has prov'd so far from lessening and healing the Differences betwixt His Majesty's Subjects of Scotland and England, that it has widened and increased them'. George I and his government were attacked and soldiers in the British army were encouraged to desert. It was a popular harangue and when it was over, 'the People with loud acclamations shouted, No Union! No Malt, NO Salt TAX!'[82]

Newspaper reporting, naturally, gave a hostile view of the Jacobite army. One referred to them 'having plundered several gentlemen's seats and committed horrible outrages'. As noted this was propaganda. More accurate was the opinion that they 'appear to be extremely dispirited and their number daily lessening by desertion'.[83] There was good reason to be unenthusiastic: they had not gained possession of Newcastle and there had been no help from overseas.

The army remained at Kelso until Thursday 27 October. They had collected the public tax revenues (£255 4s, from Alexander Potts, Town clerk, 'for the use of His Majesty King James the Eighth' and he covered himself by ensuring he had a receipt for such money) and then searched for arms; procedures they would adopt at each town they subsequently arrived at. The search was largely unsuccessful, but they did find 'some small Pieces of Cannon of different size and shape, which formerly belonged to Hume castle' and had been used in former wars with the English in the sixteenth century. Some broad swords were found hidden in the church and some small quantity of gunpowder was located, too. However, when a Jacobite, was cleaning his musket, the gun fired and accidentally injured three children nearby.[84]

Some of the cavalry left the town to go to the seat of the Duke of Roxburgh, which was nearby. They brought some hay back with them. There were also two messengers from Mar, one being Dr Arthur, who had played a part in an abortive coup de main against Edinburgh castle in the previous month, and one Mr Cunningham of Barnes. They brought intelligence (not revealed in Patten's *History*) before returning again.[85] According to Patten, the army was 'more in Number at this time, and better armed Men that at any time after'.

They were as follows:

---

82 Patten, *History*, pp.32–37.
83 *London Gazette*, 5376, 25–29 October 1715.
84 National Records of Scotland (NRS): GD1/811/9, Miscellaneous Jacobitism, Kelso receipts, October 1715; Patten, *History*, pp.37--8.
85 Patten, *History*, p.38.

Table 1. Kenmure's Lowland Cavalry

Name	Commander	Remarks
First Troop	Basil Hamilton	Nominal commander: Kenmure
Second Troop: Merse Troop	Hon. James Hume	
Third Troop	Earl of Winton	
Fourth Troop	James Dalziel	Nominal commander: Carnwath
Fifth Troop	Captain Lockhart	Composed of Carnwath's servants and paid for by Mr Auxton, an Edinburgh merchant

Patten wrote, 'These Troops were well mann'd, and indifferently arm'd: but many of the horses small, and in mean Condition'.[86]

The second contingent were the men who had crossed the Forth:

There were also Gentlemen Volunteers led by Captain Skeen MacLean, with Lieutenant David Stewart and ensign John Dunbar.[87]

Table 2. Scottish Infantry

Colonel	Commander/2nd in Command	Remarks
Earl of Strathmore (absentee)	Captain William Miller	4 companies
Earl of Mar (absentee)	Major John Forbes	4 companies
Logie Drummond (absentee)	Uncertain	3 companies
Lord Nairn	Lt. Col. Stuart	8 companies
Lord Charles Murray	Master of Nairn	8 companies
Colonel John Mackintosh	Lt. Col. Colonel Ferguson	13 companies of 50 men each

Then there were the English, 'not altogether so well regulated, nor so well armed as the Scots'.

Table 3. English Cavalry

Name	Commander	Subordinate Officer
Derwentwater's Troop	Charles Radcliffe	Captain John Shaftoe
Widdrington's Troop	Thomas Errington	
John Hunter's Troop	John Hunter	
Robert Douglas		
Nicholas Wogan		

---

86 Patten, *History*, pp.39–42.
87 Patten, *History*, pp.42–47.

There were also a number of gentlemen volunteers who were not formed into any troop. The infantry companies formed at Hexham and Morpeth are not mentioned. Patten claimed that there were 1,400 men in all, but this figure is too low and may only refer to Mackintosh's force.[88] John Sibbitt, Mayor of Berwick, put their numbers at 600 Lowland Scots and English horsemen and 1,400 Scots infantry, which would seem more accurate.[89] Cockburn's estimate of 29 October was similar, being 6–700 horse and 1,300 foot.[90] Another government source puts them at 'in all upwards of Two Thousand Men', with 200 Lowland cavalry and 400 Englishmen.[91] Yet another states there were 2,300 in total, including 1,600 Scottish infantry and 300 Lowland Horse.[92] Carpenter put the number of his enemies at 2,000.[93]

Security at Kelso was slack. When Captain Straiton and seven other well armed Lowlanders from Edinburgh rode into the town centre on 23 October, no one challenged them and they believed they could just as easily have left. One later wrote 'This made all of us, especially Straiton, very much concern'd'. If they could enter the Jacobite camp with ease, then so could enemy spies.[94]

There was great concern within Berwick about the Jacobite army's intentions. One Marchmont wrote on 22 October, 'perhaps they may think of attacking this place, which is in no strong condition'. There were only four companies of infantry and the armed townsmen at Berwick. Marchmont continued, that whilst the latter enjoyed high morale, they were untrained. Efforts were being frantically made to strengthen the town's defences, which dated back to the late sixteenth century, with the ramparts being palisaded and repaired. The difficulty was the length of the walls (about a mile long) 'which is of such extent that both the Garrison soldiers and the inhabitants of the Town would be far too few to guard, if assaulted'.[95]

The future itinerary of the Jacobite army was uncertain as far as onlookers were concerned. Sibbitt had been sending spies out constantly in October for information about the Jacobites. However, it was not always certain, noting on 20 October, 'wch [which] way they design to march I cannot tell'.[96] On the following day, one Hodham, writing from Berwick, claimed 'their design is sd [said] to be to march by the western borders of Scotland and getting into the country abt [about] Glasgow' in order to concert with Mar against Argyle. Or they might make an attempt on Berwick.[97] Loyalists noted that the nearest allies were at Newcastle, with Hodham noting 'some forces from Newcastle to march this way might doe good service' and Sibbitt had written to Scarborough and Carpenter to 'hasten their march towards Edinburgh if

---

88 Patten, *History*, pp.47–51.
89 TNA: SP54/9, 60, Sibbitt–Stanhope, 20 October 1715.
90 TNA: SP54/9, 93, Cockburn–Pringle, 29 October 1715.
91 LRO: DDX 1788/1, Plan and Account of the Battle of Preston, 1715.
92 Anon., *Annals*, II, pp.92, 117, 126
93 *Political State*, X, p.180.
94 *Weekly Journal*, 10 March 1716.
95 TNA: SP54/9, 76, Marchmont–?, 22 October 1715.
96 TNA: SP54/9, 59, Sibbitt–Stanhope, 20 October 1715.
97 TNA: SP54/9, 67, Hoddam–Lloyd, 21 October 1715.

it is in their power'.⁹⁸ Sibbitt wrote on 23 October that had the JPs arrested the leading Northumbrian Jacobites there would have been no such trouble.⁹⁹

Captain Phillips, an engineer officer, was in charge of Berwick's defences. He advocated the demolition of a number of houses just outside the town wall, presumably because otherwise they would give shelter to any attackers. This was 'absolutely necessary' for the security of the garrison, he attested. The corporation held a meeting on 17 October and agreed that some buildings in Castlegate and the Green 'must indispensably be demolished'.¹⁰⁰ Several of the owners 'readily assented' to such a proposal at this time and eventually buildings to the value of £841 10s were destroyed.¹⁰¹

As to the human defences, as early as 23 September, Laton had applied to Sibbitt to have the assistance of townsmen to guard the walls. The east gate was to be watched for strangers by two men in the day time and at night twelve men were appointed to undertake night watch, to be provided with arms and lanterns, but some men neglected this latter duty and were fined. Precautions were increased on 10 October with news of the Northumberland rising: a meeting on that day of the town's quarter sessions decreed that all male townsmen aged between 16 and 60 should take up arms or be fined. Seven days later, there was a plan to raise 10 companies of militia, of 40 men in each, officered by the corporation's officers and magistrates. They were to stand guard at night time and during part of the day.¹⁰² These defences were never put to the test. However, there does not seem to have been the remotest suggestion that the Jacobites even considered Berwick as a potential target. As with that other fortified town in the north of England, Carlisle, both probably appeared too strong to take with only limited artillery, but at this point even less well defended towns which offered even limited resistance, such as at Dumfries and Newcastle, were enough to deter them. Only where all opposition had fled, as at Kelso, would an incursion be made.

On Thursday 27 October a major decision had to be made by the Jacobites. There came news that Carpenter and his four regiments were at Wooler, 16 miles to the south east, and intended to attack them in Kelso on the following day. Carpenter had, in fact, only left Newcastle with the five troops of Cobham's dragoons and Hotham's battalion on 25 October. Four troops of Molesworth's arrived at Newcastle on the night of the 24 October; the remainder on the following day. Churchill's were expected on 25 October. They followed Carpenter on 26 October.¹⁰³

On the evening of 26 October, the Jacobites learnt this news. Among the army, there was apparently unanimity about fighting Carpenter and '300 wearied Horse and a Regiment of new levied Foot … which might have been done with little or no loss, as they were lying at three different places'. The

---

98 TNA: SP54/9, 67–68, Hoddam–Lloyd, 21 October, Sibbitt–Scarborough, October 1715.
99 TNA: SP54/9, 81, Sibbitt–?, 23 October 1715.
100 Berwick Record Office, BA/G/2/1/16, Berwick upon Tweed Corporation Guild Book, 1697–1716.
101 William Shaw and F.H. Slingsby (eds), *Calendar of Treasury Papers*, 1717 (London: HMSO, 1957), p.20.
102 *The Flying Post*, 3713, 20–22 October 1715.
103 *London Gazette*, 5376, 25–29 October 1715.

Jacobite army was stood to arms at five in the morning of 27 October. Then they waited for four hours.[104]

Meanwhile their commanders discussed what to do. Kenmure called a council of war, 'wherein it was seriously considered what course they should take'. It seems that it was attended by all the nobility present. Winton argued that they should march to the west of Scotland, not to join with Mar immediately nor to march to Edinburgh or Stirling, but 'to go and join the Western Clans, attacking in their way the Town of Dumfries and Glasgow and other Places, and then open a Communication with the Earl of Mar'. According to one Jacobite this could mean their marching to Dalkeith. Patten seems to have agreed with this course of action, writing 'Which Advice, if followed, in all probability would have tended to their great Advantage, the Kings Forces being then so small'.[105]

The English present at the meeting opposed this. Their argument was that they should 'pass the Tweed, and attack the King's Troops, taking the Advantage of the Weakness and Weariness of General Carpenter's men, who were indeed extremely fatigued, and were not above 500 Men in Number, whereof two Regiments of Dragoons were new raised and had never seen any Service.'

Patten agreed with this view, too, 'This also was Soldier-like Advice, and which, if they had agreed to, in all probability they might have worsted them, considering how they were Fatigued, and not half the number the Rebels were'. The difficulty with both these courses of action was the commanders themselves: 'there was a fate attended all their Councils, for they could never agree to any one thing that tended to their Advantage'.[106]

The second opinion was backed up by at least one Scots officer:

> It is certain that old Brigadier Mackintosh gave his opinion for fighting, and sticking his pike in the Ground, told the Northumberland gentlemen he would not stir, by there he would stay for General Carpenter, and fight him, that now he was sure to beat him, but that if they marched into England first with him at their heels, they would be sure to meet with other forces in front, and have Carpenter in their Rear, too, that if they beat Carpenter they should soon be able to fight any other Troops; and if Carpenter had the better, they had come far enough, and should make better shift with their bad Fortune there than in England.[107]

Mackintosh also noted, 'The longer they deferr'd an Engagement, the strongest Opposition they were like to meet with'.[108] Historians writing since have tended to conclude that this was a missed opportunity for the Jacobites, with numerical superiority, to defeat their enemies. The Taylers were of the opinion that in a battle, Carpenter 'would probably have been defeated with

---

104 *Weekly Journal*, 10 March 1716.
105 Patten, *History*, pp.51, 40.
106 Patten, *History*, p.51.
107 Anon., *Annals*, II, p.126.
108 Rae, *History*, p.269n.

ease'.[109] Baynes wrote, 'it would have brought the Jacobites the reputation they needed, followers would have poured in'.[110]

Yet it should be remembered that so far in the campaign in England, no one had been killed. To be the ones who caused the first blood to be shed may have acted as a brake on the Jacobite army, whose leaders were civilians inexperienced in warfare and thus reluctant to initiate violence. Their problem was that they had already lit the fuse that would eventually cause an explosion, if not now, later.

Whig contemporaries drew different conclusions from the Jacobites avoiding action, though these may have been born of complacency and contempt. James Cockburn was surprised that the Jacobites did not make a stand, and believed that this was due to 'how much the rebels are afraid of regular troops'.[111] Hotham wrote 'We have found by experience they will not stand regular troops though not one third of their number'.[112] Yet as will be seen, the Jacobite forces could fight bravely and well.

Neither of the Jacobites' plans were adopted. Instead, but not before 'old Mackintosh was at last over-persuaded, but not till they had had some very high words between them', a compromise was reached. The army marched from Kelso that day, turning south west along the border to Jedburgh, which was but 10 miles away. The decision to withdraw in face of a numerically weaker enemy cannot have failed to depress morale in the ranks. The army took four different routes; one by the Scots infantry, one by the Scottish cavalry and two by the English. The march there was not without incident. A group of men was seen ahead, over the river, so Captain Wogan went to find out who they were. If they were enemies he would fire his pistol, if friends, he would toss up his hat. However, the horsemen galloped towards him and Wogan mistook them for enemies and so fired his gun. There was alarm in the army, but not much disorder as it was soon realised that these men were friends.[113] Some stragglers surrendered to Carpenter on 28 October.[114]

The day's alarms were not yet over. On the arrival of the cavalry in Jedburgh, they heard that Carpenter's army had attacked their infantry, who had not yet arrived in the town. 'This put them into the utmost Consternation'. They mounted up and rode back towards the infantry, to relieve them. When they formed up under the cover of a hill, Patten noted 'I did then behold a great paleness in some Faces, and as much Fire and Resolution in others'. When they reached the rest of the army they found that their fears had been groundless; the alarm being caused by another party of their men having been seen, who had taken a different route. Eventually, all the men arrived safely at their new quarters.[115]

---

109 Taylers, *The Story*, p.81.
110 Baynes, *Jacobite Rising*, p.101.
111 TNA: SP54/9, 99, Cockburn–Pringle, 30 October 1715.
112 BL. Stowe Ms, 748, f.108r, Miscellaneous Original Papers on historical subjects, 1703–1739, Hotham–? 11 November 1715.
113 Patten, *History*, p.52; Anon., *Annals*, II, p.128.
114 *The Postman*, 3–5 November 1715.
115 Patten, *History*, pp.52–53.

Naturally, with the Jacobites lacking an ultimate destination, their enemies were equally in the dark as to their intentions. Cockburn wrote on 29 October, that they might march to Carlisle and Lancashire, or to Glasgow. There was no idea as to which they would pick. Carpenter, he wrote, was designing to follow them close whichever way they went.[116] On the next day he heard that Carpenter was only eight or nine miles behind the Jacobites 'his following them so close even to the fatiguing a little his troops will be of great and good consequences'.[117]

They remained at Jedburgh until 29 October, moving on because they heard that Carpenter was in pursuit and they wished to maintain the distance between them and him. Apparently Forster learnt from his friends in Newcastle that 1,000 armed men waited to join them in Lancashire, somewhat of a reduction from the 20,000 promised earlier that year. The Merse Troop had been sent to keep a watch on Carpenter's forces and to keep the Jacobite leadership informed of his movements. Carpenter's forces had crossed the border and were quartered at Downham, Mendrom, Patison, Town Yetholm, Kirk Yetholm, Monrhattle and Attanburn. The Jacobites were only eight miles from Yetholm, which was the centre of Carpenter's disposition.[118]

This news was brought to a council of war, 'where the Reasonableness of Attacking the Enemy was urged by some wise and brave men, but the Overture was rejected, upon Consideration, that we expected a better opportunity when joined by a greater Force'. They marched off in some confusion.[119] An anonymous Lowlander saw this as another missed opportunity, claiming as at Kelso, Carpenter's 'horses and men were fatigued and harassed that it would have ended … well for us'.[120]

The English faction on the council then gained precedence 'in an ill hour' and decided to cross the mountains and go to England. Captain Hunter, who knew the country well, was sent with his troops to enter North Tynedale and there secure quarters for the rest of the army. On hearing what was afoot, the Highlanders mutinied. Despite 'many Persuasions', they refused to march. It was then decided to countermand the orders given to Hunter, though oatmeal was provided for the men by the householders as ordered by the magistrates. Mr Ainsley of Blackhill and some others joined them at this stage.[121]

The army then marched south west, yet again, 10 miles to Hawick, 'a small poor Market Town'. Derwentwater, Widdrington and Forster and their relations, lodged in a house belonging to the Duchess of Buccleugh. However, the Scottish infantry, before they arrived at the town, still believed that they were destined for England. They separated themselves from the rest of the army and marched to the top of some rising ground. They rested on their

---

116 TNA: SP54/9, 93, Cockburn–Pringle, 29 October 1715.
117 TNA: SP54/9, 98, Cockburn–Townshend, 30 October 1715.
118 Anon., *A Letter*, p.3; *Weekly Journal*, 10 March 1716.
119 Anon., *A Letter*, p.3.
120 TNA: SP54/9, 107, Jacobite prisoner's experiences in the rebellion.
121 Patten, *History*, p.53.

arms and 'declared that they would fight if they would lead them on to the Enemy, but they would not go into England'.[122]

Patten believed that this action was due to Winton's advice, that they should march to the west of Scotland and join the clans there, either by crossing the Forth above Stirling or sending word to Mar that they would attack Argyle's forces at Stirling whilst he attacked from the north. The Scottish infantry would allow no one to speak to them except Winton. He had 'tutored them on this project; assuring them, that if they went for England, they would be cut in pieces, or taken and sold for slaves'. Possibly he was recalling the precedents of Preston and Worcester in 1648 and 1651 when Scottish armies had invaded England with unfortunate results. After two hours they were persuaded to continue on their march, but they maintained that they would keep together whilst in Scotland but on any indication that they would march to England, they would turn back.[123]

Once they arrived at Hawick, the Scottish infantry learnt that they would be doing guard duty that night. They saw a party of horsemen arriving, and took alarm that they were the enemy and so rushed to take up arms. The moon provided enough light for the Scottish infantry to draw up in battle order, which they did very well, but in the end this turned out to be another false alarm. Patten thought that this alarm had been given deliberately in order to test the Scottish infantry to see how they would behave when faced with cavalry and in this they passed with flying colours.[124]

The dissension among the Jacobites was known to their enemies. Cockburn wrote on the 30 October that the English were 'positive they should march into England, the Scottish infantry refused to goe saying they would be all knockt on the head'. He also recorded in another letter on that day, 'The rebels decamped in great confusion for Jedburgh, the Horse were for marching into England, but the Scottish infantry would not, so they were like to fall out among themselves'. He concluded, 'I am surprised they do not offer to make a stand against General carpenter, for tho' his dragoons are better than the rebels' horse, yet if the Highland men will stand it, their foot are far more supernumary to his, but this still shows how much the rebels are afraid of regular troops'.[125]

Next day, being the 30 October and a Sunday, Forster asked Buxton and Patten, as the two Anglican clergymen present, to provide him with Holy Communion in his chambers, which they did. He wanted all Protestants in the army to have the same benefit when it was possible to do so. That morning they marched as many as 28 miles to the south west to Langholm, 'another small market town'. That night a strong party of horsemen was sent to Eccelfechan, with orders from there to blockade Dumfries, so clearly Winton's wishes had been taken on board. This would be a prelude to the town being taken. [126]

---

122 Patten, *History*, p.53.
123 Patten, *History*, pp.53–54.
124 Patten, *History*, p.54.
125 TNA: SP54/9, 98–99, Cockburn-Townshend, 30 October 1715, Cockburn-Pringle, 30 October 1715.
126 Patten, *History*, pp.54–55.

Patten enlarged as to why the possession of Dumfries would be of great use for the Jacobites. It was a rich trading town, well suited by being on a navigable river on the Irish Sea, with good access to English and Scottish markets. There should be no problem in taking it, as it was without any regular troops or fortifications, and had only trained bands and armed townsmen to defend it. Arms, money and ammunition could be taken from there in great bulk. Possession of the town would allow support from the Highlands of Scotland, or from abroad, to rendezvous with them. He concluded, 'nothing could be a greater Token of a compleat Infatuation, that Heaven confounded all their Devices, and that their Destruction was to be of their own working, than their omitting such an Opportunity of fixing themselves past the Possibility of being attacked'.[127] A contemporary history noted 'Dumfries could not have withstood them'.[128]

These arguments were in vain because the English faction gained predominance, having been met by 'some Persons of Quality' upon a moor two miles from Langholm. They were 'positive for an Attempt on their own Country'. They expected strong support in Lancashire with allies 'assuring them that there would be a general Insurrection upon their appearing; that 20,000 Men would immediately join them'. Patten was not certain that these letters with these promises ever existed, but that 'they affirm'd it to the army, and urged the Advantages of a Speedy March into England with such vehemence that they turn'd the scale'. An anonymous Lowlander made the following remark in retrospect, 'we were deluded with lies and fair promises'. The party sent to blockade Dumfries was recalled, therefore and ordered to ride to meet the main body at Langton in Cumberland.[129]

Meanwhile, the remainder of the Jacobite cavalry was waiting for their advance guard, firstly waiting in Langholm and then marched into Ecclefechan and waited there, ready to join the advance guard towards Dumfries. However:

> … [at] about 2 in the Morning, a surprise from the General came to us, bearing that Carpenter join'd by a great many Gentry and Militia, was following us close at our heels. This, with a Story that made up of a great Opposition we were to meet with at Dumfries, so frightened us, that we must give over our Design on that place. We lay all Night there, and of our Horses and many of ourselves without Doors for want of accommodation. In the Morning we were called back to join our Foot, and the rest of the Horse who lay at Langholm last Night. When we came to the top of a muir, about three miles back, we having seen off the Advance Guard in the Morning till either they should return with the rest of the Army, or bring us word what to do; After we had waited about 3 hours, fresh News came, That the Enemy was still approaching, and Orders for us to march about another Way, and to follow the General, who was gone with the rest of the Army towards the Border.[130]

---

127 Patten, *History*, p.55.
128 Anon., *Annals*, II, p.134.
129 Patten, *History*, p.56; TNA: SP54/9, 107, Jacobite prisoner's experiences in the rebellion.
130 *Weekly Journal*, 10 March 1716.

However, before an ultimate decision was taken, the Merse trooper was told to consult with Mackintosh and Winton and upon their answer the army's fate would rest. Mackintosh was found in the middle of the river Esk and on being asked, he made the following answer, 'Why the Devil not into England, where there is had Meat, Men and Money; and that those who were deserting us, were but the Rascality of his men'. Winton was next to be asked. He was pensive at first, and then silent. When he finally spoke, he said, 'It shall never be said in History to after generations that the Earl of Winton broke off from, or deserted King James's Interest, and his Country's Good'. Then taking hold of his ears he continued, 'You, or any Man, shall have Liberty to cut these out of my Head, if we do not all repent it'.[131]

As might have been expected from their behaviour on the road to Hawick, the Scottish infantry were extremely unimpressed with this plan to leave Scotland. They may have been influenced by Winton as before, but what is certain is that they halted again and would not march on. Money and promises were made to them by the army's leaders, but many were not listening. Several hundred (Patten gave 500 as the number, Rae giving 400 and a Jacobite 300) went off in a number of different groups, 'chusing rather, as they said, to surrender themselves Prisoners, than to go forward to certain Destruction'. Nothing could be said or done to prevail on them to desist, so they went their way over the mountains northwards. Winton and most of his troop also left the army. This latter group later returned to the main body, but were still far from satisfied and Winton was never again included in council meetings. He was also never again provided with lodgings suitable for a nobleman and spent his leisure times talking to any he could find about his youthful days as a blacksmith's apprentice. Meanwhile, the cannon taken from Kelso were abandoned at Langholm, having been nailed up.[132]

Those leaving, perhaps 400 men, crossed the moors by Lockerbie, aiming for the Forth. Ten were captured at Biery hill and taken by countrymen to Dumfries. The remainder kept together and passed Moffat. Lacking food for such a number, they divided at Errrikstane, some travelling to Douglas via Crawford Moor and others to Lamington. Seen by loyalist countrymen, volunteers were gathered together and about 300 were eventually rounded up, in large and small bodies in numerous places, and were taken in captivity to Glasgow.[133] Loyalists were pleased with such news. Annandale wrote 'we may expect a good account of them in a verie little time'.[134]

This was not an auspicious start to the next stage of the Jacobite campaign, to lose nearly half of their infantry. On the other hand, there were no immediate foes in their path. Brigadier Thomas Stanwix, Lieutenant Governor of Carlisle castle, had sent a scouting party to Longtown on the day before the Jacobites arrived there, to learn of the Jacobite numbers and whereabouts. Finding they were marching towards the place, they retreated to Carlisle, taking one Graham of Inchbrachy as a prisoner. Unlike the case

---

131 Anon., *A Letter*, p.4.
132 Patten, *History*, pp.56–57.
133 Rae, *History*, pp.278–279.
134 TNA: SP54/10, 13, Annandale–Pringle, 3 November 1715.

THE CAMPAIGN BEGINS, 6–31 OCTOBER 1715

in 1745, there seems to have been no thought among the Jacobites of taking the place, though it was as weakly defended as it was in 1745.[135] There had been some reinforcements to the border town and castle, namely, the Horse Militia of the counties of Lancashire and Westmorland.[136]

However, the Jacobite march had been impressive, covering 100 miles in five days. Furthermore, they had marched 'the worst ways and weather that ever Men marched in'. Cavalrymen had carried infantrymen and their arms. Of those on foot, it was remarked 'with incredible celerity that the Foot march'd'. As to their pursuers, Molesworth's regiment was 'neither fit for so hard a march, or for service, as older Troops would have been'.[137]

Meanwhile, had they but known it, the government's forces were coming together. This was not from Carpenter, who had to temporarily call off the chase. Carpenter had reached Alnwick on 30 October and was at Jedburgh on 2 November. He had been joined by one Mr Cranstoun and 120 mounted loyalists. Carpenter stated that if Dumfries was attacked, and could stand for six hours, he would relieve it and attack the Jacobites in the rear and told a representative from Dumfries of this. Lowland loyalists also provided horses to give Carpenter's infantry greater mobility. However, it had been a fruitless experience, as Patten later wrote, 'The brave general, after his long, troublesome, and dismal marches after the Rebels, but more the Horses, for want of good Forage, returned to Newcastle'.[138] However, it was also claimed that he returned to Newcastle because 'The Lieutenant General, discovering by Intercepted Letters, that they fully designed to get possession of Newcastle', he marched back to the town.[139]

Rather, the danger to the Jacobites came from an entirely different quarter. Throughout October there had been a build up of forces in the Midlands and Cheshire. In September the decision had been taken to summon a number of regiments and battalions from Ireland to reinforce the army in England and Scotland. Of these, the battalions of Preston, Vane and Sabine and Pitt's Horse were despatched to Chester on about 10 October.[140]

Henry Prescott (1649–1719), deputy registrar of Chester, found one of the officers to be a 'vain Furioso'. The man, an Irish captain, told Prescott that 'If hee could meet with the Pretender hee would present his head in a bag to the king & parliament and make 'em easy'.[141]

On 29 October there came a letter to Major General Charles Wills (1666–1741), reading as follows:

> Whereas we judge it for our service in this juncture that the following regiments should be under your command, vizt., The Regiment of Horse of Pitt, the Regiments of Foot of Sabine, Preston and Fane, the Regiments of Dragoons of

---

135 Patten, *History*, pp.57–58.
136 Rae, *History*, p.279.
137 Anon., *Annals*, II, pp.129, 127.
138 Patten, *History*, p.89; Rae, *History*, p.273.
139 LRO: DDX 1788/1, Plan.
140 Rae, *History*, p.297.
141 John Addy and Peter McNiven (eds), 'The Diary of Henry Prescott, LLB, Deputy Registrar of Chester', II, *Record Society of Lancashire and Cheshire*, 132 (1994), p.466.

> Wynn, Munden, Honywood, Newton and Dormer, you are without loss of time, to repair to Chester, which you are to make your headquarters.
>
> As soon as you arrive there, you are with the utmost application, to inform yourself of the state of those Parts, and if you have intelligence of any insurrection, you are to march with these our forces, and attack and suppress the rebels wherever you find them.[142]

The Jacobites had fled one foe, but had another, numerically stronger, awaiting them as they pressed south, not that they were aware of this. However, as they were about to march into Cumberland and Wills' men were gathering in Chester, there would be no immediate confrontation. Yet it was not to be delayed for long as the Jacobites unknowingly went south towards their enemy.

To date the campaign had been one of shadow boxing and marked by the avoidance of conflict, usually on the part of the Jacobites, even where they had enjoyed a superiority of numbers. Difficult terrain and slower moving troops meant that the Jacobites could evade their enemies. Yet campaigns are not won by avoiding confrontation. Part of this Jacobite 'strategy' by default was due to indecision at the top level, where only compromises were possible. This state of affairs could not last forever. Neither side had done terribly well. The Jacobite forces had coalesced but had failed in any concrete objective; the British army had helped secure Newcastle but had not yet brought the Jacobites to battle. In retrospect, the Jacobites had missed their two chances of success; to attack Carpenter's weaker forces and even less forgivable, not to have either taken Dumfries or marched north to join Mar or towards Glasgow. But this would have meant missing England with its promises of mass support.

---

142 TNA: SP54/10/26, 69, George I–Wills, 29 October 1715.

3

Descent to Preston, 1–11 November 1715

It was on Tuesday 1 November that the Jacobite army, now much numerically diminished, arrived in Brampton, a small market town seven miles to the east of Carlisle, having marched south east from Longtown. On the same journey two decades ago, Celia Fiennes had written, 'I crossed over a tedious long heath to Brampton, a mile over Lime river'.[1] It was here that Forster opened his commission as general in charge, brought to him by Douglas from Mar. It was also on this day that letters from Mar arrived for Forster (addressed as being in Northumberland) and Kenmure, being transported by sea, arriving at Blyth. Duplicates of these had been intercepted, so were known by their enemies.[2]

The contents of these letters were not helpful to either man. The letter to Kenmure told him that Mar had not heard from him and he hoped he would write to him to give him the news he wanted. Mar was critical of Kenmure's lack of communication with Mackintosh, too, writing 'it was odd your lordship sent no orders or Intelligence to him, when they had reason to expect that party's coming over every day'. He hoped that Mackintosh would be of use to him and that he might meet Forster. He 'knew so little' of what was happening that he had no guidance for Kenmure, 'I must leave to yourself what is fit for you to do, as will most conduce to the Service'. He appointed Kenmure 'Brigadier of Horse' and ended wishing 'Success attend you' and that they would meet in happy circumstances.[3]

Mar told Forster about his march from Perth to Auchterarder, Argyle's counter moves and the latter's reinforcement. He explained why he had marched back to Perth, owing to supply difficulties. He talked about hoping to join Forster once he crossed the Forth. He trusted that all the Jacobite forces would join Forster. He noted that Ormonde and James had not arrived yet, but he hoped they would soon come. Again, he asked for news, 'I beg you will find some Way to let me hear from you … pray send me some News

---
1   Morris, *Journeys*, p.206.
2   Patten, *History*, p.58.
3   Patten, *History*, pp.58–60.

Facing page: The Marches in north-west England.

Papers, that I may know what the world is doing, for we know little of it here'. In fact, these letters tell more about Mar and the Jacobites north of the Forth, who had clearly very little knowledge of what was happening in England.[4] There was, 'so it was said', another letter from Mar to Forster, 'approving of his design of going into England'.[5]

It has been alleged that at Brampton that the Jacobites wished to march to Haltwistle and then on to Newcastle, but learning that Carpenter was countering that move, they did not march further.[6] Therefore the easier alternative was chosen. They expected support on marching into Cumberland, one of the most lightly populated counties in England. One Jacobite later wrote, 'Here we were to have a good many joining, which did not come to much'.[7] Another wrote, 'here we were promised great things and 1000 to joyne us, but all their promises came to nothing'.[8] A Lowlander noted, 'till we came to Lancaster, scarce one man joined us', which is a pardonable exaggeration.[9] The reason why support was expected was that in the 1690s, there had been meetings of the Catholic elite of Cumberland among the Howard, Salkeld, and Warwick families, plotting to restore James II, though these came to nothing, due to lack of opportunity.[10]

In particular, it was thought that Mr Dacre of Abbey Lanercost, who 'had promised to raise 40 men', would have joined them. However, he 'was taken with a Fortunate Fever, which hindered him from his Design'.[11] Other suspected gentlemen had long been arrested and so there was no rush of support to the Jacobite cause. Those taken into custody were Sir Robert Guldeford, Allen Askew Esq., Matthew Cragg of Camerton, Thomas Howard of Corby Castle, John Warwick of Warwick Hall, Henry Curwen of Workington and James Graham of Inchbrachy, originally from Scotland.[12] There may have been others. The suspect elite had been mostly removed from the equation, which meant that support would be limited (only 20 men from the county joined), and doubly so because those who would have led on others were absent. These arrests took place in the middle of October but there were some who protested about such treatment, Lonsdale writing 'I was desired by some of these gentlemen to move the deputy lieutenants that they might have their liberty upon their parole. I told them it was what I could not possibly do: the Northumberland men, who were all their friends, were very near'.[13]

Meanwhile Carpenter had called off the pursuit. He had reached Jedburgh by 1 November and at 10:00 a.m. on the following day heard that the Jacobites

---

4 Patten, *History*, pp.60–63.
5 *Weekly Journal*, 10 March 1716.
6 LRO: DXX 1788/1, Plan.
7 TNA: SP54/9, 107, Jacobite prisoner's experiences in the rebellion.
8 BC: 45/12/77, account of the Jacobite southern army to Preston.
9 *Weekly Journal*, 10 March 1716.
10 Monod, *Jacobitism*, p.309.
11 Patten, *History*, p.64.
12 TNA: PC2/85, pp.364, 395, Council to Carlisle, 17 April 1716, Privy Council Registers, 1714–1716; Patten, *History*, pp.67–68.
13 *HMC Manuscripts of the Earl of Carlisle* (London, HMSO: 1897), p.17.

DESCENT TO PRESTON, 1–11 NOVEMBER 1715

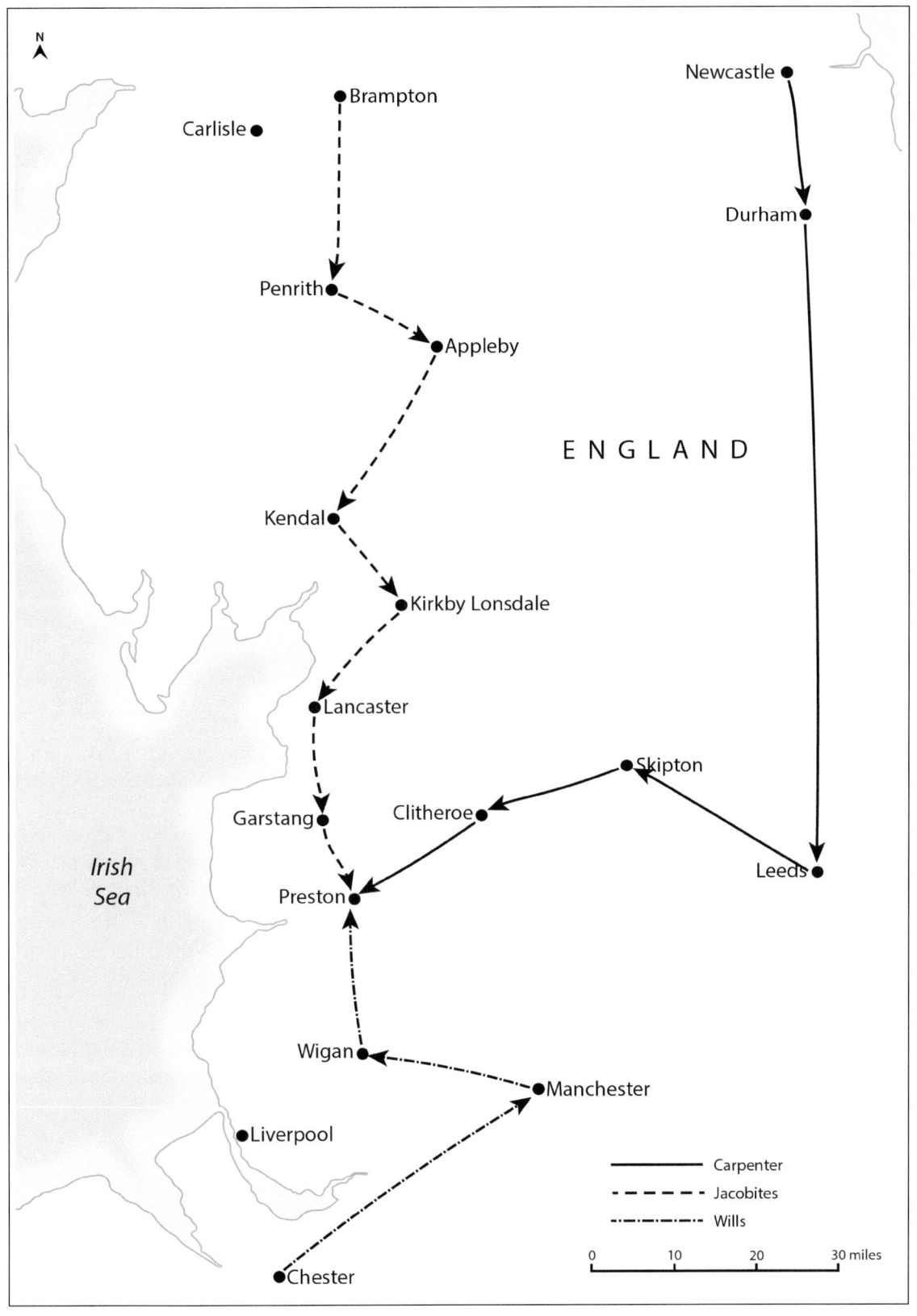

had marched towards Brampton. In turn he marched his troops over the moors and reached Elsdon late that day. On the morning of 4 November he arrived in Newcastle with his cavalry, fearful that the Jacobites might make another threat towards the town from Brampton. The infantry had marched via Wooler and came to Newcastle on 5 November. His plan then was to pursue the Jacobites on 7 November with his cavalry alone, leaving his infantry at Newcastle so he could march all the faster.[14] Unusually there was understanding among loyalist civilians for his difficulties. Liddell wrote on 8 November: '… am sorry Gen[eral] C[arpenter] should have met with a foyle. Had he pursued the same route the bogg trotters took, I am satisfy'd he could never have come up with them, must have ruin'd the young horse and indeed am apt to believe the men would have had much ado to have subsisted'.[15]

Similarly, Argyle wrote on 10 November, that he was 'perfectly satisfied that Mr Carpenter has done all that he could be expected from him by those who know anything of this trade, but he writes me word, that he has reproaches from people who do not, wch I easily conceive who are here complained of by people who are plundered'.[16]

One reason for the pursuit being called off was because of the perceived vulnerability of Newcastle. As Liddell told Cotesworth on 10 November, 'Pray thee honest Will what is the meaning off your militia disbanding att this time off day? Doe you think your selfe safer without such an arm'd force? Or that the danger is over? For my part I think there is as much reason to be on the guard now as ever: at least till we have a better account from Lancashire and that Wills is come up with the rebels. Is your Lieuten[ant] in the miff?'[17] A wild rumour circulating in Paris had it that Mackintosh had attacked Carpenter's troops in the rear, on their way to Newcastle, killing 200 dragoons and taking the baggage including £5,000 in cash.[18]

Meanwhile, the first instance of anything that might be termed an attempt at resistance to the Jacobites' march took place on Wednesday 2 November, and their existence was certainly known about by the Jacobite army, after having marched about 20 miles south west of Brampton. Humphrey Senhouse, the High Sheriff of Cumberland, as with his counterpart in Northumberland, John Johnson, called out the posse of the county, on Penrith Fell. With him was Lonsdale, though the lord lieutenant himself was absent. There was also the bishop of Carlisle (and his daughter) and the archbishop of York, Sir William Dawes (1671–1724). As well as the posse there were also a company of the county militia.[19]

The number of men in the posse is variably estimated by contemporaries. According to Peter Clarke, clerk to Richard Craikenthorpe, a Kendal lawyer, 'By the strictest observation the numbers were twenty five thousand men'.[20] Patten

---

14 *Glasgow Courant*, issue 2, November 1715.
15 Ellis, 'Liddell–Cotesworth Letters', p.196.
16 TNA: SP54/10, 39, Argyle–Townshend, 10 November 1715.
17 Ellis, 'Liddell–Cotesworth Letters', pp.197–198.
18 TNA: SP78/160, f.144r.
19 Henry Paton (ed.), 'Journal of several Occurrences from 2nd November 1715', *Scottish History Society Miscellany*, I (1894), p.513.
20 Paton, 'Journal', p.513.

stated the number to be 14,000.[21] One Jacobite claimed there were 6,000–7,000 militia there.[22] Another Jacobite alleged 20,000.[23] Charles Owen, a Presbyterian minister, put the figure at 8,000.[24] These numbers are probably exaggerated: the strength of the Northumberland posse was about 400 and as said, Cumberland was not a populous county, though the true number is elusive.

The men were ill-prepared; Clarke refers to them as being 'but very few of them had any regular armes'.[25] Patten wrote that they were 'naked and unprepared that Multitude were of all warlike Arms and Stores'.[26] Their role, as Patten noted, was 'to stand and oppose their penetrating further into England'.[27] However, according to one source the bill hook and pitchfork armed posse was only envisaged to be acting in a mopping up role, 'and that we should have nothing to do than to pick up some of their shattered fragments which he would chop them; for such a service we were well enough prepared'.[28]

What is not in doubt is that the posse fled on the approach of the Jacobite army. One Jacobite wrote, 'But in our drawing towards them they fled like sheep'.[29] Clarke wrote that this occurred at 11 in the morning, when news arrived that the Jacobites were six miles to the north of Penrith and coming towards them.[30] According to Patten, 'as soon as a Party, who they sent but for Discovery, had seen some of our Men coming out of a lane by the side of a wood and draw up upon a Common or Moor in Order, and then advance, and that they had carried an account of this to their main body, they broke up their camp in the utmost Confusion, shifting everyone for themselves as well as they could, as is generally ye case of an arm'd, but undisciplined Multitude'.[31] Another account relates how the Jacobites sent three men among the multitude where they heard 'Lord Lonsdale and others of the officers were consulting what to do and heard then determine not to fight'. They returned to the Jacobites and told them of this. At about three in the afternoon, 400 Jacobite cavalry, with trumpets being blown headed their men. Then 300 Scottish infantry followed, bagpipers making music, followed by another 400 cavalry and finally with another 300 Scottish infantry as before.[32] Apparently one man was wounded in the arm by being shot. Orders had been given by the Jacobites not to fire unless anyone resisted.[33]

Many prisoners were taken. They were soon released and as they went, all made 'joyful Huzzas cryed, GOD Save K. James and prosper his merciful Army', though whether this was because they had Jacobite sympathies or

---

21 Patten, *History*, p.64.
22 TNA: SP54/9, 107, Jacobite prisoner's experiences in the rebellion.
23 BC: 45/12/77, account of the Jacobite southern army to Preston.
24 W.E. Matthews (ed.), *Diary of Dudley Ryder, 1715-6* (London: Methuen, 1939), p.136.
25 Paton, 'Journal', p.513.
26 Patten, *History*, p.64.
27 Patten, *History*, p.64.
28 Ralph Thoresby, *Letters of Eminent Men, II* (London: Colburn, 1832), p.319.
29 TNA: SP54/9, 107, Jacobite prisoner's experiences in the rebellion.
30 Paton, 'Journal', p.513.
31 Patten, *History*, p.64.
32 Matthews, *Diary*, p.136.
33 Patten, *History*, p.66.

whether in the circumstances they thought it politic to offer thanks to their late enemies who had now released them is another matter.[34] However, one Jacobite took it to be the former, writing 'by their expressions did not seem to wish ill to our cause'.[35] Another Jacobite noted that the men fleeing 'calling aloud down with the rump', with was another Jacobite cry.[36]

Lonsdale reflected:

> I don't know whether the rout proceeded from fear or Disaffection, what makes me imagine it was a thing designed is most of the men came without any manner of arms and though the rebels knew their number to be so great they did not alter their march at all, which I fancy they would have done if they had not depended upon a great many friends who did not shew themselves.[37]

A contemporary journal had this to say a month after the rout of the posse:

> But perhaps some readers will stop me here, and ask how it comes about, that if they are so few in number, or in so poor a condition as they are at present, that they have been suffered to pass at Penrith, where the Militia of Westmorland were assembled, I shall return no other Answer than this, That the Militia is a Thing mightily cry'd up, but not a Force to be rely'd on for an Action.[38]

Many of those, in the early and mid eighteenth century, who disliked standing armies as a potential tool of tyrants (harking back to the use of such by Cromwell and James II in the previous century), as well as being expensive and a source of corruption, thought that the militia was an inexpensive and politically safe method of national defence. After all, in theory men were meant to train for the militia on an annual basis, but few, if any did so, because, in peacetime, it was seen as an unnecessary waste of time and energy. Therefore the militia as an effective tool for defence went into abeyance, only to be called up when there was a crisis and then was found wanting, as seen here. Only as a rhetorical device by opposition politicians did it have any use.

Lonsdale thus concluded, 'The county is entirely without defence and I am very much afraid these Rebels won't be stopped till they meet with a Regular Force.'[39] Townshend agreed, telling him, 'His Majesty is very sensible of your lordship's having done all that could be expected, and that it is not possible on a sudden and upon the first assembly of the people of the country, to raise a sufficient force to oppose them'.[40] What was needed were the regular troops.

The county militia remained in being, scattered around the towns of the county. The clerk of Westmorland noted, 'both proved useless … ye want of

---

34 Anon., *A Letter*, pp.4–5.
35 TNA: SP54/9, 107, Jacobite prisoner's experiences in the rebellion.
36 BC: 45/12/77, account of the Jacobite southern army to Preston.
37 BL, Add.Mss. 63093, f.61v, Blakeney Collection, Vol. XV, Miscellaneous Letters and state papers, 1685–1827, Lonsdale-Townshend, 3 November 1715.
38 Jarvis, *Jacobite Risings*, p.112.
39 BL.Add.Mss. 63093, f61v, Lonsdale–Townshend, 3 November 1715.
40 TNA: SP44/118, p.116, Townshend–Lonsdale, 8 November 1715.

constant intelligence of ye notions of ye rebels & ye late disarray of ye people by our wise game laws & several false reports designes and spread away ye people'.[41] Lonsdale noted, 'The Militia is almost throughout ill armed, but I don't know how that can be remedied at present, for they can't be provided with better in this country, and it will be a long time before new ones can be had from London. We have ordered them to throw away their pikes and get firelocks in their place, and also to put the arms they have into the best condition that is possible'.[42]

Some reflected on Lonsdale's cowardice, but Patten justified his actions as being taken to 'prevent the Effusion of so much Blood and innocent Lives, which would have been of bad Consequence, and no Service to his Master's Interest'.[43] Yet had they stood their ground, the Jacobites would have retreated, 'as it hath beene acknowledged by diverse of them'.[44]

This had the great effect of boosting Jacobite morale, 'the Rebels were greatly animated by their sudden and disorderly separating over the whole Country'. The Jacobite horsemen took many horses and arms that the posse members had left behind them. The infantry joined the cavalry and they halted on the moor, before drawing up in order of battle 'that they might enter the Town in a good Figure'.[45]

At three that afternoon the Jacobite army entered Penrith, 'a handsome market town, populous, well built and for an inland town, has a very good share of trade'.[46] According to Patten, it was 'the richest and most plentifull of that part of the country, they refreshed themselves very comfortably'.[47] Finding the 'plentifull' dinner that had been prepared for the bishop and his followers, they availed themselves of it.[48] They proclaimed James as King, received the excise money and gave receipts for the same. However, according to one Jacobite this was mostly wasted, 'the sume was spent on treats and Regails & paying Foot but no care taken of intelligence'.[49] A party of cavalry, perhaps 200 strong, under Henry Oxburgh, was sent to Lowther Hall, belonging to Lonsdale, which was three miles from the town, to find the said lord. He was not there, having left for Appleby castle following the debacle with the posse. They took provisions and horses from the property, but did not harm the sole residents of the house, two old women. They were later accused of defacing statues there and damaging the gardens and trees. Provisions, though, were scarce in Penrith. The gentry paid for their quarters in the town, but the others paid little or nothing. Any arms found were also

---

41 BL.Add. Mss., 37721, f.40v, Extracts from rate books etc. for Westmorland, 1598–1722, Memorandum on militia, 26 October 1715.
42 *HMC, Carlisle*, p.18.
43 Patten, *History*, p.65.
44 Paton, 'Journal', p.513.
45 Patten, *History*, p.65.
46 Rogers, *Defoe, Tour*, p.552.
47 Patten, *History*, p.66.
48 Anon., *A Letter*, p.6.
49 TNA: SP54/9, 107, Jacobite prisoner's experiences in the rebellion.

confiscated by the Jacobites, but no one suffered physically.[50] Defoe later commented 'they offered no injury to the town, only quartered in it one night and took what arms and ammunition they could find'.[51]

Patten, who knew the country well as he had been curate at Penrith in 1704, was sent to take a party of horsemen and seize the bishop. Apparently the latter was returning to his palace, Rose Castle, when Patten was despatched. However, Forster countermanded the order and decided that collecting money was more important. So he sent Patten through Penrith and to Eamont Bridge, where he was told he would find his brother-in-law, Mr Johnston, collector of the salt tax. Johnston had to be captured, along with his papers and money and brought before the army. However, he escaped before Patten and his men arrived.[52]

Patten wrote that the 'Town is very loyal', but there was ambivalence in loyalties. Some townsmen told the Jacobites that John Patteson, a lawyer, had hidden his arms. Likewise, there were weapons held by Sir Christopher Musgrave of Edenhall. Mr Whelpdale, a JP, and other principal townsmen, when they heard of the Jacobite advance, decided 'wisely to consult their own Interest and Safety, by shewing all manner of Civility to their Enemies; Prudence and Necessity obliging them to act that Part, which Force constrain'd them unwillingly to comply with'. On their part the Jacobites behaved well, 'the inhabitants cannot charge them with any Rudeness, Violence or Plunder in the least'. Some Jacobites, seeing there was a Presbyterian meeting house in the town, asked Forster if they could pull it down or burn it (such chapels had been destroyed by Jacobite mobs in Lancashire and elsewhere earlier that year). Forster refused them, stating 'That he was to gain by Clemency, and not by Cruelty'.[53] Forster understood political realities; that for his force to cause destruction would not lead any doubters to join them and would confirm in the minds of their enemies that the Jacobite army was lawless and unruly.

Whilst in Penrith, the Jacobites arrested several loyalists, including Thomas Wybergh, a militia captain, one Senhouse (presumably the county sheriff or one of his relations) who clearly had not fled far enough after the debacle of the posse at Penrith Fell. Mackintosh stole Wybergh's watch. Learning that Stanwix at Carlisle had captured a kinsman of the Master of Nairn, they proposed an exchange for him with Wybergh but Stanwix refused. Little did the Jacobites know it, but at this time the Carlisle garrison was being reinforced by two companies of Chelsea Pensioners, who marched there via a route within three miles of the Jacobite army.[54] According to Clarke, at this stage the Jacobite army numbered 1,700 men, so rather less than they had at Kelso, due to the desertions of a few days earlier.[55]

---

50 Paton, 'Journal', pp.513–514; Anon., *A Faithful Register of the Late Rebellion* (London: T. Warner, 1718), p.240.
51 Rogers, *Defoe Tour*, p.552.
52 Patten, *History*, p.66.
53 Patten, *History*, pp.66–67.
54 Patten, *History*, pp.67–68.
55 Edinburgh University Library Special Collections, Laing Mss. 257, f.2v, Journal of the rebellion of 1715, by Peter Clarke.

Finding there was little to subsist them in Penrith, the army marched southward for the next town along the main road: Appleby, which was 10 miles away to the south east. On the march one man joined them, but left on the next day. Appleby was 'once a flourishing city, now a scattered and decaying and half demolished town'.[56] There, James was proclaimed and the excise taken, as before. They stayed there two nights ('to no purpose' wrote an anonymous Jacobite) and left on the morning of Saturday 5 November, towards Kendal. One man joined them on this journey, Francis Thornburrow, son of William Thornburrow of Selfet Hall, near Kendal. The older man sent a servant to wait on his son, who was wearing a red coat.[57]

Little did the Jacobites know it, but another local force had been raised to resist them. Joseph Symson (1650–1731), a merchant of Kendal, wrote on 3 November that Lonsdale, who he described as the man 'who may truly be styled the northern hero … warm in the defence of King George and this Country against Popish tyranny and slavery' had ordered that the Westmorland posse gather itself together on that day. Symson was certainly enthusiastic, telling Peter Desitter, his London friend, 'I am, with my second son and a servant, well armed, just going to mount with my neighbours in defence of His Majesty King George and the Protestant religion'.[58]

Unfortunately for him, Symson's information was faulty and out of date. He believed that on 3 November the Jacobites were 60 miles away on the Scottish border, when they were actually at Penrith. He also had no idea that Lonsdale and the posse and militia at Penrith were dispersed, for he went on to write that the Westmorland posse hoped to join their Cumberland counterparts on the 3 or 4 of November. He was also supremely confident that they would deal with the enemy, 'I hope so many thousands well armed with courage, cheerfulness and weapons that the enemy dare not stand.'[59] It is presumed that the Westmorland posse disbanded on 3 or 4 November as there is no more mention of it.

The army's six quartermasters reached Kendal on the same day, at noon. Celia Fiennes wrote that it was 'a town built all of stone, one very broad street in which is the market cross, it's a good trading town, mostly famed for the cottons'.[60] Two hours later the horsemen arrived there. Mackintosh was at their head and 'looked with a grim countenance'. He lodged at Alderman Lowry's house in Highgate Street. An hour later the infantry entered Kendal. The weather had been poor for a few days already, with a great deal of rain, but on 5 November, 'it rained very hard this day'. So the infantry did not draw their swords, show their flags nor did they beat their drums. Only the six bagpipers made any sound.[61]

---

56 Rogers, *Defoe's Tour*, p.551.
57 Paton, 'Journal', p.514; BC: 45/12/77, account of the Jacobite southern army to Preston.
58 S.D. Smith (ed.), *The Letter Book of Joseph Symson, 1711–1720* (Oxford: Oxford University Press, 2000), pp.342–343.
59 Smith, *Letter Book*, p. 343.
60 Morris, *Journeys*, p.191.
61 Paton, 'Journal', pp.514–515.

The army made for the market square and at the cross, the royal proclamation was read, twice in English, 'the reader of it spoke very good English without any mixture of Scottish tongue'. Clarke was among the crowd observing the spectacle. He recalled that the statement read, 'Whereas George Elector of Brunswick has usurped and taken upon him the stile of the king of these realms, etc …' and included the sentence, which Clarke particularly recalled, 'Did immediately after his fathers decease become our only and lawful liege'. Not all were equally impressed; a Quaker standing next to Clarke did not put his hat back on after the ceremony and so a Scottish soldier lunged at him with his halberd, but missed and no one was hurt. The crowd and soldiers dispersed'.[62]

Derwentwater stayed that night with his servant in 'The Sign of the White Lyon', in Strickland Street, the publican being Mr Fletcher. The other Jacobite lords were housed at The King's Arms in the same street, a place where Celia Fiennes stayed in 1698 and recorded that Mrs Rowlandson, 'she does putt up the charr fish its best of any in the country'.[63] Its publican was Thomas Rowlandson, who was mayor of Kendal that year. Forster lodged at Alderman Simpson's house.[64]

That evening a search was made for tax money. Kendal's bellman was ordered to tell the town's tanners and innkeepers to come and pay what excise they owed, 'or else that they denied should be plundered by Jack the highlander'. The citizens complied and paid in a total of £80 and a few shillings. Receipts were given. At 6:00 p.m. Rowlandson was put under arrest as he refused to tell where the arms of the militia were located: amounting to 60 muskets which had been sent from London. It was thought he should know because he had been a lieutenant in the same body.[65]

Symson, presumably overcoming his strong antipathy towards the Jacobites, and acting in his role as a leading citizen of Kendal, spoke to Derwentwater and Forster and probably Kenmure, assuring them that the information they had about Rowlandson was faulty. At which, Forster 'swore we were all rogues' and since the arms were not delivered up, then Symson should join Rowlandson as a prisoner. However, after another impassioned vindication of the truth, Symson avoided arrest.[66]

Symson then met one Sanderson, who observed that Symson was concerned, and asked him what the matter was. On being told, Sanderson asked Symson to accompany him, but he refused, not believing that the Jacobite leaders would believe him. Sanderson did not take no for an answer and so dragged the reluctant mercer to the Jacobite leaders again. Sanderson talked to them 'very friendly' and stated, 'You may depend upon what Mr Symson tells you to be true. I'll pawn my life he will not tell you a lie'. This softened their attitude but did not help the mayor. Sanderson had joined the Jacobite army and on Symson telling him that he was concerned for both his

---

62 Paton, 'Journal', p.515.
63 Morris, *Journeys*, p.191.
64 Paton, 'Journal', p.515.
65 Paton, 'Journal', p.515.
66 Smith, *Letter Book*, p.425.

sake and his wife's, the new recruit 'shook his head and told me he could not help it'.[67]

According to Clarke, next day, the Rev. William Crosby, Vicar of Holy Trinity church of Kendal, went to meet Derwentwater and Forster to ask to have Rowlandson freed and he was. Forster also had a painful experience at the hands of his godmother, Mrs Bellingham, who was also lodging at Simpson's house. When he went to visit her, 'she met him on the stairs, gave him two or three boxes on the eare, and called him a rebel and a popish toole, which he tooke patiently'.[68]

On 5 November, the town's gunsmiths had been working all night, for little or no pay. There were rumours that the militia arms that the Jacobites wanted were stored in the parish church of Holy Trinity. On that morning Highlanders broke into the church and hoped to find them, and also looked in the vestry. Although they found no weapons, they did see the church plate and ornaments in the vestry, but left without taking them. It seems that the gentlemen in the army were well behaved and paid for their lodgings, but the majority of the Scottish infantry did not.[69]

At eight in the morning of 6 November, the infantry marched out; again without drums beating or flags flying; only the bagpipers making a noise. The cavalry waited at Forster's lodgings. The lords, Mackintosh and Forster received them, 'hats in their hands'. Mackintosh, as on the previous day, had 'a grim countenance', whilst the others, along with the horsemen, 'were disheartened and full of sorrow'. When they marched out they were not in ranks. A journeyman weaver joined them.[70]

They then went to Kirkby Lonsdale, which was but a short march away, but which meant travelling over 'steepe strong hills all like rocks'. It was a smaller place, so on arriving there, the horsemen were quartered in the town and the infantry in villages nearby. As usual the proclamation was read out and the excise collected. That afternoon, Patten read prayers in church, it being Sunday, and the vicar had already departed. One Guin carved out King George's name and replaced it with that of James 'so nicely that it resembled print very much and the alteration could scarce be perceiv'd'. There were a number of volunteers at this town: John Dalston and another gentleman from Richmond, Charles Carus and his two sons, Christopher and Thomas; all Catholic gentlemen of Hatton Hall. Carus told his new friends that the town of Lancaster, their next destination, 'had left of making any preparations for a defence'.[71]

On the way to Lancaster on 7 November, the army drew up on a hill and there they stood, resting on their arms for some time, so as to rest the infantry. Whilst they did so, Charles Widdrington, the lord's second brother, came riding from Lancashire, northwards and towards them. He had welcome news, learnt on his trip to Lancashire, where he had been for

---

67 Smith, *Letter Book*, pp.425–426.
68 Paton, 'Journal', pp.515–516.
69 Paton, 'Journal', p.516.
70 Paton, 'Journal', p.516.
71 Paton, 'Journal', p.516; Patten, *History*, p.70.

the last few days (he had left Manchester earlier in the day). According to Patten, 'he return'd with the news of their Chearfulness, and Intention to join them with all their Interest, and that the Pretender was that day proclaimed at Manchester, where the Town's People had got Arms to furnish a Troop of Fifty Men at their sole charge, besides other Voluntuiers'.[72]

According to one source, 'that place was well affected and severall thousands of men well armed were ready and would actually have joyned us'.[73] Another source stated that Manchester would not only provide 800 recruits but was also 'a place not only full of people, but also the country round of very populous, provisions plentifull, a river for the opening a communication with their friends in Staffordshire, whence likewise they expected another revolt'.[74] Forster announced that James III had been proclaimed in Manchester and that 4,000 armed men awaited them there.[75]

This news was clearly widely distributed among the army and Patten then related:

> This roused the Spirits of the Highlanders, and animated them exceedingly; nor was it more needed, for they had often complain'd before, that all the Pretences of Numbers to join them were so little, and that they should soon be surrounded by numerous Forces. But on the News they pluck'd up their Hearts, gave three Huzzas and then continu'd their march into Lancaster.[76]

Such anticipations of support were shared by the government, for James Craggs, MP, later wrote, 'the rebels in two or three days time would certainly have been joined by as many thousands well armed and mounted'.[77] Townshend had once written they 'reckon themselves sure of' such support.[78]

The reason why such support was expected was probably on both religious and political grounds. Lancashire was one of the most Catholic counties in England, with about a tenth of the population (compared to about one–two percent as a national average) still adhering to the old faith, numbering perhaps 16,000–17,000 people in all. Among these were a significant number of landowning families, with, in 1718, there being 469 estates owned by Catholics in Lancashire, or about a third of the land in the county valued at over £27,000.[79] Contemporary observer John Macky wrote that in Lancashire there was 'more of the Roman Catholick Religion in this County, than in any three in England'.[80]

In 1715 Catholics lived under numerous worldly burdens because of their faith. There were the penal laws dating back to the late sixteenth century,

---

72 Patten, *History*, p.71.
73 TNA: SP54/9, 107, Jacobite prisoner's experiences in the rebellion.
74 Anon., *Annals*, II, p.133.
75 *Weekly Journal*, 10 March 1716.
76 Patten, *History*, p.71.
77 *HMC Townshend*, p.170.
78 *HMC Townshend*, p.174.
79 Hibbert–Ware, 'Memorials', p.244; B.G. Blackwood, 'Lancashire Catholics, Protestants and Jacobites during the Rebellion of 1715', *Recusant History* 22/1 (1994), pp.42, 47.
80 John Macky, *A Journey through England*, II (London: J. Pemberton, 1722), p.153.

which made non-attendance at Anglican churches on Sunday an offence for which one could be fined. Catholic churches were illegal, as was holding mass. The Test and Corporation Acts of 1661 and 1673 barred Catholics from holding public office at local or national level. They could not become officers in the army or navy, or sit in Parliament or attend university. In his short reign, 1685–1688, James II had tried to change all this, but had been unable to do so. De facto, there was often a degree of local toleration as regards the penal laws, but not always as in 1713 a Lancashire clergyman had tried to have John Dalton and another seven Catholics condemned for recusancy, though on that occasion failed.[81]

There were some in the north west of England among the clergy who were fearful about Catholicism in the county. In the aftermath of the abortive French invasion of 1708, bishop Nicholson wrote of:

> … popery has advanced by very long strides in late years in this country and too many of our magistrates love to have it so. At the very time the French were on our coasts and our people daily expected news of their being landed, the wealthier of our papists, instead of being seized, were cringed to with all possible tenders of respect'.[82]

Likewise, the Rev. Samuel Peploe (1668–1752), Vicar of Preston, wrote in 1715 to his bishop:

> I beg leave to acquaint your lordship that there are three townships and part of another in this parish, which lie three, four and five miles from this church, and have no other convenient place of public worship, that by this unhappy situation they have been still exposed to temptations and popery, which is too prevalent in these parts of your lordship's diocese, and are thereby an easier prey to the priests of that communion, we having no less than six of these men in the one parish. From my first coming to this place I have wished for some hopeful remedy against this growing evil.[83]

Townshend was concerned, too, writing to Argyle on 8 November, 'this march of the rebels into a county full of papists and disaffected persons by whom they will probably be joyned'. He added that the Jacobite advance 'has occasioned some confusion here [in London], and has had a bad effect on publick credit and it will be some time before Mr Wills who commands in those parts can have a sufficient Body together for reducing them, and can be joined by Carpenter'.[84]

---

81 G.H. Holmes, *Making of a Great Power, Britain, 1660–1722* (Harlow: Pearson, 1993), pp.455, 457; John Gillow (ed.), *The Tyldesley Diary, the personal record of Thomas Tyldesley during the years 1712, 1713 and 1714* (Preston: Publisher Unknown, 1873), p.115.
82 *VCH Cumberland*, II (London: Archibald Constable and Co. Ltd, 1905), p.104.
83 *VCH Lancashire* VII (London: Constable and Co, 1914), p.77n.
84 Leeds University Library Special Collections, Townshend Papers, f.35v, Townshend-Argyle, 8 November 1715.

As in Cumberland, there had been plotting among the Lancashire gentry in the 1690s in favour of James II. These included the Towneleys, Tyldesleys, Daltons, Butlers, Winckleys, Cliftons, Gerards and Hothersalls. The Tyldesley family had a long history of supporting the Stuarts. Edward Tyldesley's great grandfather, Sir Thomas Tyldesley had died, fighting for Charles II, at the battle of Wigan Lane in 1651 and his son (Edward's grandfather) and grandson were also supporters of the Stuarts. They had been forming an embryo secret army to restore James II. Now was the opportunity for them and their descendants. Under James II many of these Catholic gentry had received what was due to them as landed gentry; being JPs, which had been denied to them since the reformation, gains lost after 1688.[85]

There had been discussion there about defending Lancaster because Sir Henry Hoghton (1679–1768), an MP for Preston, JP and deputy lord lieutenant, 'a Gentleman of known good intentions and steddy Loyalty to the Protestant succession' had brought the county militia into the town, 600 strong. The county's lord lieutenant, Edward Stanley, the tenth Earl of Derby (1664–1732), had written to his deputy lieutenants on 27 September to convene a meeting in order to raise the militia. They did not do so until 29 October, which was tardy compared to their contemporaries in Cumberland and Northumberland. Those meeting at Preston included Derby, Hoghton and five others. Hoghton was appointed as the colonel and it was decided that they should summon the militia from Amounderness and Lonsdale. The infantry would be armed with muskets, bayonets and cartouche boxes and the cavalry with 'such arms and furniture as are wanting to make them compleat'. They would meet again at Preston on 3 November.[86] A group of 15 deputy lieutenants urged Derby to have Captain William Leigh of the 2nd regiment of Foot Guards train the men but it is not known whether he was able to do so in the time allotted.[87]

With Hoghton was Francis Charteris (1674–1732), JP of Hornby Castle and self styled 'Colonel', a Scot and cashiered from the army on four occasions, and they thought that the bridge, 'handsome and strong' in Lancaster over the River Lune should be destroyed in order to hinder the Jacobite march south. However, the townsmen were unwilling to have this done for they argued that it would not hold up the Jacobite army because the river was low and so could easily be crossed by infantry and cavalry. Furthermore, it would be expensive to repair the bridge 'so strong and fine as before'. It would also disrupt trade which needed a bridge to allow carts laden with goods to come and go.[88] All that was done was that the pavement and north arch of the bridge had been taken up.[89]

Thwarted, the loyalists then turned to how they might deny the Jacobites anything that might be useful to them. They soon found that there was a ship of

---

85 Monod, *Jacobitism*, pp.310–314.
86 J. Lumby (ed.), 'Calendar of the deeds and papers in the possession of Sir James de Hoghton', *RSLC*, 88 (1936), p.112.
87 LRO: DDHU/53/42, Plea of 15 deputy lieutenants to Derby, 1715
88 Patten, *History*, pp.71–72.
89 Paton, 'Journal', p.517.

about 500 tons five miles up the river, owned by Mr William Heysham (1666–1716), a Lancaster MP and Robert Lawson (1652–1736), a Lancaster Quaker. On board were six cannons (four described as being 'very good' and two as being 'small'), some blunderbusses and some small arms. Hoghton suggested that the weapons be removed and then used to defend the bridge against the Jacobites. Lawson was sent for, but 'he positively refused' Hoghton's request. He was further pressed and finally resolved that he would not part with the artillery unless Hoghton would give him a bond for £10,000 to insure the ship against any damage that the Jacobites might do it. He was convinced that if the Jacobites took it they would burn the cargo and the ship. Patten assumed that the Jacobites would have stolen and destroyed the ship because of their animosity towards Hoghton.[90] For them profits trumped politics.

Following this second rebuff, Hoghton asked the mayor, aldermen and common council that they might meet him in the afternoon, to discuss the matter further. They met, with Charteris and Charles Rigby, JP, 'who were also zealous for His Majesty's Interest'. They proposed that the cannons on the Robert be removed for the army's use. This was refused. The three loyalists formed a Commission of the Peace and they then produced a warrant for seizing its cargo and arms. Lawson was forced to acquiesce as they had the power of the law on their side.[91]

Hoghton now learnt that the regiment of Stanhope's dragoons, stationed at Preston and advised (perhaps by the commander of the said dragoons) to march to Lancaster, had had no orders to do so, so remained where they were. He also found that the Jacobite army was 16 miles away and so he decided to march south with the militia, to Preston. He lacked the men to defend the town and could not use the guns he had hoped to before leaving, he asked that Lawson sail his ship down the river so the Jacobites would be unable to take the cannons on board. Perhaps predictably, Lawson refused.[92]

On either the way to Lancaster, or that night that the Jacobites had reached it, on 7 November, a party of Jacobites, led by Oxburgh, went to Hornby Castle, Charteris' home, only a few miles distant. Doubtless he was aware of their proximity and so ensured his own absence. His provisions and horse were taken by the Jacobites. Charteris later announced that 'they committed several Disorders, to the Owner's great loss'. According to Patten, this was done to ingratiate himself with the government and that 'he could never make out the Loss; nor was there any truth in the Charge'. Apparently £3 6s 8d of wine and beer was drunk and Oxburgh insisted that this would be reimbursed when James was crowned King. In fact, it could have been far worse; if Scotsmen had gone there, 'they would not have scrupled to set it on fire, so well is he respected by them … on account of his own personal character, which is known not to have been very acceptable to those who are acquainted with him'. This is a reference to Charteris' reputation as a cheat at cards and a seducer of women.[93]

---

90 Patten, *History*, p.72.
91 Patten, *History*, p.73.
92 Patten, *History*, p.73.
93 Patten, *History*, p.74.

Civilians were apprehensive as the Jacobite army approached. William Stout (1665–1752), a Quaker shopkeeper of Lancaster, recalled in his autobiography, 'Last year and this was a time of much trouble and danger, on account of the Rebellion, in which we were in feare of being plundered or worse, but Almighty Providence preserved us'.[94]

Lancaster was a town not favoured by travel writers. Celia Fiennes had written, 'it is old and much decayed' and Defoe that it 'has little to recommend it … a more decayed port (for no ships of any considerable burthen) … little or no trade'. However, the former did admit that 'the streets are some of them well patch'd and of a good size'.[95] Yet Patten wrote that in 1715 that it was 'a Town of very good Trade, very pleasantly seated'.[96]

It was at 1:00 p.m. that the Jacobite vanguard arrived at Lancaster. The weather may have lifted or the army believed the promises of imminent mass support, and they marched in in good spirits, 'swords drawn, drums beating and colours flying, and in their ranks with the bagpipes also playing'. As always they went straight away to the market place and read the royal proclamation aloud. Among the crowd was Christopher Hopkins, a stationer. He was making a note of the strength of the Jacobite army, but was spotted and taken prisoner before Forster. Forster had him taken along as a prisoner.[97]

At Lancaster a number of recruits came to join the army, mostly from country seats nearby, rather than from the town itself. The gentlemen who did so included Albert Hodgson of Leighton Hall, John Dalton of Thurnham Hall, Richard Butler of Rawcliffe and George Hilton from Cartmel in Westmorland. The only townsmen recorded by Clarke as enlisting were Edmund Gartside, a barber and an unnamed joiner, both of whom were Catholics, but there were actually several others as noted below. The two just mentioned were appointed quartermasters.[98]

According to Patten, 'While we were in this Town our Number increased considerably … in that time a great many Lancashire Gentlemen joined us, with their Servants and Friends'. However, this was not an unalloyed blessing, as Patten continued, 'they were most of them Papists; which made the Scots gentlemen and the Highlanders mighty uneasy, very much suspecting the Cause; for they expected all the High Church Party to have joined them'.[99] Most of the Scots were Protestants and so would have preferred Protestant allies. Another Jacobite also complained of this, 'I don't believe that above six gentlemen joined us here, and in fine non but papists did joyne us, which did us more harme than good'.[100] This may not have been correct: of the eleven men from Lancaster who later surrendered, two were gentlemen and nine commoners; the religious denomination of these men is not recorded.[101]

---

94 J.D. Marshall (ed.), 'The Autobiography of William Stout, 1665–1752', *Chetham Society* (1967), p.176.
95 Rogers, *Defoe, Tour*, p.549; Morris, *Journeys*, pp.189–190.
96 Patten, *History*, p.71.
97 Paton, 'Journal', p.517.
98 Paton, 'Journal', p.517.
99 Patten, *History*, p.78.
100 BC: 45/12/77, account of the Jacobite southern army to Preston.
101 TNA: KB8/66, Baga de Secretis.

There were other indications of enthusiasm, too. Owen recounted how 'at Lancaster where the mayor and aldermen when the rebels came towards the town, met them there in their robes and when they came in proclaimed the Pretender at the market in formality'.[102]

Among the rank and file there were mixed remarks made at Lancaster. Charles King remarked that, riding from Kendal to Lancaster had been a tedious day's march, while James Maloney said 'he hoped to dine on Christmas day at St. James' with King James.'[103]

Catholic support for the Jacobite cause was not enough: there were too few Catholics. Protestant support was crucial. Patten stated the Jacobites' disillusionment thus:

> Indeed, that party, who never are right hearty for the Cause, 'till they are Mellow, as they call it, over a Bottle or two, began now to shew us their Blind-side; and that is their just character, that they do not care for venturing their Carcasses any further than the Tavern. There indeed, with their High Church and Ormond, they would make Men believe, who do not know them, that they would encounter the greatest Opposition in the World; but after having consulted their Pillows, and the Fume a little evaporated, it is to be observed of them, that they generally become mighty Tame, and are apt to Look before they Leap, and with the Snail, if you touch their Houses, they hide their Horns.[104]

There was also discussion about what to do with the prisoners in the castle, which was the county gaol. On the Jacobites' arrival, these men 'gave loud Huzzas'. At first it was unanimously decided that all should be set free; mostly debtors and those awaiting trial for criminal cases. On a second consideration, though, it was concluded that only those accused of crimes against the state should be freed, but that the others would have King James' pardon speedily. Prominent among these was the man who led the rioting in Manchester in June, Thomas Sydall, a blacksmith having been the 'mob colonel'. He was clearly a respected figure in Lancaster, too, because when he and the unnamed 'mob captain' stood in the pillory on market days, 'no person was allowed to fling anything at them'. John Wilkinson, an apothecary, was the other Jacobite prisoner. The two joined the Jacobite army and were allowed to keep their former titles.[105]

That evening a search was made, as always, for both money and arms. Leonard Jackson, the town's sergeant at mace, was obliged to accompany the Jacobite adjutant in the expedition, 'to demand arms of the several inhabitants of the said town'. The Vicar's house provided three following pieces, a pair of pistols and a sword. Henry Coatley's resulted in a pair of pistols, a pocket pistol and a sword. Edward Cole's a small sword, Widow Medcalfe's three swords and Mr Gibson's a pair of pistols and a sword. These and others produced, in total, 20 'long' guns, over 60 swords and 'a great

---

102 Matthews, *Diary*, p.136.
103 TNA: KB8/66, ff.107, 113v, Baga de Secretis.
104 Patten, *History*, p.78.
105 Patten, *History* p.79; Paton, 'Journal', pp.517–518.

number of pistols'. Elizabeth Cortley of Lancaster was ordered to surrender arms and the recorder told her 'You had better deliver them quietly than have your house plundered for them' and she gave up a pair of pistols and a small pocket pistol. Apparently, the mayor, the recorder, two bailiffs, two sergeants and the bell man, Henry Hodgson, attended.[106]

Money was received from the innkeepers 'but it did not amount but to a very little'. Six Scots then went with Richard Parkinson, the mayor, to make a house to house search for weapons. Householders were threatened with being plundered by the Scots if they refused to comply. Although, Clarke claimed that little was found, with some located at the Rev. Robert Fenton's house. Although payment was not given for these finds, the gunsmiths 'were well employed in cleaning guns and pistols' and were paid. Little gunpowder was found in the shops and the barrel of it owned by Samuel Satherwaite had already been disposed of down a well.[107]

Fenton's behaviour was seen as distinctly equivocal. Although he would not read prayers for the Jacobites, allowing Patten to do so, 'It seems he was not so averse to it, any more than some of his Brethren; but he wanted to see how the scales would turn before he could think of venturing so far'.[108] Stout gives an explanation for Fenton's behaviour, describing his father's character thus, 'a man of high and austere deportment, and disdained all Protestant Dissenters … a great exacter of his demands from his own poor hearers and Dissenters, by prosecution and law'. Stout added 'his sone James [had] much of his disposition'.[109]

In the evening, Forster and Patten had dinner at the Recorder's house in Lancaster. The Rev. William Paul of Horton on the Hill, Leicestershire, and John Cotton of Cambridgeshire joined them there. The latter two explained who they were and offered to join the army. Paul told Forster, taking him to one side, about Carpenter's marches, stating that he was then at Barnard Castle in Durham, but 'that his Men and Horses were sore fatigued and the like'.[110]

The Jacobites remained in Lancaster on the following day. Forster had a proclamation issued to the effect that there was a reward of £30 if Ralph Fairbrother, a Lancaster resident, who had ridden out with Christopher Hopkins to Newcastle to give General Carpenter a list of the Jacobite army, could be apprehended. This may appear to have been a case of closing the stable door once the horse had bolted.[111]

Whilst in the town some of the Jacobites were employed more usefully. The custom house books were examined to see whether any money was to be found there. None was, but a consignment of claret and brandy had been recently taken. Those appointed from the Jacobite army for this examination made good use of some of this and kept the remainder for future use. Then a detachment was sent to Sunderland Point to locate the ship already mentioned

---

106 TNA: KB8/66, Baga de Secretis.
107 Paton, 'Journal', p.518.
108 Patten, *History*, p.75.
109 Marshall, 'Autobiography', p.170.
110 Patten, *History*, p.77.
111 Paton, 'Journal', 518.

which was armed. They found it and removed the six cannons (and perhaps one of the blunderbusses was the one was later found in the possession of a Jacobite soldier).[112] The Jacobite who had claimed that spending two days at Appleby had been wasteful, made a similar comment about the stay in Lancaster, but added a supposed reason for it, 'In Lancaster we lay two dayes, and I'm perfectly persuaded that these delays were to give the eneimie tyme (for had we got to Manchester we had done our business)'.[113]

That morning at 10 the Rev. Paul and Derwentwater had the church bell rung to summon the faithful to church. Whilst the bell was being rung, Paul took a prayer book and erased the names of Queen Anne and Princess Sophia with King James and his mother. Many attended the service and Paul took the opportunity 'instead of praying for King George prayed for his new Majesty by the name of King James, and instead of George, Prince of Wales, he prayed thus'.[114]

That afternoon, the gentlemen of the army enjoyed themselves, as Clarke noted 'This afternoon the gentlemen soldiers dressed and trimmed themselves up in their best cloathes for to drink a dish of tea with the laydys of this towne. The laydys also appeared in their best riging, and had their tea tables richly furnished for to entertain their new suitors.'[115]

A little money was also found, when the mail was opened and a bill payable by the postmaster for £50 was secured. Two Catholic priests, whether with the army or not, discussed religious matters with Fenton. As ever, there was no damage to property in the town and the gentlemen always paid their dues. However on leaving, they were 'very sorrowful to part with their new loves'.[116] The Rev. Paul was sent on 9 November by the army to Derbyshire, with letters for Jacobite gentlemen in that county.[117]

Patten thought that leaving Lancaster was a missed opportunity. He regretted that either the army could not have stayed there or at least have left a garrison there.[118] Another contemporary expanded on this theme, 'They had done well for themselves if they had staid for some Time, or at least secured the Town, which was a Port, and had an old Ruined castle, part of which is standing, was capable of being made a place of Arms and to have been put into such a Posture of Defence, as that they could not have been taken sword in hand'. In comparison, Preston was deemed 'an open town, and not capable of being put into a Posture of Defence'.[119] Celia Fiennes noted that the castle occupied a commanding presence 'the castle which is just by, but on a very good ascent from the rest of the town and so is in open view, the town and river lying round it beneath; on the castle tower walking round the battlements I saw the whole town and river at a view'.[120] John Dalton

---

112 Paton, 'Journal', pp.518–519.
113 BC: 45/12/77, account of the Jacobite southern army to Preston.
114 Paton 'Journal', p.519.
115 Paton 'Journal', p.519.
116 Paton 'Journal', pp.519–520.
117 Patten, *History*, p.75.
118 Patten, *History*, p.78.
119 Anon., *Annals*, II, p.132.
120 Morris, *Journeys*, p.189.

apparently remarked, 'The Business is now done, we have nothing to do but to march to Preston'.[121]

One reason for leaving was that they had learnt that Carpenter was marching towards them.[122] According to Patten, Forster saw Carpenter's troops as his prime and perhaps only enemy. So much so, that, 'Mr Forster spared neither Pains nor Cost to be acquainted with all General Carpenters' Motions, of which he had constant and particular Accounts every day, and sometimes twice a Day'.[123]

Yet they left Lancaster on 9 November with a degree of optimism, despite the news that Paul had brought Forster about their enemies. Advancing would allow all those others in Lancashire, who had promised their support, to join them, as well as evading any pursuers (even though they outnumbered the latter). After passing through Preston they could reach Warrington bridge and from there march to Manchester 'where they had great Assurances of great numbers to join them'. From Manchester they could then reach 'the great and rich Town of Liverpool', which would be cut off from any relief, once Warrington bridge was secured.[124] In contrast to Appleby and Lancaster, Liverpool was the richest town in the north west of England, 'one of the wonders of Britain … an opulent, flourishing and increasing trade … it is in a fair way to exceed and eclipse it [Bristol], by increasing in every way in wealth and shipping'.[125] Celia Fiennes wrote 'it's a very rich trading town, the houses of brick and stone built high and even, that a streete quite through looks very handsome, the streets well pitch'd; there are abundance of persons you see very well dressed and of good fashion; the streets are faire and long, its London in miniature'.[126]

However, Liverpool was being defended by its inhabitants. Merchants, traders and others in the adjoining districts gathered there, taking their best effects. Along with numerous sailors, they 'took all possible Precautions for the Defence of that Important Town'. Some of the routes to Liverpool were flooded and that which was not was blocked by entrenchments, defended by 70 cannons. Ships were kept at a distance from the shore, so could not be plundered. Townsmen were divided into companies and organised by William Crisp, the county sheriff's brother.[127] However, Defoe noted that there were no regular defences, being an open town and that 'they could have been glad of walls and gates … it would have fared but very ill with Leverpoole; who could have made but little resistance against an armed and desperate body of men'.[128] It is also worth noting that there had been a Jacobite demonstration in the town in the previous year.[129]

---

121 Anon., *Faithful Register*, p.270.
122 Rae, *History*, p.318.
123 Patten, *History*, p.80.
124 Patten, *History*, p.79.
125 Rogers, *Defoe, Tour*, p.540.
126 Morris, *Journeys*, p.184.
127 Rae, *History*, p.317.
128 Rogers, *Defoe's Tour*, p.541.
129 *Post Boy*, 3004, 7–10 August 1714.

Hopkins, who had abetted a spy, had been arrested and brought along with the Jacobites, but he was dismissed two miles out of Lancaster. This incident convinced one Jacobite that Forster was wholly inept. Apparently this Jacobite, William Dunlop, seized Hopkins and delivered him to an officer who then brought him to Forster, 'by whome he was severaly reproved and chastened'. The officer was then told to keep a strict watch on the man during the forthcoming march. But when he made to do so on the next day he found that Forster had had him released and this should have been 'enough to convince any man of Forster's' incapacity for command'.[130]

They also brought along the six cannons, mounted on carriage wheels taken from Hoghton's own coach, and the brandy, intended for the Highlanders, with the latter being all drunk by the time they reached their next destination: Garstang, half way between Lancaster and Preston, which was a small market town. This, and a number of country houses, were where the infantry slept that night, but the cavalry were able to push on and reach Preston by nightfall on 9 November.[131] It was dismal in the final stages of the march, though, 'proving rainy and the Ways deep'.[132] The journey between Lancaster and Preston was 20 miles.[133]

They were joined by Roger Muncaster, a Protestant lawyer of Garstang, a man 'of very good sense and natural parts' (either at Garstang or at Preston) along with a few 'poore papists'. They also received excise money that evening. On the next day, 10 November, the infantry arrived at noon and marched straight to the cross. There was a welcome for the Jacobite army there, as a hostile newspaper noted 'When they came to Town, the disloyal Inhabitants receiv'd them with the Ringing of Bells, Illuminations, &c, and forced those who were averse to their Proceedings, to do the like. They proclaimed the Pretender that Night with Huzzas'.

Allegedly the Jacobites looted the town, though this may only mean that they took the public money as usual. Those opposed to the Jacobites fled. Principal among these was the Rev. Samuel Peploe, a staunch enemy to Catholicism (despite the legend that he remained and faced down a potentially aggressive Jacobite at his church). He went to Wigan.[134]

As ever, public money was taken and the proclamation read. There was some recruiting; principally Richard Towneley and Mr Shuttleworth 'as also did aboundance of Roman Catholicks'. Towneley rode into Preston at the head of a retinue, swords drawn and flags flying. Patten wrote, 'Here, they were also joined by a great many Gentlemen, with their Tenants, Servants and Attendants, and some of very good Figure in the Country, but still all Papists'. Only 46 men from Preston itself are known to have enlisted, but there may have been others.[135] Of more importance were others from the neighbouring

---

130 TNA: SP54/9, 107, Jacobite prisoner's experiences in the rebellion.
131 Paton, 'Journal', p.520.
132 Patten, *History*, p.79.
133 Morris, *Journeys*, p.188.
134 *Original Weekly Journal*, 355, 19–26 November 1715.
135 TNA: KB8/66, Baga de Secretis; Patten, *History*, p.80, Paton, 'Journal', p,520.

parishes, too, and a Jacobite wrote '200 well armed but all papists joyned'.[136] Another contemporary claimed the figure was 1,200.[137] After the battle, there were many witnesses who recalled men riding into Preston in groups, mostly armed with swords and pistols, a few with muskets, arriving on the morning of 12 November. There may even have been a Catholic priest, one John Barrow, among them.[138] The newcomers were cheered by the Jacobites already in the town.[139] Meanwhile, William Shafto set to recruiting men and apparently enlisted 100, giving them 18 pence each.[140] Some of the newcomers tried to find lodgings at the Anchor Inn, but there was only stabling there, so went to the Mitre for a room instead.[141]

The Sign of the Mitre inn on the market square seems to have been the Jacobite headquarters, as billeting was organised from there. Efforts were made to acquire further military supplies, as the army only had 48 pounds of gunpowder on their arrival into the town (enough for about 200 men to fire 10 musket balls each), as Walter Tunstall, the quartermaster, went to Mr Gradwell's house, asking the quantity of gunpowder he had in his warehouse. He was told that the county militia had already been supplied with 300 hundred weight and so little was left. However, a barrel of between 100–120 hundred weight was located and Tunstall paid £5 for it. Apparently there was 500–600 hundred weight more, but this was hidden; a local gunsmith recalled burying 45 pounds worth of powder.[142] Tunstall also collected excise payments at the Mitre.[143]

The dismay felt that most of the English recruits were Catholic may have been threefold. Firstly most, if not all of the Scots were probably Episcopalians and may have shared the general Protestant suspicion of Catholics. Likewise, some of the English Jacobites were Anglican Tories and had expected more of their fellows to join the cause, but did not. Finally, a strong Catholic element in the Jacobite army made it easier for their enemies to cast all of their army in that vein and so handed a strong propaganda weapon to them. Yet according to Ryder, 'The papists don't rise much to join them as was expected'.[144] The number of Jacobites who joined the army on the march through the north western counties is unknown, for many slipped away before the surrender, but one contemporary source gives it as being 1,500.[145]

The Jacobites seemed in high morale. On 9 November, James Singleton shouted 'God bless King James the third and down with the Rump Rump Rump Rump'. Others were heard to 'bragg of ye great numbers that would shortly joyn them'.[146]

---

136 TNA: SP54/9, 107, Jacobite prisoner's experiences in the rebellion.
137 Anon., *Annals*, II, p.142.
138 TNA: FEC1/1585, Towneley and Tildesey, informations, 1715–1716.
139 TNA, TS23/34, 1, Treasury Solicitor Miscellanea, 1715–1723.
140 TNA: KB8/66, Baga de Secretis.
141 TNA, TS23/34, 3.
142 TNA: FEC1/1585, Towneley and Tildesley; KB8/66, f.15r, Baga de Secretis.
143 TNA, TS/23/34, 3.
144 Matthews, *Diary*, p.135.
145 TNA, TS23/34, 1.
146 TNA: FEC1/1585, Towneley and Tildesley.

There was at Preston, as in Lancaster, a social dimension, 'The laydys in this towne, Preston, are so very beautyfull and so richly atired that the gentlemen soldiers from Wednesday [9 November] to Saturday [12 November] minded nothing but courting and feasting'.[147] This was severely criticised by one Jacobite who wrote 'they applied only in feasting & revelling & playing the fool, but not one farthing on intelligence'.[148] This is not surprising, however, as Macky noted that Preston 'by its Situation, the Handsomeness of the Streets, and the Variety of Company that come there for the Conveniency of Boarding, is reckon'd next to St. Edmunds' Bury in Suffolk, Ludlow in Wales and Beverley in Yorkshire, the prettiest Retirement in England'.[149] Lancashire gentlemen in their diaries at this time often refer to visiting the place and it being a centre for social gatherings. Unused to the urgency of matters military, it is no surprise that they spent their time enjoying local society.

There had been some other apparently good news at Preston, too. The Jacobites learnt that Stanhope's regiment of dragoons, having been raised in Leicester, had been stationed in the town, but on hearing of the Jacobite march towards them, they rode away. Patten wrote 'This encouraged them exceedingly, and made them imagine that the King's Forces would not look them in the Face'. Clearly the Jacobites did not wonder why a regiment was all alone.[150] Apparently Forster claimed there were none of their opponents nearby 'except a few scatter'd troops that would infallibly fly on our Approach as those at Lancaster and Preston had done'. Thus it made sense to remain at Preston 'for the Conveniency of our friends coming in to us about this Place'.[151]

It is not clear when the Jacobites first knew of any opposition towards them to the south. There was an initial resolution to march out of Preston on 11 November and an order was given to that effect that afternoon. This was countermanded and so they stayed in the town on that day. Apparently this was because 'This Day's stay was very necessary for the conveniency of our Friends coming in to us about this Place'.[152] They had no idea that there were any enemies in the neighbourhood. Forster had been paying to have Carpenter's force's movements monitored and apparently heard reports once or twice a day about their whereabouts.[153]

The Lancashire Jacobites assured him that 'no Force could come near them by Forty miles but they could inform him thereof'. This promise 'made him perfectly easy on that side, relying entirely on the intelligence he expected from them'.[154]

Yet according to the Merse trooper, Forster did know of Wills' forces being nearby. This fact, if fact it is, is not alluded to by Patten, though as he is always Forster's advocate it is perhaps not surprising that he does not mention it but throws the blame on the army's lack of intelligence on

---

147 Paton, 'Journal', p.520.
148 BC: 45/12/77, account of the Jacobite southern army to Preston.
149 Macky, *Journey*, pp.153–154.
150 Patten, *History*, p.79.
151 *Weekly Journal*, 10 March 1716.
152 *Weekly Journal*, 10 March 1716.
153 Patten, History, p. 80.
154 Patten, *History*, p.80.

THE SECOND BATTLE OF PRESTON, 1715

The Right Honourable George, Lord Carpenter. Mezzotint by John Faber, Jr, after Johan van Diest (1719 or after). (NPG D11252. Courtesy of the National Portrait Gallery)

the Lancashire Jacobites. The Merse trooper alleged that on 10 November, 'There were received certain Notice of General Wills being in Wigan, Twelve Miles distant from us, with Two Regiments of Dragoons, who lay Night and Day at their Horse Heads'. They were prepared to retreat if attacked by the Jacobite army, but Forster advocated inactivity, despite the claim that 'We had an opportunity of cutting off the Enemy, yet general Forrester would not allow us, nor suffer us to march towards Manchester'.[155]

According to the same source, similar news came on the following day, at seven in the evening of 11 November. Derwentwater received a letter from a nobleman, possibly the Catholic Lord Molyneux, telling them that at noon on that day Wills had been joined by a further seven regiments (this was not so) and so had resolved to march to Preston. Forster was informed about the letter's contents, and 'he appeared dispirited, and then, as at all other times, very unfit for such an important Command. He had nothing to say'. Instead, he passed the letter to Kenmure. The latter did take notice of it and summoned the army's senior officers, who went to Forster's lodgings. There they found him 'in Bed without the least Concern'. A council of war was held, presumably sans Forster, and the decision was to send a cavalry patrol to Wigan and advance parties of infantry to the bridges over the rivers Darwen and Ribble, which were on the road just south of Preston, towards Wigan. The rest of the army was to be told to prepare themselves for battle. However, 'to our great surprise, these orders were countermanded by Forrester'.[156]

The crucial point was the bridge at Warrington, on the road from Manchester to Liverpool, as Defoe noted. This bridge over the Mersey was also seen as significant strategically in 1745. Defoe wrote thus of it:

> … stately stone bridge, which is the only bridge of communication with the county of Chester, it is on the great road from London leading to Carlisle and Scotland, and in the case of war, has always been affair, so as to have made themselves masters of it, it would have been so again, and on that account the King's forces took special care, by a speedy advance to secure it.[157]

Concerns about the Jacobite advance among the civilian magnates in northern England such as Cholmondeley, Lonsdale and Carlisle resulted in letters being addressed to Townshend in the first week of November; regrettably

---

155 Anon., *A Letter*, p.5.
156 Anon., *A Letter*, p.5.
157 Rogers, *Defoe's Tour*, pp.543–544.

their content is unknown, but Townshend tried to reassure them. Initially Townshend had assumed that the Jacobite army, on leaving Kelso would have retreated to Scotland, pursued by Carpenter's men, who would join Argyle at Stirling, and that Wills, with five regiments of dragoons, one of horse and three of foot, setting out on 31 October, would be quartered so as to deter any Jacobite activity in Cheshire, Lancashire, Staffordshire and north Wales, and together with the militia, 'We hope very soon to break the measures of the rebels'.[158] This former scenario did not materialise.

On 8 November, he told Lonsdale that the Jacobites 'will be hindered from penetrating much further, so that what has hitherto happened ought not to give the least discouragement or uneasiness to the honest gentlemen of the country'. This was because the forces under Wills and Carpenter would be sure to 'put a stop to the progress of the rebels' as he told Cholmondeley. On 12 November he told Brigadier Stanwix, 'We expect soon to have a further account of them from Wills', which was to be proved.[159]

Lieutenant General Charles Wills. Mezzotint by John Simon. Published by Edward Cooper, after Michael Dahl, c.1700–1725. (Courtesy of the National Portrait Gallery, NPG D19943)

Meanwhile, the Jacobites' enemies were active. On 5 November Wills had been at Wigan and heard news that the Jacobite army had crossed into England and was marching south towards Lancashire. He summoned his forces to meet him at Warrington on 10 November. Hitherto they had been quartered in Shropshire, Worcestershire, Cheshire and Staffordshire.[160] There was a regiment of dragoons at Manchester on 5 November and Edmund Harrold (1678–1722), a wigmaker there, noted in his diary on that day, 'Church ringing and b[on]fires this night an express. [It] came to ye major of dragoons [ordering] march on [6th] in morning, wch ye did. [It was] dismal to see drums beating to horse and arms'.[161] Wills was at Manchester when he heard on 8 November that Carpenter had left Newcastle on 7 November with the regiments of Molesworth's, Churchill's and Cobham's dragoons and was marching to Lancaster.[162] The two generals were in correspondence with one another and presumably hoped to take the Jacobites in a pincer movement.

Hotham's battalion had been left at Newcastle 'where the greater part of the inhabitants are in ye Pretenders' interest' according to Hotham. He

---

158 TNA: SP44/118, pp.100–101, Townshend–Cholmondeley, Carlisle and Lonsdale, 1 November 1715.
159 TNA: SP44/118, pp.116, 117, 120, Townshend–Lonsdale, 8 November 1715, Townshend to Stanwix, 12 November 1715.
160 Rae, *History*, p.318; *Weekly Journal*, 12 November 1715.
161 Craig Horner (ed.), *Diary of Edmund Harrold, wigmaker of Manchester, 1712–1715* (Farnham: Ashgate, 2008), p.347.7/627.
162 *Daily Courant* 4386, 14 November 1715.

was convinced there would be a speedy victory, 'I doubt not but a few days' will bring an account of the southern rebels dispersing for we have found by experience that they will not stand regular troops though not one third of their number'.[163] Carpenter's men marched via Barnard Castle, Richmond, Ripon and Skipton. Lumley informed Lord Egmont on 10 November, 'there is now certain intelligence come in yt ye rebels marched yesterday from Lancaster to Preston where they give out that they expect great numbers to join them'. Carpenter had received a letter with news from Wills on the previous day and so Lumley wrote of the latter, 'His motions will in all likelihood hinder their conjunction with their friends at Wigan, who were, as well as those at Preston, to have risen and declared for ye Pretender ye day before yesterday'.[164]

Meanwhile, Townshend was writing to Honywood about an unnamed cornet or lieutenant in his regiment of dragoons, who had a brother at Oxford and had witnessed some of the Jacobite disturbances there. The officer in question had 'the character of being very well affected to the government so he need not be under any apprehension' and that Honywood should 'forthwith despatch him hither'. Honywood clearly did not do so, so there was a similar letter to him a month later. Presumably Honywood felt he needed all his men for the forthcoming battle rather than sending one to London.[165]

On this day there was a considerable number of troops briefly quartered on the town, and Harrold noted, 'We had above 1000 men quarter'd in towne. Inhabitants taken up. Some fled, others hid yenselves. All in amasement. Express [after] express to [deliver to] Genll Wills'.[166]

At nine on the morning of the 6 November, Preston's foot, 'the Scotch regiment of Foot', marched out of Chester for Warrington.[167] On 11 November, Wills marched from Manchester with Wynn's, Honywood's, Munden's and Dormer's dragoons and Preston's foot to Wigan. Harrold made another diary entry:

> This day is gone Genll Wills and his men towards camp to meet the rebels, who are now at Preston, where they have proclaim'd Jms ye 3d, and pray'd for him in ye church by yir own priest, for ye minister yir wou'd not do it. Webster Jam saw ym by way if spy. I never saw so any fien men and horses in my life at one time as is gone thro' this town on this occation. O God who governs all things, give victory to the righteous and let iniquity be punished, for sin is an evil to be punished by ye judge. Do bless and preserve the Church of England in its liturgie, laws and liberty, as it now is ye law.[168]

Later that day they arrived at Wigan, where Stanhope's dragoons and Pitt's Horse were already quartered. Newton's dragoons were marching from

---

163 BL. Stowe 748, f.108r, Hotham to ?, 11 November 1715.
164 BL. Stowe 748, f.110r, Lumley to ?, 10 November 1715.
165 TNA: SP44/147, Secretaries of State: State Papers: Entry Books. Domestic. Under Secretaries' Letter Books, 1714-1724, Townshend–Honywood, 3 November 1715.
166 Horner, *Diary*, p.347.7/627.
167 Addy and McNiven, 'Diary', p.471.
168 Horner, *Diary*, p.347.7/627.

Worcester to Manchester and Wills ordered that they remain at the latter, to deter any Jacobite behaviour in the town which had seen so much in June of that year. Meanwhile, his main body had orders to march from Wigan to Preston at daybreak of 12 November.[169]

Hoghton, who was with Wills, wrote to summon local support to the Rev. Woods in Chowbent:

> The officers here design to march at break of day for Preston. They have desired me to raise what men I can to meet us at Preston tomorrow, so desire you to raise all the force you can, I mean lusty young fellows to draw up on Cuerdon Green to be there by ten o'clock to bring what arms they have fit for service, and scythes put in straight polls, and such as have not, to bring spades and billhooks for pioneering with. Pray go immediately all among your neighbours and give this notice.[170]

Another loyalist was Preston's Vicar, who left the town on the Jacobites' arrival. It was claimed that Peploe 'who so manifestly distinguished himself for his zeal and loyalty to the government when the rebels entered that town'. It is uncertain what this entailed, but presumably he provided useful intelligence to Wills and he was certainly well rewarded thereafter for services rendered.[171]

Loyalists were confident of victory, with Liddell writing, 'you may depend 'ere they be well in Lancash[ire] you will find Gen[eral] Wills ready to receive them with 7 regim[ents] off regular troops, and tis supposed Carpenter will not fail pursuing his march towards them as expeditiously as possible'.[172] Pulteney wrote likewise, 'I believe it will not be necessary to send more forces, thinking in regard those under his command, with them he will be sufficient to quell all the designs of the rebels who I hope will have the mortification to fall between both your fires'.[173] On the other hand, there was overconfidence, too, on Wills' part. Ensign Charles Colville (1691–1775) of Preston's battalion of infantry wrote 'Indeed, I have heard him blamed for not waiting for two old regiments of infantry [Sabine's and Fane's Foot] which he knew well were within a few days march of him'.[174]

On the eve of battle, last minute attempts were being made by the Jacobites to remedy their shortfall in ammunition. Richard Shepherd, a servant at Stonyhurst (home of Sir Nicholas Shureburne, a Catholic gentleman) 'did make and cast bullets ye night before Preston battle in great quantity, wch was most of ye night's work having a great provision of their muskets' lead wxh they received from John Mason as also a large melting pot', all of which belonged to his master, Sir Nicholas Shureburne. He was assisted by John Walmsley and four others. How many they made is another question. Fellow

---

169 Rae, *History*, p.318.
170 Lumby, 'De Hoghton deeds', p.113.
171 *Weekly Journal*, 11 February 1716.
172 Ellis, 'Liddell–Cotesworth Letters', p.196.
173 TNA: WO4/17, p.265, Pulteney–Lonsdale, 8 November 1715.
174 J.O. Robson (ed.), 'Military Memoirs of General Charles Colville', JSAHR, XXV (1947), p.60.

servant John Watson was busy shoeing horses of the Jacobite cavalry at this time.[175] Meanwhile, John Shaftoe had enlisted between 70–100 men (among Lancastrian recruits, presumably) and were forming them into a troop as a nucleus of a regiment he aspired to lead.[176] He gave each recruit a shilling and promised them all a horse and boots. Two brothers from Walton provided him with six horses.[177]

Despite the reluctance of the Jacobite army to fight against any serious opposition, they were now faced with a foe who was ready and willing to do so. Their options were narrowing. Wills doubtless looked forward to battle, perhaps convinced that his enemy would not stand or if they did they would soon crumble. The ensuing battle would, in fact, test the capacities of both sides to the utmost.

---

175 TNA: FEC1/340, Proceedings of communications from Thomas Rishton, 1715–1716.
176 Anon., *Faithful Register*, p.23.
177 TNA: FEC1/1585, Towneley and Tildesley.

4

The Armies

We shall now turn away from the impending battle in order to examine the men who fought it, beginning with the Jacobite army.

Unlike the case with the Jacobite army of 1745, there has been relatively little discussion of the Jacobite army of thirty years earlier. Reid lists the known units and their officers, and provides some general information about them.[1] There is some discussion about the army in England, focussing on the English component in the works of Monod and the present author (the north western Englishmen) and Gooch (the Northumbrians), with work on both nationalities in an article by the former.[2] Gooch's – and Monod's – aims were to identify and focus on the individuals who came out in revolt, rather than their military capabilities. Generally speaking, the minority of Englishmen in the Jacobite army have received far more attention than the Scottish majority.

The Jacobite army which fought at Preston was composed of three main components: the Highland and Lowland infantry from Mar's army under Mackintosh, the Lowland gentry and their servants under Viscount Kenmure and the English, mostly from the northern counties, under Forster. Historians, knowing the army's ultimate fate, have poured scorn on the force, especially its leaders. Reid makes the general observation, 'most of the Jacobite leaders in question were manifestly unfit to mount a guard on a privy'.[3] According to the Taylers, Forster was 'an even more unfortunate choice than the Earl of Mar – no soldier, and had not even the merit of personal bravery'.[4] Baynes wrote that 'Forster had few qualifications for the position. He had no military experience at all and was not especially admired'.[5] Arnold wrote 'Tom Forster had no qualifications for leadership. He had no military experience, and his martial failings will become all too apparent'.[6] According to Lenman, 'Tom Forster was quite remarkably useless at everything, except saving his own skin'.[7]

---

1 Reid, *Sheriffmuir*, pp.23–33, 155–167.
2 Oates, *Last Battle*, pp.97–105, 109–117; Monod, *Jacobitism*, pp.317–327; Gooch, *Desperate Faction*, pp.51–68; Oates, 'The Armies operating in the north of England in 1715'.
3 Reid, *Sheriffmuir*, p.78.
4 Taylers, *The Story*, p.80.
5 Baynes, *Jacobite Rising*, p.86.
6 Arnold, *Northern Lights*, p.92.
7 Lenman, *Jacobite Risings*, p.120.

There has been a lone defence of Forster. Gooch argues that he was not expected to be a military leader; the Jacobites were expecting substantial support from overseas and within Newcastle itself, as well as more assistance from the English Tories and Jacobites. He was a man let down by others, but was personally flawless. Finally, he merely bowed to the inevitable when faced with overwhelming odds.[8] According to Szechi, 'He had no military experience and an indecisive character' and notes that he and Mar both needed expert professional advice but that neither man received it.[9]

A Jacobite song, *An Excellent New Song on the Rebellion*, collected in the nineteenth century is unambiguous in the following verse:

> Lord Derwentwater to Forster said
> Thou hast ruin'd the cause and all betray'd
> For thou didst vow to stand our friend.
> But hast prov'd traitor on the end
> Thou brought us from our own Country;
> We left our homes and came with thee,
> But thou art a rogue and traitor both,
> And hast broke thy honour and thy oath.[10]

Leadership

There were two leaders of the army and a number of other senior figures within the command. Almost all were in post due to their social, political and religious status, not military experience or ability. Mar had determined that when the army was in Scotland, they would be led by a Scotsman (Kenmure) and when in England by an Englishman (Forster). However, as to the latter, Mar was following James Stuart's order of 14 October that Forster should be commander in chief until Ormonde arrived.[11]

As with historians, contemporaries on both sides tended to disparage the Jacobite leadership. An anonymous Lowlander wrote 'our Generals and Lords were all of a piece, either Rogues or Cowards, save two, Derwentwater and Wintoun', adding 'our Generalls Courage was so great that they never durst look any body in the face and altered their resolutions every half hour … were not ten minutes of one mind.'[12] Apparently the two exceptions, and Lord Nairn 'were all very tight and firme'.[13]

The Scottish leader was William Gordon, the Viscount Kenmure. According to Patten, 'He was a grave, full-aged Gentleman, of a very ancient family, and he himself of extraordinary Knowledge and experience in Publick

---

8   Gooch, *Desperate Faction*, pp.83–84.
9   Szechi, *1715*, pp.171, 195.
10 M.G.H. Pittock (ed.), *The Jacobite Relics of Scotland collected by James Hogg* (Edinburgh: Edinburgh University, 2003), pp.104–105.
11 *HMC Stuart Papers*, IV, p.453.
12 BC: 45/12/77, account of the Jacobite southern army to Preston.
13 TNA: SP54/9/107, Jacobite prisoner's experiences in the rebellion.

and Political Business, though utterly a stranger to all Military Affairs; of a singular good temper and too Calm and Mild to be qualified for such a Post'.[14] The Master of Sinclair was also critical, writing 'I shan't dispute with any that my lord Kenmure was a very honest man, but as unfit for that province as any man of that rank can be supposed to be'.[15]

The English leader was Thomas Forster, MP of Atherstone in Northumberland. He was from gentry stock, educated at Newcastle School and then at St John's College, Cambridge, before becoming county sheriff in 1703 and one of the county's two MPs in 1708, elected as a Tory. He was later unflatteringly described thus, 'of a Middle Stature, inkling to be Fat, well shap'd, except his Mouth wide, his Nose pretty large, his Eyes Grey, speaks the Northern Dialect'.[16] Patten, as his chaplain, defended his reputation:

> I cannot but justify him against the many Aspersions he lies under … It must be own'd he was no soldier, nor was the command given to him as such, but as he was the only Protestant who could give any Repute to their Undertaking, being of note in Northumberland, of an ancient family, and having for several years been member of Parliament for that county, and therefore very popular: For if the Command had been given to either of the two lords, their characters, as Papists, would have discouraged many of the people, and being improved against the Design in general.[17]

Lady Cowper was convinced that Forster's social connections were key to his position: 'I conjecture that it was for the sake of his uncle [Nathaniel Crewe, bishop of Durham] and Aunt that he was made General, and not at all from the Fitness of the Thing for he had never seen any Army in is life'.[18]

Derwentwater made a similar remark:

> What could we do better? The Catholics were not to appear at the Head of the Business; High Church was to do it. And who could we in Northumberland pick out to please the High Church better than Mr Forster, Knight of the shire who represented them all?[19]

Another contemporary comment suggests that Forster's Anglicanism was crucial: '… the Earl of Derwentwater was the chief Person there, yet he being a papist, it was feared it would have fear'd some of the High Church party from joining them, if he had been the General'.[20]

Contemporaries critical of Forster were also scathing. Scottish loyalist, John Clerk of Penicuik, wrote that Forster was 'an idle, drunken senseless

---

14 Patten, *History*, p.39.
15 Scott, *Memoir*, p.255.
16 Patten, *History*, p.108.
17 Patten, *History*, p.97.
18 Cowper, *Diary*, p.57.
19 John Oldmixion, *History of England during the reigns of William and Mary, Anne and George I* (London Publisher Unknown, 1735), p.616.
20 Rae, *History*, p.239n.

man, not good enough to lead a company of militia'.[21] Rae referred to Forster as a 'cowardly general'.[22] Contemporary historian John Oldmixion wrote likewise, deeming him 'an illiterate half witted country squire … so ignorant and worthless a person'.[23] Even an ally, Miss Hodgson of Tone, was critical, 'he was a pig-headed fool', despite being a good horseman.[24]

Instead, Forster took counsel elsewhere, 'he always submitted to the Counsel of Colonel Oxburgh', who 'has got the Character of Brave and Bold: He has given signal Instances thereof Beyond Seas; but we all must say, we saw very little of it'.[25] The latter was a landed Catholic Irishman who had served in James II's army in 1695–1700, and was styled colonel. According to Patten, he 'was of a good, mild, merciful disposition, very thoughtful and a mighty zealous man in his Religion, quiet in his Conversation, and more of the Priest in his Appearance than the Soldier'. He also noted, 'in our case that he either wanted Conduct or Courage, or perhaps both: He was better at his Beads and Prayers than at his Business as a soldier'.[26] Apparently he was the commander of the English forces, under Forster and rode at the head of the cavalry on the march.[27]

Forster also sought counsel with another, Patten noting 'Besides the influence of Colonel Oxburgh, my lord Widdrington had too great Prevalence over Mr Forster's easy temper: and this Lord we thought understood so little of the matter, that he was as unfit for a General as the other; for tho' the Family of Widdrington be fam'd in History for their Bravery and Loyalty to the English Crown, yet there is little of it left in this Lord, or at least he did not shew it, that ever we could find'. Widdrington was William Widdrington and was a Northumbrian Catholic nobleman, who had no experience of soldiering.[28]

Forster was a politician and not a soldier. As such he was a good figurehead leader to head the English Jacobites and may well not have expected to even have had to fight a battle, as in the changes of regime in 1660 or 1688. He was not unaware of his limitations, though. However, his choice of adviser may well have been unsound and he was certainly viewed by the army as being its commander, especially at the moment of the final crisis in Preston and this was not a role he was fitted for, as he was to acknowledge.

The other principal figures were all noblemen. Best known among these was James Radcliffe, 3rd earl of Derwentwater. He was a wealthy young man, recently married and with an heir, owner of large estates in the north of England. He was popular among his tenants and neighbours. However, he was a Catholic and had known James Stuart as a child when he had lived at the exiled court; indeed James II had raised his grandfather to the peerage

---

21 J.M. Grey (ed.), 'The Memoirs of Sir John Clerke of Pencuik', *Scottish History Society*, series 1, 7 (1892), p.91.
22 Rae, *History*, p.239.
23 Oldmixion, *History*, p.616.
24 Baynes, *Jacobite Rising*, p.91.
25 Patten, *History*, p.98.
26 Patten, *History*, pp.119, 97.
27 Anon., *Faithful Register*, pp.240–241.
28 Patten, *History*, pp.97–98.

in 1687. He was a genuine Jacobite but could not be its movement's leader because of his faith. Patten wrote of him:

> He was a Man form'd by Nature to be generally belov'd; for he was so universal a Beneficence, that he seems to live for others. As he liv'd among his own People, there he spent his Estate, and continually did Offices of Kindness and Good Neighbourhood to every body, as Opportunity offer'd. he kept a House of generous Hospitality and noble Entertainment, which few in that Country do, and none come up to. He was very charitable to poor and distressed Families on all Occasions, whether known to him or not, and whether Papist or Protestant.[29]

There were also a number of Lowland noblemen: George Setoun, the Earl of Winton, 'of a very ancient family, wants no Courage, nor so much Capacity as his friends find it for his Interest to suggest', Robert Dalziel, the Earl of Carnwath, 'singularly good in his Temper, and of an agreeable Affability, and delivers himself very handsomely in his Discourse'. Then there was William Maxwell, Earl of Nithsdale.[30]

There were two other principal military advisers to the Jacobite leadership. One was Mackintosh, who had some military experience. Patten claimed that he was a very avaricious man and was motivated by plunder: 'His Avarice and Covetousness very much discover'd Man: For it is well known that he made false Musters of his men, and gave them in far more numerous than they were ... Besides several small spirited Actions of taking Bribes. [31]

After being critical of Kenmure, as noted above, Sinclair wrote this of Mackintosh:

> ... yet less qualified for it, for he had neither rank nor any distinguishing thing about him except ignorant presumption and ane affected Inverness English accent, not common, indeed amongst Highlandmen; and it may be allouued to quote the character that a ladie gave of him, who I wish most of our men had resembled either in sense or any other thing, I mean my ladie Nairne, who, regrating heartielie her husband's being concern'd where Mackintosh was Commander, said, he had been herding of Highland cattle this eight and tuentie year, that he had turned ox himself.[32]

He also noted:

> ... under the command of one who had no pretensions to know anything of service ... the world had no better opinion of that time than they have at present, and who had nothing to recommend him but that his chief, the Laird of Mackintosh, who all lookt on to be a very weak man, imagin'd him wiser than himself, and delivered up himself and his Clan up to his dispoasale; all of which, if consider'd, and that the Brigadier had not creedite for thirtie pounds in the countrie ... it will look

---

29 Patten, *History*, pp.47–48.
30 Patten, *History*, pp.39–41.
31 Patten, *History*, p.14.
32 Scott, *Memoir*, pp.255–256.

odd how so many Lords and Gentlemen trusted themselves to him, or that as had the face to choose him for such a command.[33]

Some of the junior officers, however, were men of a military background. Captain James Dalziel had been an officer in the British army and was a half pay officer in 1715, resigning his commission on the onset of the campaign. Captain Philip Lockhart was a half pay officer, having served in Lord Mark Kerr's regiment. Thomas Errington of Beaufront 'had been formerly an Officer in the French Service, where he had got the Reputation of a good Soldier'. Robert Talbot was another Irish Catholic who had fought in the French army, 'he was accounted a very good soldier'.[34] Major Nairn, another veteran, 'was by many thought the best soldier among them' and John Shaftoe had been a captain in Frank's battalion in the recent war in Spain. However, Ensign John Erskine of Preston's battalion had 'the character of a soft half witted person'.[35] Richard Harris was another ensign from that same battalion who was in the Jacobite ranks; both were to find themselves on the opposing sides to their former colleagues at the battle.[36] William Brereton had been a major in Jones' horse in the recent war.[37] Not all officers were so; the Honourable James Hume was 'not very capable of having the Command of a Troop, as well on account of his Age, as other Incapacities'.[38]

Many of these men were motivated by strong political and religious principles. English Tories sought political power, Scottish nationalists wanted an end to the Union, Scottish Episcopalians wanted a return to the episcopacy and English Catholics wanted toleration and an end to the penal laws. A Stuart restoration could lead to all of these. More specifically, Carnwath 'was brought up under the Tuition of One who made it his study'd Care to instill the Principles of Hereditary Right, passive Obedience, and non Resistance into his Mind … an entire Affection of the Liturgy and Worship in use in the Church of England'. Richard Gascoigne, an Irish Catholic, 'was bred a Roman; according to his principles was zealous for the Chevalier, and a declared Enemy to the Revolution'. A letter from Ireland noted that Oxburgh's character and 'Inclinations to the Pretender; which made him appear as Irreconcilable to the Protestant Interest'.[39] As far as is known, all the officers of the Jacobite army were gentlemen, social and political standing were key to their being officers; they were men who could bring others to the field by their influence and coercive ability.

The Jacobite army was disparaged by the contemporary press, being described as being made up of 'Papists and many of them are servants and fellows of the meaner sort'. Furthermore, they were said to be 'not indifferently armed especially the Horse'.[40] Another hostile contemporary comment, about the Jacobite Lowland forces was as follows, 'many of 'em were their neighbours;

---

33 Scott, *Memoir*, pp.156–157.
34 Patten, *History*, pp.40, 41, 48, 110.
35 Anon., *Faithful Register*, pp.22–24.
36 *London Gazette*, 5385, 26-29 November 1715.
37 Charles Dalton, *English Army Lists, VI* (London: Eyre and Spottiswoode, 1904), p.254.
38 Patten, *History*, p.39.
39 Patten, *History*, pp.40, 117.
40 *London Gazette*, 5376, 25–28 October 1715; 5378, 5–8 November 1715.

that they were Swearers, Foreswearers, Drunkards, Thieves, Whoremasters, in short the vilest Wretches that ever infested their Neighbourhood'.[41]

Recruitment and Finance

Many men came to the Jacobite army as part of a group led by a gentleman or nobleman. Derwentwater brought his smith and groom along with him (Simon and George Dickson of Corbridge).[42] Sinclair wrote, 'My Lord Nairne and his son brought in their owne men, and some of the Duke of Athole's Highlandmen'.[43] Derwentwater arrived with friends and servants.[44] Richard Towneley arrived in Preston with between 16–60 men, half mounted and half on foot; Sir Francis Anderton had eight horsemen with him.[45] Some men may have been happy to have come along: Sinclair wrote of those recruited by Nairn and Lord Charles Murray (younger brother of the better known Lord George Murray), 'the Athoile men, who were naturallie well inclined to the cause'.[46] Patten recounts how a group of keelmen were marching to join the Jacobite army of their own accord, without any obvious leader, presumably as volunteers.[47]

Yet many of the men in the Jacobite ranks had been compelled to serve therein. Mar had written to his baillie on 9 September, bemoaning the lack of recruits coming in voluntarily and wrote, 'so I will be forced to put other orders I have into execution'. To be specific, he wrote:

> … let my own tenants in Kildrummy know, that if they come not forth with their best arms, that I will send a party immediately to burn what they shall miss taking from them: And they may believe this not only a Threat, but, by all that's sacred, I'll put it into Execution, let my Loss be what it will, that it may be an Example to others.[48]

James Menzies later petitioned that he had been forced to join the Jacobite army under 'a warrant of fire and sword against all who would not join the Highlanders'. He was captured at night time and taken prisoner to Perth 'where he was very harshly dealt with and threatened with death and destruction of his house and tenantry unless he would comply'. He had been badly treated when crossing the Forth. William Mackintosh asserted he had been 'partly forced and partly deluded into the rebellion, having been forced from his home and taken to Perth'.[49]

Many men offered similar defences at their later trials and so there may be a suspicion that for some these were excuses in order to escape the noose

---

41 *Flying Post*, 3731, 1–3 December 1715.
42 TNA: KB8/66, f.95v, Baga de Secretis.
43 Scott, *Memoir*, p.50.
44 Patten, *History*, p.19.
45 *St. James Evening Post*, 72, 12–15 November 1715.
46 Scott, *Memoir*, p.35.
47 Patten, *History*, pp.28–29.
48 Rae, *History*, pp.193–194.
49 TNA: SP35/7, ff.37r, 43r, State Papers Domestic: George I, Menzies-George I, 1716.

thereafter. But not in all cases, as with Failie Ferguson, who was acquitted because:

> … who proved not only that he was forced into the Rebellion, but that he was brought along under a Guard, having refused to come; and also that he attempted several Times to desert, but was prevented, and was threatened to be hanged, if he offered it again, and that they offered him a Lieutenant's Commission, but he refused it.[50]

This may well have been the case with some of the English recruits, too. Thomas Carus, a Lancashire gentleman, claimed that his father pressurised him into taking part in the campaign, 'both urged and constrained your petitioner … to goe along with them … threatened to turn his wife and tender infants out of home and let them starve unless he would goe along with them'.[51] It is not known how far some of the men were influenced by others into action. That some were seems inescapable. Thomas Errington claimed that as a tenant of Derwentwater he was obliged to take part in the campaign due to 'the many obligations he laid under by being tenant to several lead mines'.[52]

Yet when on the scaffold, some Jacobites attested their loyalty to the Jacobite cause in no half hearted manner. John Bruce, a Scot, claimed 'I am not asham'd of that cause for which I die but rejoice that I am worthy to be a sacrifice for the vindication of the undoubted Right of my Lawful and Natural liege Lord King James the Third, and the expiring Liberties of my dear Country'.[53] Likewise, Derwentwater was later to declare:

> I have made bold with my loyalty, having never any other but King James III for my lawful and rightful sovereign: him I had an inclination to serve from my infancy, and was moved thereto by a natural love I had to his person, knowing him to be capable of making his people happy … I intended to … serve my King and country, and that without self interest, hoping by the example I gave, to have induced others to do their duty … to the service of my King and Country, and the re-establishment of the ancient and fundamental constitution of these Kingdoms, without which no lasting peace or true happiness can attend them.[54]

According to Lady Cowper, one of the Jacobites was a fanatical hater of Protestants. This man was Richard Shuttleworth, 'He was famous for saying he hoped in a little Time to see Preston Streets running with heretic Blood as they do with Water when it had rained twelve Hours'.[55]

Many of the recruits may have joined due to links of family, neighbours and friendship with others. This certainly seems to have been the case in England. Charles and Peregrine Widdrington were brothers to Lord Widdrington (who

---

50 Rae, *History*, p.379.
51 TNA: SP35/7, f.30r, Carus–Townshend, 1716.
52 TNA: SP35/5, f.173r, Errington–Prince of Wales, 31 May 1716.
53 *Weekly Journal*, 13 October 1716.
54 *Political State of Great Britain*, XI (1716), p.239.
55 Cowper, *Diary*, pp.84–85.

was cousin to Derwentwater) and Edward Tyldesley's father's diary mentions at least a score of Jacobite gentry who were to participate, along with his son, in the campaign. Walter Tancred, though from Yorkshire, 'was Companion to the Lord Widdrington in all his Country Diversions'. Richard Towneley was Widdrington's brother-in-law. Charles Radcliffe was the younger brother of Derwentwater. William Shaftoe of Bavington was allegedly 'brought into the Rebellion through the Instigation of his Lady' and brought his son with him. Brothers Edward and James Swinburne both came in. Dr Alcock had been overheard making Jacobite remarks and so, not wanting to be tried for these, joined the Jacobite army.[56] Lady Cowper wrote, 'some Sons drawn in by their Fathers, and Mr Shafto by his Son, who forced him to take arms'.[57] Lower than the social scale, four members of the Cowp family of Walton, all of whom were weavers, enlisted, and as shall be noted many men came from certain parishes, all of whom probably knew each other. There were four Scottish Rutherfords, all doctors and it is hard to suppose they were all strangers to one another.[58] It is less difficult for new recruits to engage in warfare if they are doing so with their friends and neighbours.

For many of the English, politics, religion and family background may have been crucial. Given the limited evidence available, they were overwhelmingly Catholic; about 75 percent overall being so, and this was even more so in Lancashire, though less so from the north east where Protestant gentry were in a small majority. Many had had fathers who had supported James II and had plotted against William in the Lancashire conspiracy of the 1690s, and/or ancestors who had fought for Charles I in the civil wars. The grandfathers of both John Dalton and Edward Tyldesley had been killed fighting for the Royalist cause in 1643 and 1651, respectively.[59] George Hilton (1673–1725) was a Catholic gentleman from Westmorland. Apart from being a Catholic, he was impoverished, separated from his wife and known to have a violent temper and a fondness for drink. He was thus an ideal candidate to take part in such a risky undertaking.[60]

The Scots, incidentally were almost wholly Protestant and probably mostly Episcopalian, which Church had been made illegal in 1690. Nationalism and religion were their two major motivations. John Loveday, an English traveller in Scotland in 1732, noted 'All in general with the utmost freedom damn the Union; as unanimous, in saying no good of King William, all remember the Darien affair and the Massacre at Glencoe'.[61] As has been noted, there was friction between the Scots and English and this was on both religious and nationalistic grounds.

There were baser motives, too. According to Sinclair, the Highlanders were motivated by the hope of loot from successful war, 'The Highlandmen would

---

56 Patten, *History*, p.109, 113, 115.
57 Cowper, *Diary*, p.78.
58 TNA: KB8/66, Baga de Secretis.
59 TNA: KB8/66, Baga de Secretis; Monod, *Jacobitism*, pp.317–327.
60 Anne Hillman (ed.), *The Rake's Diary: The Journal of George Hilton* (Kendal: Curwen Archives Trust, 1994).
61 Sarah Markham (ed.), *John Loveday of Caversham, 1711–1789* (Salisbury: Michael Russell, 1984), p.135.

rise out of hopes of plunder and would doe as they had always done'.⁶² A similar motive was ascribed to one Clavering, a relative of Lady Cowper, who wrote 'A desperate Fortune had drove him from Home in hopes to have repaired it'.⁶³

There were also volunteers, as Patten related when on his way, alone, to join the Jacobites on 19 October in Northumberland. He met a number of unarmed keelsmen and after realising they were not militia, asked them their business, 'They answered … We are Scotsmen, going to our Homes to join our Countrymen that are in Arms for King James'. One of them then said 'I'll drink his Health just now: So with his Bonnet, which he dipt into a Runner, he said, Here is King James' Health; which all his Partners did'.⁶⁴

An insight into recruiting was provided by one John Tattersall. On 6 November, Towneley was holding open house at Towneley Hall, near Burnley, and plying guests of all social grades with drink. Two days later, with the Jacobite army at Lancaster, he told the assembled throng 'such as would take up arms and goe with him he would be glad of their company and such as would not might go home'. However those preferring the second option were barred from doing so. Towneley and Shuttleworth, at noon, 'took ye rest along with them, driving them as sheep before them'. On reaching Haslingdon, Tattersall escaped at night time.⁶⁵

As well as men, armies require money. Regular armies are paid for by governments who raise money by taxation and loans to pay for wages, uniforms, equipment, arms and ammunition. Without money an army turns to banditry who create resentment and anger among the population which they rob. Yet the Jacobites had no such resources at their back. They could only pay from the funds belonging to themselves, but these were limited to that which they had to hand and could carry with them. This may have happened in the first few weeks of the campaign until Kelso was reached.

There was another way and that was seized upon from Kelso to Preston. Patten recorded that at Kelso the Highlanders 'failed not here, as well as in all Places, to demand all the Publick Revenues, viz., of Excise, Customs, or Taxes'. These were taxes on both property (Land Tax) and on certain goods which were sold (Customs and Excise taxes), and which were collected locally before being transmitted to the Exchequer in London.⁶⁶

James Ossington acted as the collector of these monies for the Jacobite army. He later recalled how he kept 'all the accounts' and 'having the trouble of paying the men, as well as providing the money and a great many other things'. It seems that the men were paid sixpence a day, which was an improvement on the threepence that Mar paid the Scots. Ossington noted 'I proclaimed the King in Northumberland, Cumberland, Westmorland and Lancashire, and collected all the public moneys and duties of all kinds and gave receipts under

---

62 Scott, *Memoir*, p.26.
63 Cowper, *Dairy*, p.62.
64 Patten, *History*, p.29.
65 TNA: FEC1/1585, Towneley and Tyldesley.
66 Patten, *History*, pp.37–38.

my own hand to every person for the use of King James'.[67] In all £379 5s 8d was collected in Westmorland, Cumberland and Lancashire.[68]

The Scottish infantry were paid sixpence a day from 1 November.[69] Winton paid his cavalry eighteen pence or two shillings a day, though of course, they had a horse to maintain, too.[70]

Equipment and Tactics

The Jacobite army had to build up an arsenal from scratch: there were no arms from abroad nor any major capture of arms from government stockpiles. Gentlemen, of course, had their own swords and pistols. Macky wrote in the next decade of Highland gentlemen, 'They have a Ponyard Knife and fork in one sheath hanging at one side of their Belt, their Pistol at the other … with a great Broad-Sword by their side'.[71] Not so the bulk of the men. There were complaints in the building up of the army in Scotland that their weaponry was poor, but this should have come as no surprise. Sinclair makes many references to the lack of arms and ammunition, particularly to those of Strathmore's battalion. In September they had come to Perth 'with such armes as they had, all more for shew and countenance than use'. When they were about to cross the Forth, 'much the greatest part, wanted flints … being Low Countrie men, they had neither suords, or pretended to make use of any'.[72] More generally, he noted, 'most of our armes were good for nothing, there was no method fallen on, nor was the least care takne [taken] to repair those old rustie brokne [broken] pieces, which it seems, were to be carried about more for ornament than use, tho' gunsmiths were not wanting'.[73]

On 2 October 1715 there had been a raid on the ships at Burntisland which had managed to obtain 354 muskets and a quantity of gunpowder and musket balls, but for an army of several thousand, clearly this was small beer.[74] On the eve of the expedition over the Forth, Sinclair bemoaned the fact that they were being sent 'so badlie armed, and without pouder'.[75]

John Sibbitt, mayor of Berwick, who had a close watch kept on the Jacobite army as it marched into the north of England, noted that Mackintosh's men 'arrived with musket, sword and target according to the Highland manner', but that 'they have neither ammunition nor provisions but what each man carries himself'.[76]

---

67 *HMC Stuart Papers*, III, pp.300.
68 Jarvis, *Collected Papers*, p.187.
69 Patten, *History*, p.58.
70 *Penny London Post*, 412, 16–18 December 1745.
71 Macky, *A Journey through Scotland*, p.190.
72 Scott, *Memoir*, pp.43, 143.
73 Scott, *Memoir*, p.81.
74 Scott, *Memoir*, pp.98–100.
75 Scott, *Memoir*, p.156.
76 TNA: SP54/9, 107, Jacobite prisoner's experiences in the rebellion.

Clarke noted that the Scottish infantry bore swords, and that their quartermasters had targets, sword and either a gun or a brace of pistols.[77] Sergeants may have borne halberds, as in the regular army, as a Scot armed with one menaced a Quaker at Kendal.[78] They had flags, drummers and bagpipers.[79]

The English were variously armed: from poor to good. Robert Douglas reported that at the end of October, 'few or none well armed, all the greatest part altogether without armes; that their horses were light hunting horses, and hunting saddles and snaffles made up their accoutrements; that there was scarce a cutting sword amongst them … several, yea numbers, who had joyned and returned home for want of arms'.[80] Another contemporary observed, 'They were ill armed, some had swords and no muskets, some had muskets and no swords, some fowling Pieces, some pitchforks, some no weapons at all'.[81] Yet on the other hand, an anonymous Lowlander noted that some of the recruits joining in the following month consisted of '200 well armed men'.[82] Another anonymous Lowlander remembered this differently, 'not 200 Horse, the half not Arm'd and a very few Foot, not arm'd at all'.[83] At Hexham it was noted that of a company of English Jacobite infantry, they 'found means to arm them very well'.[84] The Jacobite cavalry were deemed to be 'armed with swords and pistols' and 'well armed', riding with drawn swords.[85] At their trials, both Widdrington and Derwentwater both attested to the inadequacy of their arms; the former alleging that his men had 'no Arms, but his common fowling pieces and wearing swords and fewer horse than he had constantly kept'. Derwentwater claimed, 'I was wholly unprovided with men, horses, arms and other necessaries'.[86] Some of the horses ridden by the Jacobite cavalry were only coach horses and thus not those able of mounting any type of offensive cavalry action. Some of those joining, such as a group of keelsmen, were unarmed and the Jacobites could not offer would be infantry recruits any arms. Muskets were hard to come by, therefore.[87]

As to the Lowlanders, who made the much of the cavalry, 'they were much better horsed for the purpose, because they had strong ruff horses, and were all very well armed: which I understood, well armed in comparison of the English'.[88] Winton's horsemen were mostly armed with swords and pistols.[89]

A list of a small portion of the Jacobite army gives their arms as noted by witnesses prior to the battle. Of those 13 Scottish gentlemen noted there: four were armed with sword and target, three with sword and pistol, two carried muskets, one a bayonet and three seemed to be unarmed. Of 12 Scottish rank and file, seven were musket armed, one carried a sword and target, one a

---

77 Paton, 'Journal', pp.514–515.
78 Paton, 'Journal', p.515.
79 Paton, 'Journal', p.515.
80 Scott, *Memoir*, p.191.
81 Anon., *Annals*, II, p.136.
82 BC: 45/12/77, account of the southern Jacobite army to Preston.
83 *Weekly Journal*, 10 March 1716
84 Anon., *Annals*, II, p.76.
85 Patten, *History*, pp.17, 19.
86 Anon., *Faithful Register*, pp.56, 67.
87 Patten, *History*, pp.21, 29.
88 Scott, *Memoir*, p.191.
89 *Penny London Post*, 412, 16–18 December 1745.

THE ARMIES

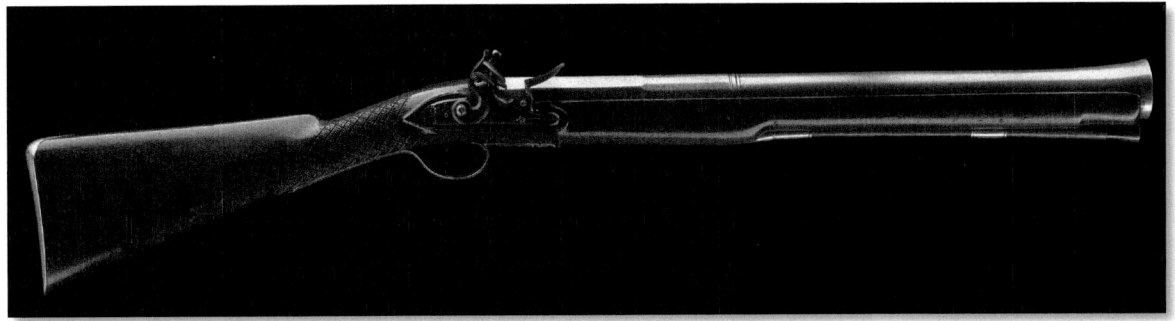

Blunderbuss taken from a Jacobite by a British soldier at Preston. (Courtesy of the National Museum of Scotland, NMS X2015.143)

sword, one a drum and two did not carry arms. In contrast, of the 14 English gentlemen noted: six were sword armed, five had a sword and pistol, one a musket and sword, one was unarmed and the other had unspecified arms. The dozen English rank and file were less well armed: three had a sword and pistol, three had swords, one a musket, one a sword and musket and four were unarmed. How representative this sample of about two percent of the army is, is another question, but it does suggest the English were least well armed, but even so three quarters were armed and a higher proportion of the gentry were so. Of the Scots, a few were unarmed, but many were musket armed.[90]

The general shortage of weaponry was evident from the fact that in the march through north west England, searches for such were made at the towns in which they stopped. At Kendal the mayor was taken prisoner for not telling where the militia arms were. On hearing that the arms were stored in the parish church, the Scots broke into it in search of them. On a weekend the town's gunsmiths were ordered to work 'very hard … for little or no pay'.[91]

There are no known uniforms for the Jacobite army, but the Scots wore blue and white cockades, the English red and white cockades. Winton had five servants in his own livery.[92] Apart from Strathmore's battalion, all the other Scottish infantry seem to have worn Highland dress whether they were Highlanders or not and apart from Mackintosh's command, most were not. This may have been as much a political as a fashion statement in identifying Highlander with Jacobite.[93] Highland dress was described by Macky in 1728 thus, the gentlemen 'dress'd in their slash'd short Waistcoats, a Trousing (which is Breeches and Stockings of one Piece of strip'd Stuff) with a Plaid for a cloak and a blue Bonnett'. Their followers wore 'belted Plaids, girt like Womens Petticoats down to the Knee: their Thighs and half of the Leg all bare'.[94] Some English rank and file were described as going to the Mitre inn in Preston to obtain liveries and two men are described as wearing Towneley's livery, but there are no indications what these were or how many men wore

---

90 TNA: KB8/66, Baga de Secretis.
91 Paton, 'Journal', pp.515–516.
92 *Penny London Post*, 414, 20–23 December 1745.
93 Jenn Scott, *I am minded to rise: The clothing, weapons and accoutrements of the Jacobites in Scotland, 1689–1719* (Solihull: Helion, 2020), p.46.
94 Macky, *Journey through Scotland*, p.190.

them; most descriptions of English Jacobites merely refer to the wearing of the appropriate cockades in their hats.[95]

Some Scottish battalions carried flags and had musicians, but by no means all and there was a Northumberland bagpiper. The colours of both Mar's and Logie Drummond's battalions were taken at Sheriffmuir so clearly the fragments of these forces at Preston did not have them.

Attempts were also made to acquire artillery, as has been noted, whether the guns taken in the Lowlands, dragged along and then spiked, or the guns taken from the ship moored at Lancaster. The calibre of the latter guns and the quantity of the ammunition is unknown, but they were deployed at Preston. There were no trained gunners, however, and a sailor was employed to operate them. There were four sailors listed among prisoners taken after the battle, so he was probably one of these.[96]

A little training seems to have taken place. Sinclair complained that of the Scottish battalions, only Strathmore and Panmure took any trouble 'disciplining their regiments'.[97] The Englishmen in the army had been constantly on the move, but some received some training. Captain Talbot, once a regular soldier, 'at several places' drew up his men and disciplined the troop. Major Nairn, another veteran, is recorded as doing likewise with his men.[98] Robert Pilkington later swore 'He saw Mr [Edward] Tyldesley disciplining and exercising his said troop'.[99] In the first instance, it is presumed this involved showing men how to load and fire their muskets, judging by the level of musketry during the battle, and the second may have involved sword or pistol drill.

The traditional view of Jacobite tactics is that, lacking training and discipline, it was a simple rush to melee; such had happened at Killiecrankie in 1689 and was to happen, to an extent, at Sheriffmuir in 1715. Cameron of Lochiel described the Highland method of war to Viscount Dundee in 1689. After noting that warriors in classical times commonly used broadswords and targes, he then stated:

> The Highlanders are the onely body of men that retain the old method, excepting in so far as they have of late taken the gun instead of the bow to introduce them into action: That so soone as they are led against the enemy, they come to within a few paces of them, and having discharged their pieces in their very breasts they throw them down, and draw their swords: That the attack is so furious, that they commonly peirce their ranks, putt them into disorder, and determine the fate of the day in a few moments.[100]

Yet they were also able to use their firepower as well as their melee ability. On their march to Appleby, rabbits were shot in Whinfield Park and Patten

---

95 TNA, TS23/34, 1.
96 TNA: KB8/66, Baga de Secretis.
97 Scott, *Memoir*, p.52.
98 Anon., *Faithful Register*, pp.259, 22.
99 TNA: FEC1/1585, Towneley and Tildesley.
100 J. MacKnight (ed.), *Memoirs of Lochiel* (Glasgow: Maitland Club, 1842), p.251.

remarked that they 'are exceeding good marksmen'.[101] When Lord Forrester was fired upon at Preston, 'he received several wounds'.[102]

Sinclair, as a former regular soldier and a Lowlander, had a poor opinion of the Highlanders, readily admitting 'no man of the partie has so bad ane opinion of Highlandmen as I'. Negatively he thought 'they are capable of doeing in a plain field, against regular troops, depends on accident, or the irregularitie of the troops and they never will be brought to attack anie who have the best cover, nor will the wit of man bring them to stand cannon which has ane astonishing influence over them.'

Yet he thought that they could be effective: 'but where they are invested, and see no retreat, I am of opinion that none are capable to make a more vigorous defence in a breach, for they fire as well as any, from under cover, against attackers, and in the melee, which must hapne in a storm, their sabres are dangerous weapons'.[103]

The other issue, as we have seen, was that there was a lack of trust between the Scots and the English and this was noted by Sinclair, noting what Robert Douglas declared:

> … the Scots seem'd afraid, when they should come to action, of the English running away from them on their fleet horses; and it was impossible it could happen otherwise, for those who have no armes, and have means of getting off by their fleetness of their horses, will and must doe it; or, if they be shut up in a toun, without armes, will discourage those who have armes.[104]

The Jacobite battalions seem to have been organised along the lines of regular troops, into companies commanded by captains, with junior officers and NCOs and even musicians. The formations below described indicate this.

However, the Highland part of the army was a minority; being restricted to Mackintosh's regiment of just over 300 men. Most of the army were Lowlanders and English whose approach to combat was far similar to that of their enemies; in relying principally on firepower, though their training, if they had any, was rather more rudimentary. The Lowland Scots in this instance mostly wore Highland dress but their fighting style would not emphasise melee.

The High Command and staff of the Jacobite army were Thomas Forster, William Mackintosh, the earls of Nithsdale, Carnwath, Widdrington and Derwentwater and Viscount Kenmure. Forster had the Rev. Patten as his chaplain and Peregrine Widdrington and Charles Wogan as his ADCs. Henry Oxburgh was his military adviser. William Tunstall was the army's Paymaster General and Quartermaster General, with William Calderwood as Quartermaster General to the Scots. William Raine and Henry Widdrington were other quartermasters. James Ossington was collector of taxes. John Crofts was the adjutant. They numbered 17 in all. Englishmen were predominant in this grouping.[105]

---

101 Patten, *History*, 68.
102 Patten, *History*, p.85.
103 Scott, *Memoir*, p.130.
104 Scott, *Memoir*, pp.191–192.
105 Patten, *History*, pp.107–119.

As to the men, their known social composition, largely based on prisoner listings, was as follows:

Table 4. Social Composition of the Jacobite Army

Occupation	Number	Percentage
Doctors and physicians	30	1
Farmers	29	1
Husbandman	80	5
Labourers	292	16
Nobility and gentlemen	546	29
Servants	363	20
Shoemakers	20	1
Tailors	25	1
Weavers	61	3
Yeoman	187	10
Others/unstated	237	13
Total	1,870	100

Table 5. Parish/County of Origin

Parish	Number	Percentage (of whole army)
Alvie, Inverness	23	2
Blair, Perth	23	1
Duirinish, Inverness	37	2
Dull, Perth	38	2
Dunlichity, Inverness	56	3
Edinburgh, Midlothian	31	2
Fortingall, Perth	46	2
Glamis, Angus	39	2
Inverness, Inverness	19	1
Kilmuir, Angus	18	1
Logierait, Perth	47	2
Moy, Inverness	21	1
Preston, Lancashire	46	3
Walton, Lancashire	41	2

Table 6. Counties of Origin: Scotland

County	Number	Percentage (of Scots in the army)
Aberdeen	56	3
Angus	124	8
Berwickshire	29	1
East Lothian	23	1
Fife	12	1
Inverness	244	14
Midlothian	60	3
Perth	229	13
Roxburgh	20	1
Others/unstated	194	11
Total	991	53

Table 7. Counties of Origin: England

County	Number	Percentage (of English in the army)
Cumberland	20	1
Durham	25	1
Lancashire	474	25
Northumberland	233	13
Yorkshire	11	1
Other counties/unstated	121	6
Total	884	47

There were also nine Irishmen and one Dutchman (half of one percent); included in the 'Other English' totals.[106] A number of the men were elderly: at least 39 were aged between 60–77.[107] However, of a sample of 24 of the Lancastrians, one was 57, four had been born in the 1660s, three in the 1670s, five in the 1680s and eleven in the next decade, the youngest three being in their teens.[108] Oxford student Lionel Walden was aged 20.[109] The men were overwhelmingly drawn from Invernesshire, Perthshire, Lancashire and Northumberland, with a small number of parishes in each providing very many men, probably many of whom were drawn out by landowners. Most were gentry, servants and labourers.

---

[106] TNA: KB8/66, Baga de Secretis.
[107] TNA: SP44/120, p.25, List of prisoners, August 1716, Secretaries of State, State Papers, Entry Books, 1716–1721.
[108] International Genealogical Index.
[109] *Oxford University Alumini IV* (1886), p. 1554.

THE SECOND BATTLE OF PRESTON, 1715

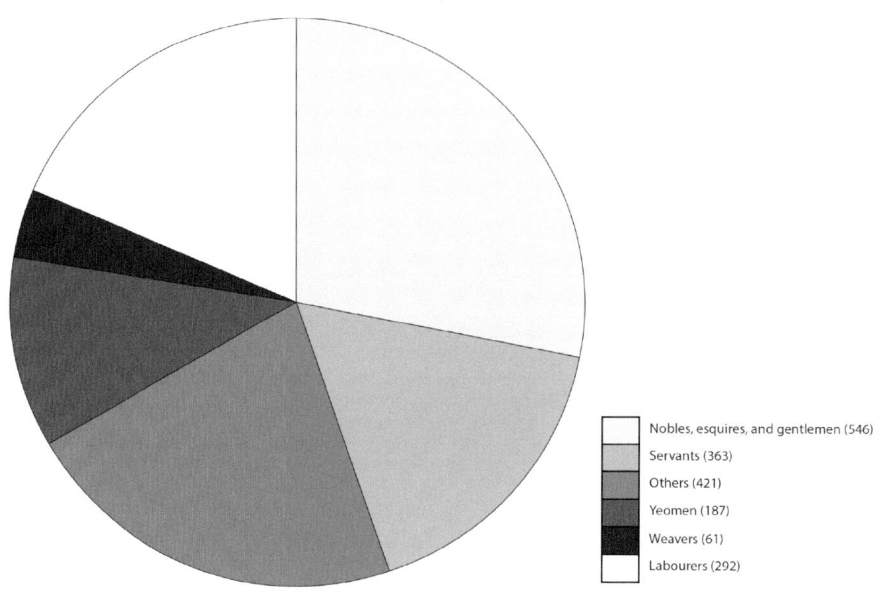

Occupations of Soldiers in the Jacobite Army

Jacobite Origins

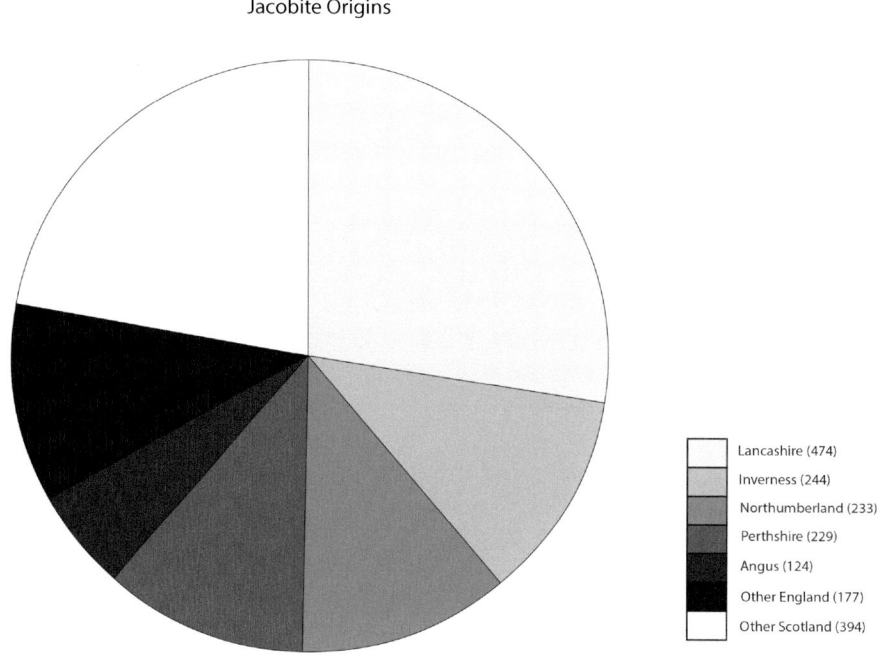

The Commands

Much had changed since Patten made his account of the different units at Kelso. Some companies no longer existed and some men were not in any unit. We are able to know the composition of the army because of the circumstances in which it came to an end. The manuscript lists of prisoners taken after Preston and who were distributed to prisons in the north of England, have survived and list names of men, parish and county, occupation and where known, regiment and troop/company, and they form the bulk of the information given below. Listings of gentry, nobles, officers and servants taken to London for trial were listed in newspapers.

A detailed breakdown of the Jacobite forces can be found in the appendix but a summary is as follows:

Infantry

Table 8. Earl of Strathmore's Battalion

Name of Unit	Number of Men
Officers	14
Captain Douglas'	34
Captain Miller's	34
Captain Balfour's	35
Captain Scrimson/Scrimshaw's	33
Unidentified	2
Total	152

Table 9. Earl of Mar's Battalion

Name of Unit	Number of Men
Officers	7
Forbes' company	31
Innes' company	3
Total	41

Table 10. Logie Drummond's Battalion

Name of Unit	Number of Men
Officers	7
Men	2
Total	9

Table 11. Earl of Nairn's Battalion

Name of Unit	Number of Men
Officers	29
Captain Stuart's	70
Captain Robertson's	38
Captain MacGruther's	10
Unidentified	31
Total	178

Table 12. Lord Charles Murray's Battalion

Name of Unit	Number of Men
Officers	26
Captain Stuart's	9
Captain Robertson's	25
Captain Menzies/Minneries'	37
Unidentified	8
Total	105

Table 13. Mackintosh's Battalion

Name of Unit	Number of Men
Officers	52
Colonel Mackintosh's company	23
Lieutenant Colonel Farquharson's company	11
Major Mackintosh's company	14
Captain Angus Mackintosh's company	43
Captain Lachlan Mackintosh's company	19
Captain Duncomb Mackintosh's company	13
Captain William Mackintosh's company	13
Captain MacBean's company	15
Captain Shaw's company	23
Captain MacQueen's company	10
Captain Lachlan MacLean's company	7
Captain MacGillivray's company	40
Unidentified	18
Total	301

Cavalry

Table 14. Lowland Scottish Cavalry

Name of Unit	Number of Men
Viscount Kenmure's Troop	17
Captain Hume's Troop	22
Earl of Winton's Troop	34
Earl of Carnwath's Troop	16
Captain Lockhart's Troop	16
Gentlemen Volunteers	39
Tindale Troop	10
Total	154

Table 15. English Cavalry

Name of Unit	Number of Men
Earl of Derwentwater's Troop	22
Earl of Widdrington's Troop	20
Captain Hunter's Troop	23
Captain Douglas' Troop	26
Captain Wogan's Troop	30
Captain Sawhill's Troop	18
Captain Talbot's Troop	26
Dalton's Troop	20
Townley's Troop	14
Tyldesley's Troop	20–60
Total	219–259

Note that at least three other English troops are known to have existed, John Dalton's, Inglesby Thorpe's and John Langdale's but prisoner lists do not designate these Lancastrian men so these troops have not been listed here.

Table 16. Others (men not known to have been attached to any military unit)

Type	Number
English nobility and gentry	180
English servants and followers	430
Scottish nobility and gentry	90
Scottish servants and followers	76
Total	776

Grand Total
Command: 17
Formed infantry: 786 (six battalions)
Cavalry: 373–413 (17 troops)
Others: 776
Total: 1,952–1,992

Table 17. Summary of Prisoners[110]

Type	Number
English noblemen and gentry	75
Servants and followers	83
Others	305
Scots noblemen, gentry and officers	143
Other Scots	862
Captured elsewhere	21
Total	1,489

To this must be added the 10–28 men killed whose identities are not known. This is an absolute minimum and does not include the men who escaped on the night after the first day's fighting; according to Patten.

On the whole, the Scottish infantry was rather more socially and geographically homogenous than the cavalry forces. Many would have known the others in their units from birth. Unlike the case with the British army, there were considerable numbers of gentlemen in the ranks. The majority of the Scots were from the Lowlands, not the Highlands, with only one clan regiment, making the clansmen a distinct minority within the Jacobite army, for the majority of the clans did not join the Jacobite army in Scotland until early November, shortly prior to the battle of Sheriffmuir.

The overall strength of the Jacobite army at Preston has been rarely estimated by those writing about it. Many do not give any figure. A recent writer has plumped, without giving reasons, for '1,400 or so' and later '1,500 or so'.[111] Paul Monod gives 2,500.[112] Gooch puts the figure between 3,000–4,000.[113] Others, such as Baynes, Reid and Szechi wisely avoid making an estimate of any kind. Contemporaries gave diverse figures, ranging from a press report of 1,400, which Lionel Walden, a member of that army later said, to the Duke of Berwick estimating 2,000, and another at between 2,000–3,000, up to a maximum of between 4,000 and 5,000 in another, with Rae estimating their numbers at being over 4,000.[114] As Patten noted, 'so

---

110 Patten, *History*, p.143.
111 Jonathan Worton, *The Battle of Glenshiel* (Solihull: Helion, 2018), pp.28, 57.
112 Monod, *Jacobitism*, p.321.
113 Gooch, *Desperate Faction*, p.81.
114 *Political State*, XI (1716), p.167; *Weekly Journal*, 255, 19 November 1715; Berwick, *Memoirs*, II (1778), p.235; *St. James' Evening Post*, 73, 15–17 November 1715, Rae, *History* p.324.

many different Accounts of their Numbers have been made publick, that it is not easy to know what may be depended upon'. [115]

However, perhaps the best basis to begin with as an absolute minimum is the number of prisoners taken. Most contemporary published estimates list 1,489 men taken, and they are broken down as in Table 17, above.

Another contemporary estimate gives 1,103 Scots and 466 Englishmen, or 1,569 in total.[116] Both, as noted above, would seem to be underestimates.

The figures cited above lead us to number the staff at being 17, Mackintosh's infantry command to 786 men split into six very unevenly numbered battalions. The English cavalry numbered 219–259 in nine troops with an unknown strength of a further one, the Lowland cavalry were 154 strong, of seven troops. Then there were 610 English and 166 other Scots. Add this to the 10–28 unidentified fatalities then we have an approximate number of between 1,962–2,020 men.

These figures derive from several listings of prisoners; those sent to London, mostly gentry and their servants and the officers were listed in *The London Gazette*, *The Faithful Register* and Patten's *History*, though not all gentry officers were sent to the capital. There is also a single sheeted contemporary document titled *A List of the most Considerable of the Scots and English taken prisoners at Preston 13th November 1715*, printed in Edinburgh by one John Moncur in 1715. There are also manuscript lists of those assigned to four different locations in the north west as prisoners. The total here is 1,297. There is also a manuscript 'list of the persons against whom informations are taken at Preston' in the aftermath of the battle: mostly from Lancashire and mostly Catholic and amounting to 329. Some of these names are on the previous manuscript lists but by no means all. There are also constables' returns giving 84 men who had escaped from Preston but who had been with the army previously (most of these men are listed in the previous list).

Then we come to the difficulty of not knowing how many men escaped before the final surrender on 14 November. Patten writes that this was 'a great many'. A reference in the west riding quarter sessions provides an estimate of as many as 1,500.[117] Another contemporary estimate is 2,000.[118] Perhaps an approximate number of just over 2,000 men is a realistic estimate for the total Jacobite strength, though it may have been several hundred more. This number may be an over estimate of actual combatants as medical men and servants may not all have taken part in the actual combat. By contemporary standards this was a low number for an army; Monmouth had about 3,000 men at Sedgemoor in 1685 and Mar had almost 10,000 at Sheriffmuir 30 years later.

---

115 Patten, *History*, p.39.
116 Anon., *A List of the most Considerable of the Scots and English Nobles and Gentlemen* (Edinburgh: John Moncur, 1715).
117 West Yorkshire Archive Service, Wakefield, QS10/13, p.112a, West Riding Quarter Sessions Order Book, 1712–1720.
118 Anon., *Annals*, II, p.142.

The Forces of George I

If there has been little work on the Jacobite army of this period compared to that which fought in 1745–6, there has been even less on that of their opponents. Reid has a chapter about the army generally and an appendix of the regiments involved, listing officers.[119] Szechi wrote, speaking of the forces in general, in Scotland as well as in England, 'The government's regular forces performed up to standard in most cases and the government militia and volunteers performed as poorly as could have been expected'.[120] Baynes gives a mixed verdict about the army's performance, writing that 'the squabble between Carpenter and Wills draws attention away from the gallantry of Preston's Regiment'.[121] Ironically, less is known of the British army than their enemies, as they lacked a chronicler.

If the Jacobite army was less than elite status, then the same can be said about their enemies. The great war machine that had been built up in the War of the Spanish Succession had been dismantled with the coming of peace by 1713, with less than half the battalions being retained. In 1711 there were 88,996 British troops in pay; about 30,000 were discharged in 1712 and another 35,696 in 1713.[122]

The British Army

Overview

The British Army was a relatively new institution as a standing army in 1715; indeed until 1707 it had been made up of three separate establishments and now it was two: Britain and Ireland (the Scots and the English establishments merged with the Union of 1707). Each was administered and funded separately by the British and the Irish administrations. The civilian master was the secretary at war; in 1715 this was William Pulteney (1684–1764). Military control went to the Captain General; Marlborough having being reinstated in 1714, but who was largely inactive in this period. Yet the troops could be transferred between Britain and Ireland and could fight together at home and abroad. Under the excellent leadership provided by Marlborough it had proved its worth in the War of Spanish Succession where, alongside allied Dutch and German troops, it had defeated the French armies time and time again in Flanders, but under lesser generals had had more mixed success, including two defeats, in Spain (at Almansa and Brihuega) in the same conflict. However, the coming of peace in 1713 at Utrecht meant that most of the army's regiments and battalions were disbanded as they were no longer needed in peacetime. Those remaining were scattered through Britain's newly won territories as well as being stationed in castles, towns, cities and villages at home, there being no barracks in England before 1717.

---

119 Reid, *Sheriffmuir*, pp.12–22, 169–181; Oates, *Preston*, pp.105–122.
120 Szechi, *1715*, p.195.
121 Baynes, *Jacobite Rising*, p.204.
122 Andrew Cormack, 'These Meritorious Objects of the Royal Bounty': *The Chelsea Out-Pensioners in the Early Eighteenth Century* (Self-published, 2017), p.32.

THE ARMIES

Generalmanship

Captain General of the army was the recently reinstated John Churchill, Duke of Marlborough, but he had little role in the campaign. Reid makes no examination nor analysis of the role of the senior officers in the campaign, though an earlier historian made a damning indictment of General Wills. Szechi stating:

> By contrast, the command skills exhibited on the government side went from mediocre to good. The accolade for worst commander on the government side during the rebellion has undoubtedly to go to a professional army officer: major General Charles Wills. He was, though, very fortunate, in that if the Jacobites had responded as aggressively to his botched attacks on Preston as some of them were clamouring to do, he might have gained the special distinction of being the architect of a truly catastrophic defeat.[123]

Patten wrote flatteringly of Wills and Carpenter, perhaps naturally so, in the prologue of his book, which was dedicated 'To The Lieutenant Generals Carpenter and Wills and the rest of the commanding officers of his majesty's Forces at the attack at Preston'. He went on to state that they 'had the Honour to command his Majesty's Troops … in honour of your Courage and Conduct … to do you the Justice which is due to your Merit, by assuring the World that it was to your prudent management and unshaken Bravery, animated by the Justice of the Cause, the Signal defeat of that Day was justly owing'. He went on to write that some 'with a View to lessen the Characters of brave Men … have pretended to assert the contrary'.[124]

Wills was the junior of the two but ironically had the larger command. He had become an ensign in 1682, aged 16, in Colonel Erle's regiment of Horse, becoming a captain in 1691 then transferring to another cavalry regiment as major in Sanderson's Horse and by 1697 was a lieutenant colonel. This rapid promotion was because of the opportunities of promotion and death during the Nine Years' War (1688–1697) as Wills saw active service against the French in Flanders. When war broke out again, he was at first lieutenant colonel of Caulfield's horse, brigadier in 1707 and major general in 1709. Much of this service took place in Spain alongside General James Stanhope, who became a senior figure in government in 1714. Wills had suffered wounds in battle and had also experienced warfare in the West Indies.[125]

Carpenter had, unusually, entered the army as a private in 1672, aged but fifteen, in the Foot Guards. He became a quartermaster in Peterborough's Horse in the 1680s. By the next century he was well on his way to the heights of command, as lieutenant colonel of the Royal Regiment of Dragoons in 1703, a brigadier in 1705, major general in 1708 and lieutenant general in 1711. As with Wills, he had been wounded in battle in Spain.[126]

---

123 Szechi, *1715*, p.196.
124 Patten, *History*, preface.
125 *Oxford Dictionary of National Biography (ODNB)*, 59, pp.430–431.
126 *ODNB*, 10, p.225.

THE SECOND BATTLE OF PRESTON, 1715

Wills had three brigadiers under him. James Dormer (1679–1741) had been a lieutenant and then a captain in the first Foot Guards in 1702. He had fought at Blenheim and Ramillies. In 1708 he was colonel of Mohun's Horse and was a brigadier in 1711. In 1715 he was given a commission to raise a regiment of dragoons. Dormer was also an intellectual soldier and read widely on military matters. Richard Munden (1680–1725) had also been a captain in the Foot Guards in 1702. He was a lieutenant colonel in 1706 in Lovelace's Horse, colonel in 1708 and brigadier in 1711. As with Dormer, he fought in Flanders and took part in Blenheim and Ramillies in Flanders and then in Spain. He was also commissioned to raise a regiment of dragoons in 1715. Philip Honywood (c.1680–1752) was the third brigadier, who had 21 years' military service in 1715, obtaining his present rank in 1710.[127]

There is no doubting, therefore, that the senior officers of the British army were all experienced officers, in contrast to their opponents. Yet they were accustomed to fighting regular opponents, not irregulars, and as the Scottish army found in 1689, irregular foes did not fight in the same way and could beat regulars. The junior officers were very diverse; some were experienced soldiers, who had fought in the War of the Spanish Succession, such as Captain James Gardiner, but many were newly appointed and inexperienced, such as the 21 year old Henry Pelham of Dormer's dragoons, often appointed for political and social reasons, just as their counterparts in the Jacobite army were, though the British army had far more experienced officers. Of those we know about among the three veteran regiments, 22 had seen war service and 14 had not and the number in the newly raised units would probably be less of the former and more of the latter.

Most of the regiments were led by their lieutenant colonel: Colonels Dormer, Munden and Honywood, all of whose regiments were present at the battle, were also brigadiers and had that role in the action. George Preston was at Edinburgh castle as its deputy governor. It is not known where Stanhope, Pitt and Wynn were at this time, but there is no reference to them being at the battle.

Judging by the names of some of the officers, some were probably French Huguenots or their sons, Protestants who had fled from religious persecution in France and so had no love for Catholic Jacobites. Captain Lieutenant Marcellus La Roone (1679–1772) of Stanhope's, was born in England but had a French background. La Roone entered the Guards in 1707 as a volunteer, then in 1708 served as a lieutenant in Orkney's regiment at Oudernade and at Winnendall where he was wounded. After serving at the siege of Ghent and Tournai in 1709, his unit was transferred to Spain where, in 1710, he fought at Almanera and the sieges of Saragossa and Madrid.[128]

---

127 *ODNB*, 16, p.575; Eveline Cruickshanks, Stuart Handley and David Hayton, *The Commons, 1690–1715*, IV (Cambridge University Press, 2002), p.954; Charles Dalton, *Army List*, I (London: Publisher Unknown, 1910), p.115.
128 John Thomas Smith, *Nollekens and his Times*, II (London: Henry Colburn), pp.256–275.

Organisation

The British infantry was composed of guards and foot battalions, but the former were not involved in this campaign so can be discounted. The infantry was divided into battalions, each of 10 companies and the battalion was known by the name of the colonel proprietor, so the infantry battalion deployed at Preston was called, ironically, Preston's Foot, after General George Preston, the battalion's absentee colonel. Each company included a captain (except the three commanded by the field officers), a lieutenant and an ensign (the grenadier company had two lieutenants and no ensigns), two sergeants, three corporals and a drummer and had an establishment strength of 50 privates. There was a small headquarters staff of the colonel, lieutenant colonel, major, chaplain, surgeon and a mate, adjutant and quartermaster and a servant. Officers had a servant each. The first three of these were labelled 'field officers' and were also, at least in theory, company commanders as well, but in battle this role often fell to the company's lieutenant. There were two types of infantry; nine companies being made up of line infantry and the last being the grenadier company, made up of the steadiest men, usually veterans, and were distinguished by wearing mitred hats not tricornes. The battalion had an establishment strength of 605 men including officers.[129]

The cavalry in the British army in this period were either horse or dragoons. Both were employed in the campaign so both are of importance. As with the infantry both took their regiment's name after that of their colonel. They had a headquarters staff of colonel, lieutenant colonel, major, adjutant, chaplain, surgeon and a kettle drummer. The horse regiments were divided into six troops, grouped into three squadrons. Each troop had a captain, a lieutenant, a cornet, a quartermaster, two or three NCOs and a trumpeter (horse) or a drummer or hautbois (dragoons) and an establishment strength of 40 troopers. Dragoons, originating from the civil wars, were organised similarly, but with six troops and were technically deemed mounted infantry and troopers were paid at lesser rates; one shilling and sixpence per day compared to two and six for the horse.[130]

There was no separate Royal Artillery corps until 1716; gun crews were put together and supplied with artillery, ball and gunpowder when needed. Usually such men and equipment were found in castle garrisons. Since no artillery was used by the British army in the campaign in England, there is no need to examine them in further detail.

Equipment

The British infantryman was armed with a flintlock musket, five feet long, and socket bayonet, meaning the weapon could be fired with the bayonet attached, and also carried a sword. Sergeants carried a halberd and officers a half pike, both in addition to a sword, though both were expected to lead and direct rather than take part in melee except in self defence. Grenadiers may also have carried grenades, especially when there was a need to assault

---

129 Michael Barthorp, *Marlborough's Armies* (London: Osprey Publishing, 1980) p.12; TNA: War Office Papers concerning establishments, 1715–1716, WO24/29, pp.10a, 12a.
130 Barthorp, *Marlborough's Armies*, pp.10–11; TNA: WO24/29, pp.8a–8b.

a fortification, and had been used at Killiecrankie in 1689.

The horse were armed with a straight sword, a brace of pistols and sometimes a carbine, whereas the dragoons, whose role was seen as being 'mounted infantry' were armed with a sword, bayonet, hatchet and a carbine, a rather shorter musket than the infantry.

Tactics

The infantry battalions marched towards their enemy, stopped within musket range and then fired by platoon. Although a musket ball could carry 250 yards, effective range was about 60 yards and rate of fire was usually two musket balls per minute. Men stood in ranks of three so that in theory all could fire at once, but this led a battalion to be vulnerable if they were suddenly attacked and there was no one who could shoot. It was then divided into 18 platoons, with only six firing at one time, so those not firing could be reloading in order to keep the battalion's fire continuous.[131]

Drill books stated that once a battalion had marched into battle, the colonel's company was to be on the right and the lieutenant colonel's was on the left, with the major's to the left of the colonel's and the eldest captain's on the right of the lieutenant colonel's and so forth, with the two newest companies being in the centre of the line. Half the drummers were placed on the right and half on the left, the sergeants dispersed through the ranks and the commissioned officers at the front of the men. The commander gave the orders and the sergeants ensured these were followed.[132]

The horse were expected to engage the enemy's horse and then to threaten the enemy's infantry and artillery. Firing before charging was officially disapproved of as it reduced the impact of that charge. In a pursuit they could vastly increase the enemy's casualties as the latter fled; in a defeat they could cover the retreat of their own troops. Dragoons did a lot of the army's donkey work, with reconnaissance duties, providing escorts and preparing the way for the army's advance. They also fought on foot as had happened in Scotland in June 1689, but were increasingly seen as mounted troops, fighting alongside the better paid horse, and being used in pursuits, and in peacetime were useful for their mobility to combat smugglers and rioters.[133]

Pay

The six lieutenant generals each received £15 18s 1/4d per day, making £5,820 per annum

The six major generals each received £7 19s per day, making £2,910 per annum.

Brigadiers received £10 19s 4 3/4d per day, making £4,015 per annum

---

131 Barthorp, *Marlborough's Armies*, pp.13–14
132 Anon., *The Duke of Marlborough's new Exercise of Firelocks and Bayonets* (Unknown publisher, 1712), pp.2–3.
133 Barthorp, *Marlborough's Armies*, pp.10–11.

Table 18. Pay of Headquarters Staff

Rank	Horse	Dragoons	Infantry
Colonel	19s 6d/£356 17s	19s 6d/£356 17s	14s/£256 4s
Lieutenant Colonel	8s/£146 8s	9s/£164 14s	7s/£128 2s
Major	5s 6d/£100 13s	5s/£91 10s	5s/£91 10s
Chaplain	6s 8d/£122	6s 8d/£122	6s 8d/£122
Adjutant	5s/£91 10s	5s/£91 10s	4s/£73 4s
Surgeon	6s/£109 6s (includes horse to carry medical chest)	6s/£109 6s	6s 6d/£118 19s (includes pay for mate)
Kettle drummer	3s/£54 18s	n/a	n/a
Quartermaster	n/a	n/a	4s 8d/£85 8s
Total Cost	£2 13s 8d/£982 2s	£2 11s 2d/£936 7s	£2 7s 10d/£875 7s

Table 19. Pay of Officers and Men[134]

Rank	Horse	Dragoons	Infantry
Captain	£1 1s 6d/£393 9s	15s 6d/£283 13s	10s/£183
Lieutenant	15s/£274 10s	9s/£164 14s	4s 8d/£85 8s
Cornet/Ensign	14s/£256 4s	8s/£146 8s	3s 8d/£67 2s
Quartermaster	8s 6d/£155 11d	5s 6d/£100 13s	n/a
Sergeant	n/a	2s 6d/£45 15s	18d/£27 9s
Corporal	3s/£54 18s	2s/£36 12s	12d/£18 6s
Musician (trumpeter for horse, drummer & hautbois for dragoons, drummer for infantry)	2s 8d/£48 16s	2s/£36 12s	1s/£18 6s
Trooper/Private	2s 6d/£45 12s 6d	3s/£38	£12 3s 6d
Total	£8 7s 8d/£3,068 6s	£5 8s 6d/£1,985 11s	£2 19s 8d/£1,091 18s

Company and troop officers were given an allowance for two horses each and three for the captain, in lieu of having a servant.

The total cost of a regiment of horse per annum was £19,391 18s (£52 19s 8d per day); that of a regiment of dragoons rather cheaper at £12,849 13s (£35 2s 2d per day) per annum and that of an infantry battalion £11,812 13s per annum.[135]

Uniforms were provided by the regiment's colonel; and would provide a complete uniform on joining (costing £2 10s) and then a year later would provide replacement shirt, shoes, hat, stockings, breeches and neckerchief (costing 14s 4d). Uniforms were red. The colonel would also provide weaponry;

---

134 TNA, WO24/29, p.5a.
135 *Ibid.*, pp.8a, 8b, 10a, 12a.

THE SECOND BATTLE OF PRESTON, 1715

Colonel James Gardiner by J.T. Wedgwood, published by William Johnstone White. Engraving, published 1 November 1815. Gardiner is better known in Jacobite history for his death at the Battle of Prestonpans in 1745. (Courtesy of the National Portrait Gallery, NPG D34276.)

standardisation was not introduced until the following reign.[136]

Regiments

We now turn to the officers and men within the army. Officers and men were very much set apart from each other as far as records were concerned. The officers were listed in 'Army Lists' dating their commissions with date and ranks, and where known these have been collated. Officers bought their commissions, with the commanding officer's permission; at the formation of a new unit the commanding officer had a very free hand in his choice of officers, but thereafter was expected to offer vacancies to the longest serving officer below the immediate rank of the vacancy. Officers thus tended to be drawn from the ranks of the gentry, merchants and professional classes, as well as sons of serving or retired officers. There were also published lists of the officers in the newly raised regiments.

Details of men in the ranks, who were usually from the ranks of the skilled and semi-skilled workers, agricultural labourers and craftsmen, have been taken from lists of men to whom pensions were granted, some due to injuries sustained at the battle of Preston but most due to other illnesses and being 'worn out'. Those who were killed or died on active service or who deserted or had been in disciplinary trouble are not recorded here. Generally less is known about them than the officers.

A description of two men from Wynn's regiment, both who enlisted at Turnham Green in Middlesex, were as follows. Henry Denninson was 'red haired, round faced, freckled about 25 years of age, five foot eight inches high, born in Ireland, and by trade a taylor'. William Squire was a 'middle sized man wears a brown wig, thin face, an Englishman, a carpenter by trade'. William Ancram of Preston's was described as being 'a middle sized well fed man'.[137]

Some of these units were old established battalions and regiments but most were not. Because of the concern caused by the discovery of the Jacobite schemes in the summer, the government decided on 22 July to raise additional regiments of dragoons and battalions of infantry. In all, commissions were given to politically loyal noblemen and gentry (William Stanhope, who raised a dragoon regiment, was the younger cousin to James Stanhope, for instance) to raise 13 regiments of dragoon and eight battalions of infantry; in all, it was envisaged, 2,574 dragoons and 3,450 infantry, to supplement

---

136 Barry Lyndon, 'Military dress and Uniformity, 1680–1720', *JSAHR*, 54 (1976), pp.109–111; Andrew Cormack, 'Some remarks on the provision of cavalry swords', *JSAHR*, 93 (2015), p.307.
137 TNA: WO26/14, p.241, War Office warrants, regulations and precedents, 1712–1717; WO116/1, Chelsea Registers, 1715–1727.

the existing forces. Many of these newly raised forces did not see active service, but as we shall see, seven of these new dragoon regiments were eventually present at Preston (the forces on campaign in Scotland were all 'old' units, some brought over from Ireland). New recruits were given a bounty of 40s on enlisting.[138]

On 23 July Pulteney gave officers the following instructions:

> These are to authorise you by beat of drum or otherwise to raise so many volunteers as shall be wanting to complete the said regiment to the above number. And when you shall have listed 15 men for service in any of the said troops you are to give notice to two of our Justices of the Peace of the Town or county where in the same men who are hereby authorised and required to view the said men and certify the day of their doing so.[139]

The Right Honourable Henry Pelham by Edward Harding, published by William Coxe, after Unknown artist. Stipple engraving, published 1802. (Courtesy of the National Portrait Gallery, NPG D5491)

By the first week of August, officers had been appointed to all these units and such were listed in the government's official newspaper.[140] The men took longer to raise, but aided by the promise of a bounty of 40s per recruit, numbers came in. On 4 August, Munden reported to Pulteney that his dragoon regiment 'was near Compleat, arm'd and mounted'. On 22 August gunpowder was being issued to the new regiments.[141]

How complete all the regiments were is another question, for on 25 October there was an order to 'beat the drum' to recruit to five of Wills' dragoon regiments: Dormer's, Stanhope's, Honywood's, Wynn's and Munden's as well as the two regiments of dragoons under Carpenter's command.[142]

A constant refrain made by the Jacobites was that their opponents were inexperienced. Patten claimed they 'were, for the most part, raw, new-listed men.'[143] Another Jacobite noted 'The enemy were mostly raw green horns'.[144]

Yet some of the officers and men in these 'new' units had seen previous military service in other units in the recent wars. Many of those demobilised in 1713 may well have sought re-employment in the army in 1715. Of the 152 men that we know of (perhaps 10 percent of the whole), the median age was 44 years and the median number of years of service was 13–14, with only 11 of the 152 being new recruits. James Cowell of Dormer's had

---

138 TNA: WO4/17, p.148, Pulteney to Ordnance officers, 26 July 1715.
139 TNA: WO26/14, p.236, Pulteney to colonels, 23 July 1715.
140 *London Gazette*, 5353, 6–8 August 1715.
141 TNA: WO4/17, pp.148, Pulteney to Ordnance officers, 26 July 1715, 192, Pulteney to Munden, 12 September 1715, 175, Pulteney to colonels, 22 August 1715.
142 TNA: WO26/14, p.236, Pulteney to colonels, 25 October 1715.
143 Patten, *History*, p.86.
144 TNA: SP54/9, 107, Jacobite prisoner's experiences in the rebellion..

been at Malplaquet, as had James Scarborough. John Christie had served at Hochstedt. Peter Jennings had been at Alamanza.[145] Most, though, had never fought together and so were not as cohesive as the veteran units. Lists of men in the ranks can be found in pension records where those men survived to receive them, often decades later. The rank and file are mostly unknown as individuals, and even those known by name have no other details about them except age and length of service, but only a very few are discernible. Unlike the Jacobites they were a diverse lot: Englishmen, Scots and Irishmen drawn from throughout the British Isles. Some had previously been apprentices, at least one a husbandman and another a smith. Donald McBane, who served at Preston, later wrote that he had joined up (in 1687) because his mistress put him on short rations. Their motivations in general are unknown, but steady employment and the possibility of promotion and advancement may have played their part; some may have been influenced by religion and politics. Most men were in their 20s or 30s but a few were older and a very few were younger. The number of veteran units at Preston was limited to Pitt's horse, Preston's foot and eventually Cobham's dragoons.

Taking a sample of 70 men, it can be seen that 47 or 69 percent joined aged between 21 and 29 and 21 or 29 percent aged 30–36, with John Bavington enlisting at the grand old age of 44 and Peter Jennings joined aged 17. Service in the army, which often involved serving in more than one battalion or regiment, often involved a period of 20–30 years and many men left service in their 50s or 60s. In this sample of men granted pensions, 36 were in their 50s and six in their 60s, but wounds and disability often resulted in leaving earlier; 18 aged in their 40s and 11 in their 30s. It is also worth noting that this was very much a British army, with men coming from England, Scotland and Ireland. From 1736 parish and county as well as former occupation are routinely listed, which increases our knowledge of their backgrounds prior to army life. From a sample of 20 that we know served at Preston, there were 10 Englishmen, seven Irishmen and three Scots, which roughly equates to the proportions of populations across the three kingdoms, though of course this also relates to where the regiments were recruiting; two of the regiments at Preston had been recently based in Ireland. Their former occupations were diverse, but labourers predominated; two were former apprentices, there was a weaver, a pipemaker, a bricklayer and a tobacconist.[146]

The other concern about the army was its reliability and the Jacobites certainly hoped that it would not oppose them (Monmouth's rebels had similar hopes in 1685). Bolingbroke wrote that the Stuart court believed 'many officers of the army, and the majority of the soldiers were very well affected to the [Jacobite] cause'.[147] There were some soldiers who apparently had Jacobite sympathies. Four men in Honywood's dragoons had been arrested in Essex for 'treasonable practices' in the autumn of 1715; eventually

---

145 TNA: WO116/1–3, Royal Hospital Chelsea Disability and Royal Artillery Out Patients Admission Books, Cavalry and Infantry, 1715–1746.
146 TNA, WO116/1–3, Chelsea Registers, 1715–1746.
147 Bolingbroke, *Works*, I, p.133.

this total was a sergeant, two corporals and six troopers, and as noted two ensigns in Preston's battalion went over to the Jacobites.[148]

Army Transport

Eighteenth-century armies lacked their own transport and the British army had to rely on civilian contractors, who would be repaid after the campaign was over. There is a note of five contractors providing nine wagons for Wills' baggage and another for the Hundred of Blackburn to reimburse constables therein the sum of £300 for such services.[149]

Irregular Forces

As well as the regular forces, there were a number of locally raised forces who operated in the north of England and the Borders.

The Militia

Constituted in 1662 by the Militia Act, this provided for, in theory, the local defence of a county in cases of emergency. The county's lord lieutenant, a nobleman, would be in charge, or if incapacitated, three of the deputy lieutenants. Appointed by the Crown, these men would be politically reliable and would be substantial landowners in the county and would make up the officers of the militia. The militia were supposed to train once a year for a week, but, conditioned to years of peace, had not done so.

Each landowner had to supply men to serve in the militia, depending on the value of their estate/s. Arms were provided by the parish constables and were to be the equivalent to those used in the regular army. The men were to be paid out of the county rates. They did not have to serve outside the county boundaries.[150] Lancashire constables were busy in supplying the militia. For example, the constable for Formby spent 5s 4d to put the parish muskets in order and provided belts and cartridge boxes for another 10s 4d, cleaned a halberd for 2d and put two swords and a pike in order for a shilling. He also advanced money to parishioners who served in the militia. In Haslewood, the constable spent £10 14s 10d to buy muskets and swords, 7s 6d for cartridge boxes and paid for ten parishioners to serve a fortnight in the militia.[151]

In 1715 the principal figure in the county militia for Lancashire was not the Lord Lieutenant, the Earl of Derby, but a deputy lieutenant, Sir Henry Hoghton. The Lancashire deputy lieutenants had met on 27 September to discuss the crisis, and on 27 October ordered the militia to come into being, armed with muskets and bayonets on 3 November.[152] How well armed they eventually were, despite the efforts of the constables, is open to question, for

---

148 *St. James Evening Post*, 24–27 March 1716; TNA: SP44/118, pp.26–27, Townshend to Honywood, 2 November 1715.
149 LRO: QSP 1091/2, Quarter Sessions Petitions, 1715–1716; DP/508/1, Hundred of Blackburn, transport charges, 1716.
150 Jarvis, *Jacobite Risings*, pp.106–110.
151 LRO: PR 3360/4/1/1, Formby's Churchwardens' Accounts, 1703–1733; PR 3724/15, Haslewood's Constables' Accounts, 1714–1715.
152 Lumby, *Deeds and Papers*, p.112.

Lonsdale wrote 'The militia throughout is ill armed, but I don't know how that can be remedied at present, for they can't be provided with better ones in the country and it will be a long time before new ones come from London'.[153]

The Posse Comitatus

As a second line of defence, the county sheriff had the authority, at a time of crisis, to call out all able bodied men in the county between the ages of 16 and 60, in arms. This was primarily in the case of riots. Yet this had taken place in both Northumberland and in Cumberland in 1715. There was no provision for training or equipment and as noted, the posse at Penrith was armed mainly with agricultural implements.

The Lancashire Dissenters

In early June 1715, the Dissenters' meeting house in Cross Street, Manchester, had been destroyed by rioters. There was good reason why Dissenters should be apprehensive of the Jacobite forces and so rally to the government's cause. On occasion, Dissenters had armed themselves to defend their chapels. They did so on this occasion, too, but their arms were at best rudimentary and their fighting skills undoubtedly low. They did, however, possess local knowledge and could be of secondary value to the British army. Apparently they numbered 300 men and were armed with 'swords and pistils and guns and partly with scythes fixed to the end of straight sticks'. The men followed their leader 'General' James Woods 'having a congregation that loved him extremely and would follow him anywhere'.[154]

The overall strength of the forces fighting at Preston is unknown. Few contemporaries hazard a figure, though Berwick thought it was a mere 1,000 and as with historians discussing Jacobite numbers, few historians have tried. Michael Barthorp assumed there were 1,600 men in Wills' regiments and Monod put them at an impossible 5,000; Reid states they were 'just over 2,000 men' including the militia.[155] A contemporary source gives the combined force of Carpenter and Wills as 2,500, but it is not known if this includes the irregulars with both: probably not.[156] Each of the newly raised dragoon regiments should have numbered at 200 men, but their actual strengths may have been a little lower, for at Sheriffmuir, Argyle's dragoon regiments numbered between 166–174 rank and file, excluding officers. His infantry battalions numbered between 238 and 369 men, again excluding officers.[157] A contemporary gives Preston's infantry battalion as being 300 men strong.[158] Lionel Walden gave total army strength as 2,100.[159] The estimate of 1,600 men for Wills' force is not unreasonable, but a range of 1,400–1,800 seems more likely, excluding the militia and volunteers, who did not take part in

---

153 *HMC Carlisle*, p.18.
154 Matthews, *Diary*, p.234.
155 Berwick, *Memoirs*, II, p.235; Barthorp, *Jacobite Risings, 1689–1745* p.7; Monod, *Jacobitism*, p.321; Reid, *Sheriffmuir*, p.89.
156 *Political State*, XI (1716), p.167.
157 TNA: SP54/9, 92, return of Argyle'army, 29 October 1715.
158 Anon., *Annals*, II, p.135.
159 D.W. Rannie, ed., 'Hearne's Collectons', VI, 1717–1719', *Oxford Historical Society*, 43 (1902), p.88.

the assaults on Preston. It would seem, therefore, that the Jacobite army had a slight numerical advantage. Yet the British army who had more experienced officers and men, was better armed and equipped.

To sum up, Wills had five regiments of dragoons, all newly raised, one veteran regiment of horse, one veteran battalion of infantry, the Lancashire militia and the armed Dissenters. The civilian forces were held in reserve and so Wills had seven regular units to attack with.

5

The Battle, 12–14 November 1715

Before we can sensibly discuss the battle, it is necessary to explore the terrain and also to consider 'urban warfare' in the early modern era. Celia Fiennes visited the town less than two decades before the battle and she wrote:

> Preston stands on a hill is a very good market town … there is a very spacious market place and pretty church and severall good houses; at the entrance to the town was a very good house which was a lawyers, all stone work 5 windows in the front and high built according to the eastern building neer London, the ascent to the house was 14 or 15 stone steps large and a handsome court with open iron palisades on the gate and one each side … there were 2 or 3 more such houses in the town and indeed the generality of the buildings especially in 2 or 3 of the great streetes were very handsome, better than in most country towns, and the streets spacious and well pitch'd.[1]

Defoe notes that Preston was a major regional social centre:

> … a fine town and tolerably full of people, but not like Liverpool or Manchester; besides we come now beyond the trading part of the county. Here's no manufacture, the town is full of attorneys, proctors and notaries, the process of law here being of a different nature than they are in other places, it being a duchy and county palatinate, and having particular privileges of its own. The people are gay here, though not perhaps the richer for that; but it has by that obtained the name of Proud Preston. Here is a great deal of good company.[2]

Fortunately there are a number of maps showing the town in 1715. In its centre was the marketplace, with the town hall and market cross, and The Sign of the Mitre inn to the north eastern side. Turning off from the north west corner of the market was Friargate, with its windmill at its

---

1 Morris, *Journeys*, p.187.
2 Rogers, *Defoe's Tour*, p.548.

THE BATTLE, 12–14 NOVEMBER 1715

Map of southern Lancashire by William Yates, 1786.

extremity, on the road north to Lancaster, on which the Jacobite army had marched into the town. Travelling westwards from the south west corner of the marketplace was Fishergate, leading to the river Ribble and its fords. From the south east corner of the marketplace, which was a continuation of Fishergate, was Churchgate, which eventually swung to the south east and towards the road to Wigan. Along the south side of Churchgate, just to the east of the marketplace, was the White Bull inn and then St John's parish church (with its churchyard extending mostly to the south), and further along on the north side was Hoghton's fine town house; on the opposite side of the road was Mr Ayre's slightly less lofty house. Across each of the three main thoroughfares was the site of the Medieval gate, where incoming merchants were charged tolls. There were many smaller lanes or weinds leading off from the three main roads. To the south of Preston was the tidal River Ribble. It had one bridge across it, on the road to Wigan, but the river split so that to cross from the Wigan road meant first crossing the Darwen bridge and marching through the village of Walton before the Ribble bridge

THE SECOND BATTLE OF PRESTON, 1715

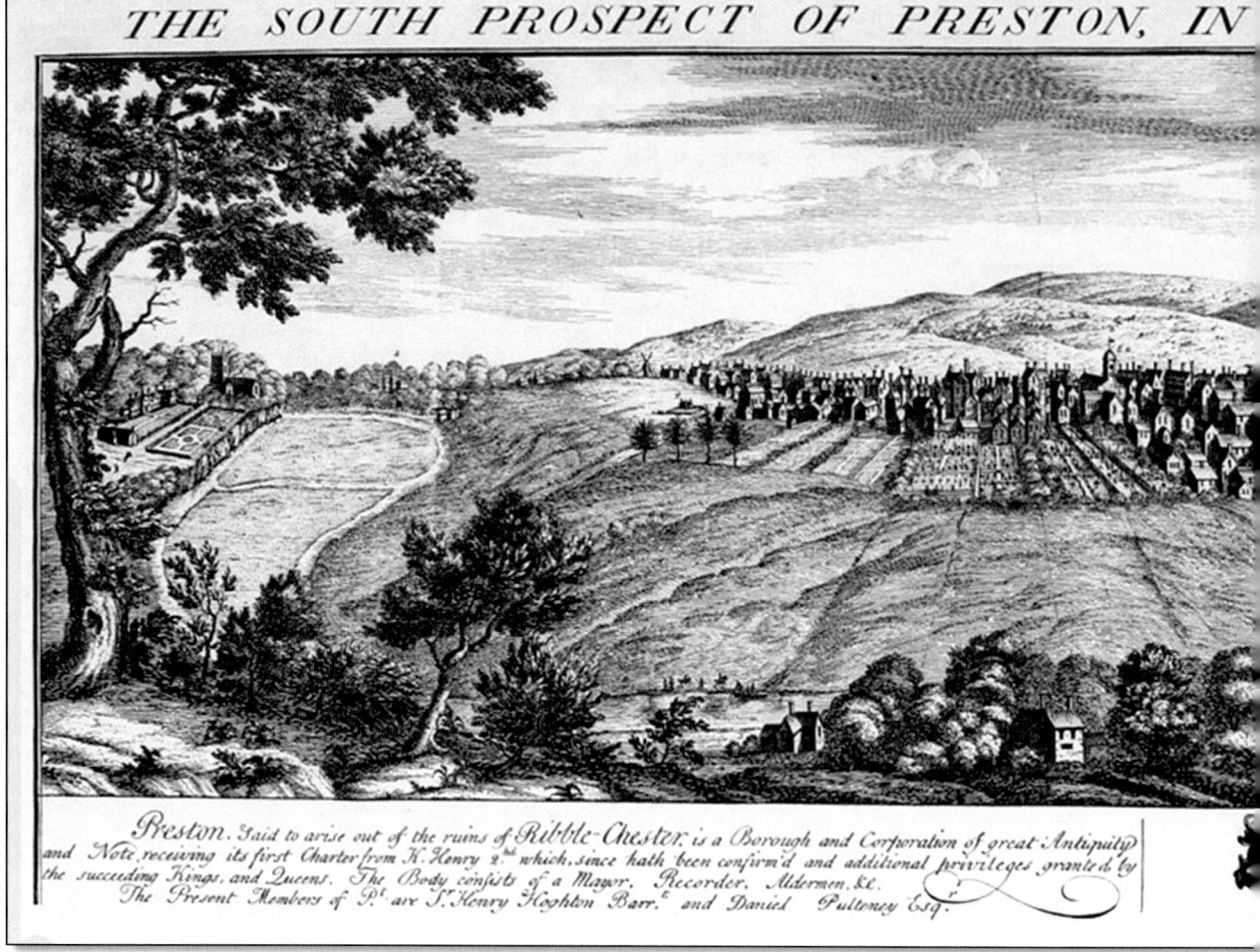

The south prospect of Preston, in the county of Lancashire. This is the view of the town that the British army would have seen on marching north towards Preston on 12 November 1715. By the Bucks Brothers, 1727.

was reached. Furthermore, there was a ferry to the west of Preston and as the river swung northwards near Penwortham there were two fords.[3]

Street fighting became more commonplace in the twentieth century as towns and cities grew and countries became more urbanised. There have been some significant battles in cities in World War Two, in Stalingrad 1942–1943 and in Berlin in 1945, as well as in many others. Modern armies train to fight in such environments, but in the eighteenth century such combat was very unusual. Armies might partially fight to gain villages, such as at Blenheim in 1704 as part of a wider battle, and walled towns might stand sieges and suffer an assault.

In Britain the most recent battle which had taken place within a town was at Dunkeld in 1689 and before that at Worcester in 1651. Hibbert-Ware, from the vantage of 1845, stated, 'Military men of the present generation will recollect, under what disadvantage, during the late war, besieging operations were conducted, whenever they were abroad as a preliminary measure, to

---

3   Royal Archives: RCIN 726092, Plan of the Battle of Preston, 1715.

THE BATTLE, 12–14 NOVEMBER 1715

take the place without'. He recalled the instance of the trouble that British infantry had seen during street fighting in Buenos Aires in 1806 and that facing Marshal Marmont's troops in dealing with revolutionaries manning the Paris barricades during the French Revolution of 1830.[4]

Urban warfare usually gives the advantage to the defender. The defenders are often far more knowledgeable about the town's layout. In this instance, Preston was well known to most of the Lancashire gentlemen – both in the Jacobite army and among the Lancashire militia and volunteers – as it was a major regional social centre, which they had often cause to visit, as noted in Lancashire gentlemen's diaries of the time. The defenders are usually able to reduce the attacker's advantages in numbers and other ways. Streets can be barricaded and fire can be directed on the attackers from windows and doorways as well as behind the barricades, so from three sides. Defenders have the advantage of cover whilst the attackers are cramped within streets and so are easy targets.

---

4   Hibbert-Ware, 'Memorials', p.135.

This was certainly the case at Dunkeld on 22 August 1689. The attacking Jacobite army numbered between 3,000 and 5,000 men, with cavalry and artillery and the defending regiment of Scottish government infantry numbered perhaps 600–700 men. The latter had only had a few days to prepare their defence of the small 'open' (that is, unwalled) town. The defence was a successful one, whereas a battle between these forces in the open would have resulted in the latter being defeated with ease. Likewise in 1679 a small force was able to repel a larger one attacking Glasgow.

Wills' force was marching northwards from Wigan to Preston and this route, albeit two decades previously, was described by Celia Fiennes thus:

> Preston is reckon'd but 12 miles from Wiggon but they exceed in length by farre those that I thought long … its true to avoid the many mers and marshy places it was a great compass I tooke and passed down and up very steep hills and this way was good gravel way; but passing by many very large arches that were only single ones but at large as two great gateways and the water I went through that ran under them was so shallow notwithstanding these were extream high arches, I enquired the meaning and was inform'd that on great raines those brookes would be swell'd to so great a heighth that unless those arches were so high noe passing while it were so; they are but narrow bridges for foote or horse and at such fords they are forced in many places to boate it till they come to those arches on the great bridges which are across their great rivers … I passed by at least half a dozen of these high single arches besides severall great Stone Bridges of 4 or 6 arches which are very high also over their great bridges.[5]

The weather on the day of the battle is unremarked on by all eyewitnesses. Thus it was certainly a dry day without any rain which would interfere with musketry. Nicholas Blundell, a Catholic gentleman of Little Crosby in Lancashire, noted in his diary, 'This Month [November] has been seasonable enough though generally very cold'.[6] Therefore weather conditions were favourable for a battle, but given the season of the year, daylight hours would be limited, with darkness falling by 4:00 p.m. and complete darkness in another half an hour and Preston was without street lights.

According to Patten, as noted in chapter three, Forster was allegedly unaware that Wills' forces were at Wigan or would be imminently arriving at Preston. That morning, Forster sent the Rev. Paul with messages to allies in Staffordshire and Leicestershire. He met Wills on his way, who stopped and questioned him. Wills had no suspicion that Paul was a Jacobite and so let him on his way.[7]

At least one detachment of Jacobite horsemen rode south east of Preston along the Wigan road that morning, presumably at daybreak. This may have been in order to garner intelligence about the enemy or, if they were in ignorance of Wills' whereabouts, could have been the advance guard of

---

5 Morris, *Journeys*, pp.186–187.
6 Frank Tyrer (ed.), 'The Great Diurnall of Nicholas Blundell, 1712–1718', *Record Society of Lancashire and Cheshire* (1970), p. 153.
7 Patten, *History*, pp.80–81.

THE BATTLE, 12–14 NOVEMBER 1715

the whole force as it prepared to march towards Manchester as planned.[8] This may have been John Leybourne and his servants as an eyewitness later observed, he saw him and 'his servants mounted their horses with all their arms and accoutrements and went into a march about half a mile out of town and afterwards came back again to Preston and one of these servants told they had been in the marsh exercising'.[9]

At nine in the morning, this detachment of scouting Jacobite cavalry returned to Preston. They told Forster that Wills was about to arrive. Hume's troop of cavalry was ordered to mount up. Forster then countermanded this action.[10] It was thought that the enemy marching towards them constituted a regiment of horse, six of dragoons and ten of infantry; the latter figure was grossly inflated.[11] These would have made the Jacobites even more apprehensive and clearly prevented any idea of a march to Manchester. According to La Roone, 'They had a design of turning off towards Manchester, but finding us so near them, retired with some precipitation to Preston'.[12]

One story circulating in the next year was that Derwentwater was:

> … exercising his men upon the marsh to the south west of Preston when he learned ye King's Forces were just upon 'em, he became very joyful, putt off his hatt and he shouted they are all for us, commanded his men into the town and rid to meet them, he met them with their swords drawn a little before they came into the Ribbald Bridge … he ridd back to towne in a great consternation and cryed we are undone they are against us.[13]

It is assumed that Derwentwater believed the army would come over to the cause of the 'rightful' King; Monmouth had believed likewise in 1685.

Always shy of making decisions, especially one that would lead to conflict, this time there could be no shrugging off military action. A retreat was not a possibility: being caught in the open by enemy cavalry might be to invite massacre; there may also have been suspicion by the Scots infantry that the Lowland and English horsemen would desert them in the crisis. A stand at Preston was thus inevitable.

The Jacobite army could fight in the fields outside Preston. Or they could fight inside the town. Forster seems to have been initially of the opinion that a battle in the open was the best option. Thus he advanced a small party to hold the main bridge and then 'went to view a ford in the River, in order for a Passage to come behind them'.[14] Presumably the plan was to fight Wills to the south of the river.

One Jacobite later wrote that they were 'resolved to goe and fight them in the open fields' and he believed that this would 'which had we done we

---

8   Anon., *A Letter*, p.5.
9   TNA, TS23/34.
10 Anon., *A Letter*, pp.5–6.
11 *Weekly Journal*, 10 March 1716.
12 Smith, *Nollekens*, II, p.270.
13 TWAS: CP3/22, Letter of Robert Cotesworth to William Cotesworth, 2 June 1716.
14 Patten, *History*, p.81.

THE SECOND BATTLE OF PRESTON, 1715

View of the River Ribble south of Preston. (Author's photo, 2019)

gain'd the day'.[15] Another explained, 'At first it was resolved to fight them in the plain fields, which more than probably would have ended gloriously for us for we were all hearty and well inclined to the work. The enemy were mostly greenhorns and much fatigued'.[16] There was a council of war among at least some of the officers (Richard Gascoigne and John Shaftoe were there) before the battle, as to what should happen; it being stated of Major John Nairn that 'when the King's forces approach'd, he gave his vote for drawing out, and fighting them in the open fields'.[17] It would appear that this option was then prepared for.

In order to facilitate a battle in the open, and to enable the rest of the army to form up and march out and across the fords, a body of infantry was placed by the bridge over the river to hold up the enemy there. According to Patten, they were 100 'choice, stout, well armed' men from Mackintosh's regiment and were led by the battalion's deputy commander, Lieutenant Colonel John Farquharson, 'a good officer and a very Bold Man'. Another Jacobite alleged that the force was that of Colonel Stewart (possibly Captain Stuart of Nairn's is meant) and 120 men. Francis Charteris alleged the force was 220 strong, made up of both infantry and cavalry. According to Patten, they 'would have

---

15 BC: 45/12/77, account of the Jacobite southern army to Preston.
16 TNA: SP54/9, 107, Jacobite prisoner's experiences in the rebellion.
17 Anon., *Faithful Register*, p.23.

defended that important pass of the Bridge to the last Drop'. It would appear that this force was an advance guard, to hold the bridge 'till the rest had advanced and drawn themselves out of the Town'.[18] Clarke also suggested that at 11:00 a.m. that morning after Wills' approach was known about, Derwentwater sent 300 horsemen (most of the army's cavalry) to the bridge 'to oppose General Wills passage over it'.[19] A detachment of cavalry rode to the south of the river, accompanied by Forster, to view the ground there and this suggests there was a plan to fight the battle to the south of the Ribble.[20]

Yet as a Jacobite noted, 'But our generals & lords were all of a piece, either Rogues or Cowards'.[21] The decision was taken, perhaps at noon, and probably by Forster, when Wills' army was seen marching into Walton le Dale, to withdraw all the forces thereabouts into the town, a cautious and defensive policy, quite in character with earlier decisions taken by the same commanders throughout the campaign. This may have been because the troops were too slow in marching out of the town and would be unable to form up in time for battle. Or it may have been due to concern about the vulnerability of infantry fighting cavalry in the open as Mackintosh later mentioned. Possibly the largely untrained and undrilled men could not be expected to perform well in the open. Patten wrote, 'This Retreat was another wrong Step, and has been condemned on all hands as one of the greatest oversights they could be guilty of'.[22] It is not certain when this retreat took place, one source suggests it did not occur until Wills' men came into view, at about 1:00 p.m.[23] It may not even have been ordered, as another account alleged, 'They never came off till the Enemy was almost within Gun-shot of them and then they thought proper to retire without any Orders'.[24] If this was true, then it suggests that the Jacobite leadership, dealing with their myriad tasks, had forgotten about the detachment they had placed at the bridge or perhaps only one knew they were there and had not told the others that they were there.

According to Patten, the river was not fordable except for a ford a long way from the bridge and that could have been covered. The bridge could have been made impassable, 'they might have barricaded it so well, that it would have been impracticable to have pass'd here, or to have dislodg'd them from it; also they had cannon, which General Wills wanted'. The bridge could have been a place where a stand could have taken; the British troops would have been exposed to fire without having any cover, whereas the rising ground made the Jacobite position strong.[25] Another Jacobite attacked this decision, 'the Ribble Bridge, which might and would have defended that important

---

18 Patten, *History*, p.81, *Weekly Journal*, 10 March 1716; BL. Add.Mss. 47028, f.104v, Dering to Egmont, 15 November 1715.
19 Paton, 'Journal', p.521.
20 *Weekly Journal*, 10 March 1716
21 BC: 45/12/77, account of the Jacobite southern army to Preston.
22 Patten, *History*, p.81.
23 *London Gazette*, 5384, 22–26 November 1715.
24 *Weekly Journal*, 10 March 1716.
25 Patten, *History*, pp.81–82.

THE SECOND BATTLE OF PRESTON, 1715

post and been of great service in galling and retarding the enemy's motions' was thrown away.²⁶ Likewise, a Lowlander claimed:

> It was thought very necessary by every body to defend the Bridge and Colonel Stewart was very fond to keep it. It was well situated by advantageous ground upon each side, and the close hedge from it to the town, that the men under Colonel Stewart could almost have defended it against Will's whole forces.²⁷

On being shown the position in 1745, Charles Edward Stuart declared that he thought it strange 'that they Should have deserted the Bridge'.²⁸

After the battle was over, Forster and Mackintosh discussed this issue. Forster stated that Mackintosh had the operational charge of the army on that day and 'had view'd the Bridge over Ribble, why did you not defend it, being a Matter of no great difficulty to have maintain'd that Important Post?' Mackintosh gave his answer thus, 'It was not maintainable, because the river was fordable at several Places'. There were indeed the two fords at Penwortham, about a mile to the west of the main bridges and also a ferry. When it is recalled that there were Lancashire men with Wills who could have told him where the river could be easily crossed, Mackintosh's reasoning was reinforced. Furthermore, as Mackintosh later noted, 'nothing more frightens the Highlanders than Horse and cannon'.²⁹ Stationing these men at the bridge only made sense if the Jacobite army was to fight outside the town: this advance guard would buy the time that the Jacobites would need to form up their army ready for battle on leaving Preston. But since the decision had been taken to fight in the town, there was no need for them to be at the bridge and so were logically withdrawn, though this was 'contrary to their inclinations, called off'.³⁰

A study of the previous battle at Preston (1648), notes that the Penwortham ford was dependant on the tide (the river flowed into the North Sea) and sometimes could only be crossed by swimmers. There was a track at Fishwick called Watery Lane which ran down to the river. It turned out that in 1648 the Penwortham ford was impassable to the Royalist cavalry.³¹ On the other hand a contemporary later wrote that 'there was only one Ford by which they could come another Way, which might have been easily defended, too: but all this was slighted'.³²

The plan to fight within the town was greeted with dismay by some, as a Jacobite later wrote, 'was it not plain madness … to coop themselves up in a town which had no walls, and where there was no provisions. But we were no better used in the defence of the town as will appear by the sequel'.³³ Despite

Facing page: The Battle of Preston. The scene shown here is entirely fictional; there was no fighting on or near to the bridge over the Ribble. (Courtesy of the Drambuie Whisky Museum, D262b)

---

26 TNA: SP54/9/107, Jacobite prisoner's experiences in the rebellion.
27 *Weekly Journal*, 10 March 1716.
28 R.E. Bell (ed.), 'Memorials of John Murray of Broughton, 1740–1747', *SHS*, 27 (1898), p.246.
29 Patten, *History*, pp.82, 104–105.
30 *Weekly Journal*, 10 March 1716.
31 Stephen Bull and Mike Seed, *Bloody Preston: The Battle of Preston, 1648* (Lancaster: Carnegie, 1998), pp.64, 73.
32 *Weekly Journal*, 10 March 1716.
33 TNA: SP54/9/107, Jacobite prisoner's experiences in the rebellion.

part of the army wanting to fight outside the town, the decision not to do so was greeted with immense activity within Preston, as Patten recounted 'During this time, the Rebels were not idle in the Town, nor did they appear in the least discourag'd, but applied themselves resolutely to their Business, barricading the Streets, and posting their men in the Streets, by-lanes and Houses, to the greatest Advantage, for all Events'.

Defending Preston had its advantages and drawbacks. On the credit side, it was built on a hill and so attackers would be tired on reaching the point of combat, whereas the defenders would be fresh. However, it was not a walled town and so had no defensive perimeter or purpose built strongpoints. As noted, there were three principal roads leading into and through the town: all were broad, ranging from 53 feet wide at the eastern end of Churchgate to 40 feet further westwards.[34]

There is no unanimity on the initial Jacobite disposition, which was presumably organised by Mackintosh. There is general agreement that most of the cavalry were dismounted and in the churchyard, clearly as a reinforcement against what would probably be the main attack from the bridge. The Merse Trooper has Douglas and Hunter's troops on the south side of the churchyard (but were later moved inside houses on Churchgate), with the bulk of the Lowland cavalry and the Northumberland gentlemen on the north side, and Wogan's troop to the west of Hoghton's house.[35] Patten has the gentlemen volunteers in the churchyard, but he may mean this to mean all of the cavalry as he does not refer to them being elsewhere. According to him, Derwentwater, Kenmure, Nithsdale and Winton were there, too.[36] However an anonymous Lowlander places only the Scots volunteers and dismounted cavalry in the churchyard and that the English were in the market place and in unspecified other place/s.[37] A later witness claimed that Towneley (who had removed his coat and was notable in his red waistcoat) and his men were on foot in the churchyard.[38] Merse Trooper notes that the English were in the market place, too, except for the dismounted Northumbrian cavalry in the churchyard.[39]

Patten goes on to note that Derwentwater stripped to his waistcoat and offered the men money to make defences and encouraged them to do so, though this might be a more general reference to motivating the men elsewhere in the town by the barricades. When that was done, he ordered Patten to mount up and be ready to bring him constant accounts of what was happening elsewhere and where the volunteers could move to reinforce any weak points. Patten was happy to acquiesce in what would be a dangerous role.[40]

---

34 LRO: DDX 194/1r, Plan of Preston with names of householders, 1684.
35 Anon., *A Letter*, p.6.
36 Patten, *History*, p.83.
37 *Weekly Journal*, 10 March 1716.
38 TNA, TS23/34, 1.
39 Anon., *A Letter*, p.6.
40 Patten, *History*, p.83.

It was noted that Winton, with sword and pistol in his hands, was on foot at the head of 200 men.[41] One Lowlander claimed that all the cavalry except Carnwath's troop was dismounted.[42]

The main physical defences for the town were five barricades across the principal streets leading into Preston. None was at the furthermost outskirts of Preston and later Mackintosh was taken to task about this, being asked, 'Why he did not make his Barricade at the extreme end of the street leading to the Town, which would have prevented the King's Forces from taking possession of the Houses below his barrier, which was a great way up the Town?' He replied thus, 'at the extreme end of the Town there were so many Lanes and Avenues, that to defend them would have required more Men than I had'.[43]

The first was a barrier near to the parish church and this was under Brigadier Mackintosh's command, but it is not clear what troops he had with him; perhaps Nairn's men as they are not noted as being elsewhere. It was probably at the site of the old Medieval bar where the road was narrowest. Two cannon were placed at this barrier. Lord Charles Murray led the men at a barrier on the eastern end of Churchgate, about 220 yards to the east of Mackintosh's barrier which led to the fields, to the south of the town. It is presumed that he had all the men from his battalion here: at least 101.[44]

On the north side of Churchgate, between the two barriers was the detached town house of Sir Henry Hoghton, an ardent anti-Jacobite and this was initially garrisoned either by one Captain Innes of Mar's regiment and 50 men, or by Captain MacLean and his 37 gentlemen volunteers, depending on whether Patten and an anonymous Lowlander or the Merse trooper is believed (Patten claimed the gentleman volunteers were in the churchyard). This was an important site, as the Merse trooper explained, 'whose battlement and balcony did command the Head of the Hollow Way, that leads from the Bridge to the Town, and the Street in the Mercat-Place, and a great part of the Neighbouring Fields: This House had a Garden at the back of it, with a High Brick wall'. It was, therefore, a stronghold in miniature and thus a valuable asset to the defenders.[45]

The third barrier was called the Windmill and that was on the road leading from Preston to Lancaster (Friargate), to the north of the town. Colonel Mackintosh was in command here, with his own regiment, so about 301 men. Further southwards down Friargate and not much to the north of the marketplace was another barrier, by which were posted two cannons. Finally, there was a barricade to the south west of the town, on Fishergate, the road to Liverpool, commanded by Major Miller and Captain William Douglas, so composed of the remaining men of Strathmore's battalion (about 152 men). There were two more cannons placed here. A sailor was in

---

41 Anon., *Faithful Register*, pp.129, 139.
42 *Weekly Journal*, 10 March 1716.
43 Patten, *History*, p.104.
44 Patten, *History*, p.83.
45 Anon., *A Letter*, p.6.

charge of the cannon at Murray's eastern barricade.[46] John Langdale and his 'troop' of Lancastrians were said to be at Friargate, but also near to the marsh, which would place them at Fishergate.[47] One Jacobite wrote that the cannons were 'charged with small bullets', presumably some form of canister.[48] Of these roads into the town, the widest and thus most difficult to defend was Churchgate (now known as Church Street) which led to the bridges.

No one ever stated what the barriers were made of. Such were common in street fighting in the revolutions in Europe in the nineteenth century. They did not feature in the Dunkeld battle. It must be conjectured that they were made up of furniture from houses, perhaps including doors and tables and chairs, carts and any street furniture that could be found. As barriers against artillery they were flimsy, but as defences against infantry these makeshift defences were effective enough. Their opponents certainly thought so, with the town said to be 'strongly barricaded' and the inner barrier was 'very strong both by Nature and Art'.[49] Apparently on learning of these, Wills sent a messenger to Liverpool to ask for two or three cannons 'to force the barricades'.[50]

The remainder of the Jacobite army may have acted as a mobile reserve to exploit any opportunities or plug any gaps.[51] Certainly some of the cavalry, such as Talbot's troop, were dismounted, but as we shall see, not all were.[52] There were also some Jacobite reinforcements from Stonyhurst on the morning of the battle. John Walmsley, a servant, rode with the Stonyhurst troop to Preston and Thomas Watson delivered horses to 23 men that morning.[53]

Some of the Jacobite leaders seem conspicuous by their absence, such as Forster, Widdrington, Oxburgh and Carnwath. After the battle, a visitor to Preston wrote the following, 'The maids of Genll. Forster will take their oaths on't that he was in Bedd with a sack posset in the hottest time of the action'.[54] Likewise, Widdrington was nowhere to be seen, and according to Patten, adopted a similar tactic, 'he was never seen at any Barrier, or in any Action but where there was the least hazard'. These two were not alone, Patten referring to 'some of which kept themselves warm in a Chimney-Corner during the Heat of the Action'.[55] There certainly seems to have been a lack of overall command or co-ordination, and with the luxury of interior lines, this was certainly a missed opportunity; one Jacobite claimed 'no orders at all was given, but everybody did as he pleased'.[56] A Lowlander remarked, 'our cowardly officers, when there was use for them, either could not be found, or when got, would not command'.[57]

---

46 Patten, *History*, p.90.
47 TNA: FEC1/1585, Towneley and Tyldesley.
48 *Weekly Journal*, 10 March 1716.
49 *London Gazette*, 5384, 22–26 November 1715.
50 Smith, *Nollekens*, II, p.271.
51 Anon., *A Letter*, p.6.
52 Anon., *Faithful Register*, p. 259.
53 TNA: FEC1/310, communications from Thomas Rishton.
54 TWAS: CP3/22, Robert to William Cotesworth, 2 June 1716.
55 Patten, *History*, p.98, dedication.
56 LRO: DDXX 2244/1, Partial Account of the trial of the Jacobite prisoners at Liverpool, c.1716.
57 *Weekly Journal*, 10 March 1716.

Meanwhile, Wills' men had begun their march from Wigan at daybreak. They marched in the following order: a captain and 50 men of Preston's foot as the vanguard (though Patten referred to dragoons being in the vanguard), then the remainder of this veteran battalion supported by a captain and 50 men from an unspecified regiment of dragoons. This was unusual: cavalry were conventionally the vanguard of any regular force, riding ahead in order to locate the enemy and then giving notice to the rest of the army, their speed allowing them to do so. Perhaps Wills did not think his dragoon regiments, all of whom were newly raised, would have been capable of the task or perhaps he deemed them unreliable. The horse, of course, would not have been expected to have undertaken such work.

Following the vanguard were the three brigades of cavalry that Wills had formed his horse soldiers into. The first was Honywood's brigade, formed of his own regiment and Wynn's. Second was Dormer's, consisting of his own regiment and Pitt's Horse and finally Munden's brigade of his own men and the men of Stanhope's regiment. The baggage train made up the rear and was guarded by 50 dragoons. Apart from Stanhope's and Pitt's, all had marched the day before.[58] Not mentioned in this array there was also the county militia led by Hoghton, consisting of cavalry and infantry.

Some miles from Preston the little army was met by Messrs Wood and Walker, two Dissenting ministers from Lancashire, with their armed congregations, 'a considerable party'. The two ministers explained to Wills that 'they were ready to take any Post his Excellence was pleas'd to assign them'. Wills reviewed the men and told them 'That after he was come to Preston, he would assign them a post'. Nothing else of any note occurred in the long march.[59]

It was about one in the afternoon that they arrived at the bridge over the Ribble, having crossed the Darwen bridge and marched through Walton. They were then only a mile from Preston itself. Wills' advance guard ascertained that the Ribble bridge was undefended. Wills was surprised, because he believed 'that the Rebels would have made their greatest effort at that Place'. He therefore suspected that there might be an ambush laid on the lane that led to the town. This was lined with hedges and as Patten wrote, 'The Lane is indeed very deep, and so narrow that in several places two men cannot ride a-breast'. Indeed, there had been allegedly fierce fighting here in the battle of 1648 when large stones had been hurled down the lane at advancing troops and 'if Oliver [Cromwell] himself had not forced his horse to jump into a Quicksand he had luckily ended his days there'.[60]

Wills presumably sent out scouting parties, perhaps made up of Preston's infantrymen, and 'caused the Hedges and Fields to be view'd and the Ways laid open for his Cavalry to enter'. Finding no sign of the Jacobite forces here, he then jumped to the incorrect conclusion that the Jacobites had fled and were in full retreat to Scotland, though he thought that the latter was

---

58 Rae, *History*, p.318; Anon., *Annals*, II, p.136.
59 Rae, *History*, p.318n.
60 Patten, *History*, p.82.

impossible.[61] Possibly the remainder of the troops may have rested after their long march, as it was 18 miles along the road from Wigan to Preston.

The little army then began to march uphill towards Preston. The advance guard, however, soon returned with the news that the Jacobites were ready to fight 'with a resolute Countenance'.[62] Mackintosh and Forster reviewed the situation, they briefly being located in the same building, the latter remarking:

> … he will attack, and beat us all, if we do not look about us: still Forster laugh'd, when Mackintosh, looking out of the window, seeing some of the new men that came out of the country pass by, Look ye there, Forster, says he, are yon fellows the men ye intend to fight Wills with: Good Faith, sir, and ye had 10,000 of them, I'd fight them with 1000 of his dragoons … They were ill armed, some had swords and no muskets, some had muskets and no swords, some fowling pieces, some pitchforks, some no weapons at all.[63]

Meanwhile, others were worried about the imminent battle. John Shaftoe, for one, was described thus, 'he seem'd somewhat concern'd, yet he appeared at the Barrier with courage enough'. John Ferguson, of Mackintosh's battalion, armed only with a short sword, refused to go to a barricade when commanded by a captain to do so, and so was placed under arrest in a guard house.[64]

The initiative was now firmly in Wills' hands. According to Patten, 'he had nothing to do but to prepare for an Attack, which he went about immediately'. Part of his army was sent through a gate to the fields to the north of the town. The remainder was also deployed in the enclosed fields to the south east of Preston, where they could be formed up into lines to attack the Jacobites, for the main road itself was very narrow, especially for cavalry and only allowed a frontage of three or four men. His plan was to attack the Jacobites in the town, but was also ready to counter any attempts at sallies or escape.[65]

Wills could see that the entrances to the town were barricaded and defended with cannons. There were to be two main assaults. One was to be on the south east of Preston, on the Wigan road. This was to be made by Preston's battalion of infantry led by Lord Forrester. Supporting them were a captain and 50 men from each of the five dragoon regiments, led by a colonel, lieutenant colonel and a major. These 250 or so men were all dismounted: dragoons often fought on foot as well as on horseback. In their rear were the bulk of Honywood's dragoons, all mounted, presumably to deter or oppose any sally by the Jacobites. In overall command of these troops was Brigadier Honywood. This force was perhaps about half of Wills' command, possibly about 600 strong in all.[66]

---

61 Patten, *History*, p.82.
62 Patten, *History*, p.82.
63 Anon., *Annals*, II, p.136
64 Anon., *Faithful Register*, pp.23, 245.
65 Patten, *History*, pp.82–83.
66 Rae, *History*, p.319.

THE BATTLE, 12–14 NOVEMBER 1715

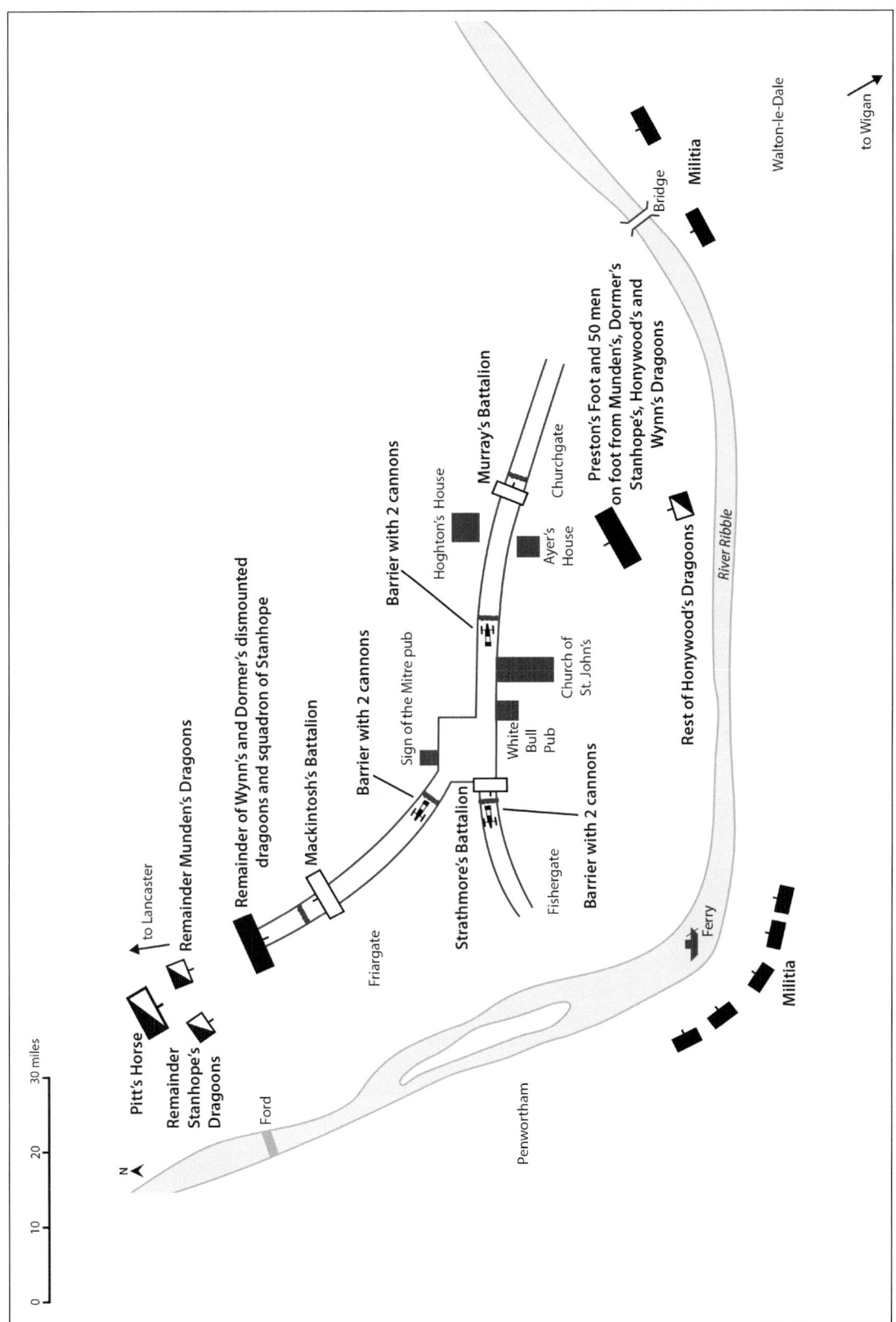

The Battle of Preston, Day 1

Table 20. Officers in Charge of Each Troop

Regiment	Captain	Lieutenant	Cornet
Honywood's	Hussum	Mitchell	Gardiner
Wynn's	Smith	n/k	n/k
Munden's	Howard	Dawson	O'Bryan
Dormer's	Newcomen	Lasale	Delahay
Stanhope's	Deleuze	Leighton	Durell

They were accompanied by Colonel Pierson, Lieutenant Colonel Nassau and Colonel Solomon Rapin.[67] Meanwhile, as La Roone later wrote, 'all the dragoons were dismounted, and the horses were linked together and put into adjacent fields with a sufficient number of men to take care of them'.[68]

It is possible that grenades were used in the assault, as would have been customary in siege warfare by men of the grenadier company of Preston's. Such occurred at Killiecrankie in 1689, and again here, as later. A grenade was uncovered during excavations in the nineteenth century. It had failed to explode, so if this was typical, they were clearly of little use.[69]

They may have waited until their fellows were in position elsewhere. Wills had the remainder of his army march around the north of the town so that they were amassed in the vicinity of Friargate. The remaining men from Wynn's and Dormer's dragoons and a squadron of Stanhope's, were there ordered to dismount (perhaps about 350 men in all). Brigadier Dormer would lead them here. In support, as elsewhere, were mounted troops; the remainder of Munden's dragoons, a squadron of Stanhope's and the entirety of the fully mounted Pitt's horse, under the command of Munden, were to act in support of the foot soldiers, wherever possible.[70] The cavalry could have stopped a Jacobite counter attack, but otherwise they were not being utilised. Pitt's horse, divided into two squadrons, was in support of the assault troops.[71]

The non-regular forces who had marched with Wills had not crossed the bridges over the Ribble. They had remained to the south. Once Wills had arranged his main forces, he sent word back to them. They were to 'keep the Bridge of Ribble, to prevent the Rebels escaping that way, or their Friends coming from that side to join them'. It will be recalled that both sides expected that the Jacobites would receive considerable support from Manchester and though Wills had ordered Newton's dragoon regiment to garrison the town to prevent anyone doing so, they were marching from Worcester on the previous day so may not have arrived there yet. A contemporary map shows two companies of foot militia being stationed between the Ribble and the

---

67 *St. James' Post*, 74, 17–19 November 1715.
68 Smith, *Nollekens*, II, p.271.
69 Charles Hardwick, *History of the Borough of Preston* (Preston: Worthington and Company, 1857), p.229n.
70 Patten, *History*, pp.83–84.
71 RA: RCIN 726092.

Darwen and the other two companies and the two troops of horse militia to the west of the junction of the two rivers, stationed behind hedges directly to the south of the town; the whereabouts of the Dissenters is not shown.[72] Yet another contemporary map shows the bulk of the militia guarding a ford to the south-west of the town.[73]

It is not certain where Wills posted himself; the account below suggests he was near Preston's battalion. It seems that all his men were committed to the attack; apart from those ordered to support each assault, there was no other reserve. His orders were 'to march, and gain the Ends of the Town, and set the Houses on Fire, to dislodge, by that Means, the Rebels from their Barricade, and to make such Lodgements for their Men, as to prevent their sallying out upon them, or making their Escape'.[74]

Ensign Colville of Preston's foot later remarked:

> I must do that justice to our General, who as I observed before has been blamed for not waiting for more troops [two infantry battalions in Wills' command had not yet arrived and he did not wait for them], that being posted on the Grenadier Company and having thereby an opportunity of hearing the General's orders and remarks, that when we came to the Ribble Bridge and found the bridge and hollow way not defended, he said that people must surely be in a confusion else they would surely have defended their strong post, and therefore I will attack them and not give them time to think.[75]

As noted in the previous chapter, Wills has been condemned for attacking the town, though this has been made with hindsight. A cautious man might have waited for Carpenter's cavalry and for the two battalions of veteran infantry which were part of his command. Yet as also noted there were political concerns that the Jacobite army might gather more support and become more dangerous if they were not extinguished. Engaging in any aspect of warfare is taking a risk; whether it is justified is judged by results and that is not possible to know in advance. It can also be argued, as Carpenter was later to do, that the attack was made because of Wills' personal ambition, wanting to win without his co-general's aid and so take all the glory of victory for himself and in so doing be promoted to lieutenant general.

There was also the question of time. To *begin* a battle in the afternoon on an autumnal day meant that the hours of daylight were very restricted. There would only be two hours in which a conclusion could be reached: thus no time for subtlety in tactics. It is possible that Wills believed the Jacobites were low in morale and that one attack would lead to their utter collapse; after all they had avoided conflict earlier in the campaign and had retreated into the town earlier that day. Regular soldiers often despise irregulars and underestimate them. Yet even poor troops, when their backs are to the wall and are well entrenched, can fight fiercely in defence.

---

72 Rae, *History*, p.319n; LRO: DDX 1788/1, Plan.
73 RA: RCIN 726092.
74 Rae, *History*, p.319.
75 Robson, 'Military Memoirs', p.16.

THE SECOND BATTLE OF PRESTON, 1715

The Battle of Preston, by Pet. Schenck. This is the only known contemporary picture of the street fighting that took place at Preston in 1715. (Courtesy of the Drambuie Whisky Museum, D251)

The question is, where did the first attack take place. It might seem logical for a force that had crossed the river and was marching therefore, towards the eastern part of the town that Murray's barricade on Churchgate would have been under attack and indeed one contemporary states that this is what happens.[76] However, the bulk of the other eyewitnesses clearly state that it was Mackintosh's barrier, near to the church that was attacked, and additional evidence for this comes from the fact that artillery fire was used against the attackers and Mackintosh's barrier had two guns. Furthermore, one statement refers to an attack on the churchyard at the same time and that was closer to Mackintosh's barrier rather than Murray's. It may seem less logical to attack an inner, not an outer barrier, but this seems to have occurred. Given that there were a number of Lancashire loyalists with Wills, including Preston's vicar, Wills was probably told of alternative routes into the town, by using the undefended side streets, or wiends.

The first attack was made, according to Clarke, at about two o'clock, though Carpenter believed it was an hour later, on the barricade in Churchgate held by Brigadier Mackintosh, so presumably the troops had entered the street by a side street (otherwise they would have had to assault Murray's barrier first), though this is not mentioned by eyewitnesses. The infantry were interlaced with the dismounted dragoons as they advanced and they presented an easy target, and that was after they would have been fired upon whilst forming ranks after having emerged into Churchgate. According to Patten, the attackers were 'met with such a Reception, and so

---

76   *Weekly Journal*, 10 March 1716.

terrible a Fire was made upon them; as well from the Barricado as from the Houses on both sides, that they were obliged to retreat', with the bulk of the casualties being presumably from Preston's battalion, for they were funnelled into the street and, according to Clarke, 'the Highlanders firing out of cellers and windows, in 10 minuits time killed 120 of them. The Highlanders also fired the 2 said ship guns, but the bullets flew upon the houses, so that no execution was done thereby'.[77]

Another comment about the ineffectual Jacobite artillery fire came from Patten:

> … the Rebels, though they had six pieces of cannon, did not much use them except at first only; in short they knew not how, having no Engineers amongst them; and a seaman who pretended Judgement and upon his own offer, took the Management of the cannon, acted so madly, whether it was that he had too little Judgement or too much ale or perhaps both.[78]

Clarke's estimate of fatalities seems far too high and is surely an exaggeration. Despite this, it is clear from these two accounts that the British troops made no headway, took casualties and were forced to retreat. First blood had gone to the Jacobites without any doubt.

There is another, and hitherto unknown and very different, account of the first attack as reported by an anonymous Lowlander. It is worth reproducing in full:

> … the first attack was commanded by Brigs Dormer and Honywood and the Lord Forrester who with Brig Preston's Regt of Foot interweaved with dragoons made the first attack at the avenue leading to the church. There were men commanded by Kenmure and the Lord Charles Murray having two pieces of cannon and an intrenchment in the street and support by Captain Lockhart and Mr Basil Hamilton's troops, made a gallant defence and caused great damage. Lord Charles killed several of the enemy with his own hand when they had lodged themselves in the churchyard and Derwentwater, Mr Murray of Shewhope Hepburn the younger of Keith Mr John Paterson and many other gentlemen behaved themselves gallantly. In short all signalled themselves. The enemy attackt very resolutely but were as well received and frequently repulsed upon foot also which their foot began to fall off and keep at a little distance whereupon a body of their horse advanced. To meet which Captain Lockhart marched upon his horse and the two bodys came to close work with sword and pistol in which we had not one man killed, butt we killed several; of their men and our Gentry mauled the Enemy bravely with their broadswords. The dispute lasted a long while. But at length the enemy left away before Mr Lockhart's Troop which was on our right whereupon that captain with a great deal of courage and conduct, calling to his men that the day was their own then immediately went off to his right and marched at them found ym galloped around the Enemy. And again formed his men between them

---

77 Paton, 'Journal', p.521.
78 Patten, *History*, p.90.

and their Foot, attack and drove them before him. In the mean time the Enemy's right seeing their left give way, fled in great confusion trampled down their foot, whereupon Mr Basil Hamilton wheeled about to the right with his troops and advancing to the other side of Captain Lockhart's troop was playing and some of our foot seeing the advance on the said syde so that we drove them up into a corner, took about 50 prisoners with their officers who were now brought into the town and so secured. In short the enemy was soundly beat above 180 killed and their officers.[79]

This description is of especial interest because it shows that the fighting spilt over into the churchyard and suggests that the first assault was a two pronged attack, on both the barricade and the churchyard. It is also of note for this is the only recorded battle between opposing cavalry in the entire Jacobite campaigns of 1689–1746 and it shows that Jacobite cavalry could and did beat their opponents.

Honywood and Forrester (and possibly Wills) as the senior officers there had to rethink their approach to the attack. The accounts are confused and neither of the former officers wrote about this stage of the battle. Two different tactics were adopted; one being the result of taking advantage of a Jacobite error.

The first was deliberate arson; unusual because destruction of civilian property was usually something that generals were reluctant to authorise as any damage was their responsibility. Be that as it may, a small party of soldiers was sent to burn the barns and some of the houses at the far east of Churchgate street. Property set on fire here included Richard Myer's house, worth £76 and his barn with £27 10s worth of corn in it, William Wall's two houses worth £100 in total, Edward Stanley's house worth £116, Thomas Molyneux's house worth £56 and William Hayhurst's property and others.[80] Fearful that the flames would spread westwards, the Highlanders retreated further into the town along Churchgate, abandoning the furthest barricade to the east. Fortunately the winds were blowing northwards, 'which had it been south, the judicious are of opinion that most of this towne would have been burnt'. Such had occurred at Dunkeld in 1689 with only three houses surviving.[81]

Another opportunity emerged for the attackers. Some of Preston's officers discovered, or were told, about another way into Preston from Wigan, and this one was unbarricaded and undefended. There had been Jacobites placed at Hoghton's house and at Ayre's, but they had been withdrawn, perhaps to act as an immediate reserve during the assault on the Churchgate barrier or perhaps due to fears of the fire spreading. In particular, Hoghton's town house was abandoned and this became a topic of great controversy among the Jacobites, just as the abandoning of the Ribble bridge earlier had been.[82]

---

79 TNA: SP54/9, 107, Jacobite prisoner's experiences in the rebellion.
80 TNA: FEC1/246–250, Preston, Original claims for losses, 1718.
81 Paton, 'Journal', p.521.
82 Patten, *History*, p.84.

As usual, Patten stated where responsibility lay, 'Mr Forster cannot be blamed for this Oversight, but it must be charg'd upon the Brigadier, who when the Regiment of Preston's made this brave and bold Attempt, withdrew His Men from those Houses'.[83] However, an anonymous Jacobite wrote that it was Forster who gave the withdrawal order and that Innes 'at first refused to obey without a written order for by justification which Forster sent him'.[84] Another anonymous Jacobite noted that he was not certain who gave the withdrawal order, but that he had heard that Forster was responsible.[85] Whoever was at fault, Hoghton's house were abandoned. This was probably because these were forward positions which had now become isolated and thus vulnerable. It may also have been because troops were needed from these places to meet the main attacks on the Churchgate barricade.

Patten noted that once Forrester had scouted the situation and noted the abandoned property he sent men to seize it, but this meant running the gauntlet of Jacobite fire from the barrier at the church, only 70 yards away:

> It was a very desperate attempt, and shews him [Forrester] an Officer of an undaunted Courage. Whilst this was doing, the Rebels from the Barrier, and from the Houses on both Sides, made a terrible fire upon them, and a great many of that old and gallant Regiment were kill'd and wounded: The Lord Forrester received several wounds himself. Beside the damage they received on that side, they were sore galled from some Windows below them.[86]

Those firing from buildings included that by Douglas' and Hunter's men. According to Patten, Douglas distinguished himself by being 'very vigorous at the Action at Preston where he and his men were possess'd of several Houses and did a great deal of Harm to His majesty's Forces from the Windows'. Hunter behaved likewise, he 'behav'd with great Vigour and Obstinacy at Preston, where he took possession of some Houses during the Attack, and galled that brave Regiment … making a great slaughter out of the Windows'. He added there was return fire from Preston's battalion, 'but did little Execution, the Men being generally cover'd from the Shot: and delivering their own shot securely, and with good Aim; yet some were killed and some wounded'. These wounded included 'two Gallant gentlemen', Peter Farquharson of Rochaly, 'a Gentleman of infinite Spirit', being shot through the bone in the leg, and one Mr Clifton, 'a gallant and thoroughly accomplished Gentleman', shot through the knee. They were both removed from the scene and taken to the nearby White Bull, being used as a makeshift field hospital. Thomas Brereton was also hit by several musket balls.[87]

Eventually Honywood had men from Preston's battalion occupy Hoghton's house and some of the dragoons occupied Ayre's house which was almost

---

83 Patten, *History*, p.84.
84 TNA: SP54/9, 107, Jacobite prisoner's experiences in the rebellion.
85 *Weekly Journal*, 10 March 1716.
86 Patten, *History*, p.85.
87 Patten, *History*, pp.49, 85–6.

THE SECOND BATTLE OF PRESTON, 1715

Church Row. Looking down Church Street towards the location of the two large houses, later occupied by British troops. (Photograph by Charles Singleton, 2022)

opposite and never occupied by the Jacobites.[88] The Merse trooper noted, 'I saw a Regiment of Foot possess themselves of Sir Henry Hortoun's House, and a strong Detachment of Dragoons on Foot possess another House opposite to Hortoun's' by passing through Hoghton's gardens.[89]

Derwentwater and Lord Murray ordered men from the latter's battalion to engage their enemy at Hoghton's house. The latter had entered the property by the gardens and were initially there, until driven into the house by Jacobite musketry. The Merse trooper was convinced that there was a necessity to retake the house. In his memoir he wrote:

> I desired that the said House should be demolished by Two pieces of Cannon that were ready charged on the Front of the Churchyard, and that the Earl of Derwentwater and Lord Charles Murray should jointly attack the Enemy without the Town. I went for Orders to General Forrester, who would by no means allow of it, saying That the Body of the Town was the Security of the Army.[90]

This failure to act was to have deadly effects for the Jacobites. As Patten noted, 'And from these two Houses came almost all the Loss of the Rebels sustained during the Action'.[91] Colville wrote that 'from which we had a full view of the rebels and soon made them quit their post [presumably meaning Murray's barrier]'.[92] It is presumed that troops could fire from upper windows down on Jacobites seen in the streets and even behind barricades, and so lacked the cover that they had against troops on the ground. Meanwhile, the approaches to these two houses were strengthened by the throwing up of breastworks on Honywood's orders. This was in part to prevent any Jacobites from sallying out against them or escaping.[93]

There was a further attack in this part of the town, at four o'clock according to Clarke. It was the last action in this part of the town that day as light was rapidly fading. He wrote that the Jacobites were firing from dykes, gardens,

---

88   Rae, *History*, p.320.
89   Anon., *A Letter*, p.6.
90   Anon., *A Letter* p.7.
91   Patten, *History*, p.84.
92   Robson, 'Military Memoirs', p.60.
93   Rae, *History*, p.320.

walls and hedges, and of the 300 attackers, 140 were killed, or so he wrote in his typical exaggerated way.[94]

Patten gave additional details. Murray 'behaved very gallantly, but being very vigorously attack'd, wanted Men'. He asked Patten to let Derwentwater know of his need. The peer sent 50 gentlemen volunteers from the churchyard 'to reinforce him, who came in very good Season'. There was a lull in the fighting, so Patten was ordered over the barricade in order to see what the attackers were doing. They saw him in his clergyman's costume and failed to suspect him to be a Jacobite combatant. He was not fired upon, but soon returned to let Murray know that another attack was being prepared.[95]

Patten deemed that the defensive works were all but impregnable: 'nor, had they been all old Soldiers, could they have beaten Lord Charles from that Barrier, which was very strong, the number they had slain from the Barn-holes and Barrier itself added very much, so that at last the Officers themselves thought fit to give it over'.[96]

This was presumably Mackintosh's barrier. At this point the street, judging by Kuredon's 1675 map, was about 50 feet wide; space for about 14 men to fire, but the attackers were at a severe disadvantage: not only where there the enemy to their front, behind the barrier, but there were enemies to their flanks (from houses), probably at several levels of height. The amount of firepower against them was far more than that which they could reply to and all their enemies were behind cover. It was an almost impossible task against resolute men.[97] However, Colville alleged that the Jacobites firing from buildings were less than accurate because they 'did not hurt us as they durst not look out of the windows to take their aim'.[98]

It has been alleged that the Jacobites missed an opportunity here to exploit their enemies' disarray. Mackintosh was later asked 'Why he did not sally out himself with his Men? Or why he would not obey Mr Forster, who would have had the Horse to have sallied out?' Mackintosh replied:

> … if his Foot had sallied out, they might by that means have been parted from the Horse, and so left naked to have been cut off: Besides, nothing more frightens the Highlanders than Horse and Cannon. As for obeying Mr Forster, in the letting the horse sally out, he said, If the Horse had attempted any such thing, they would have gone through the fire of his Men; for they were afraid the Horse design'd such a Thing and would have been able to have made a Retreat, and left them pent up in the Town.[99]

Patten (although no one else mentioned his presence) also claimed that Forster was present at the barricade here, and 'He shew'd several times Forwardness enough for Action, and particularly that he was very far from

---

94 Paton, 'Journal', p.521.
95 Patten, *History*, p.86.
96 Patten, *History*, pp.85–86.
97 LRO: DDX 194/1r, Plan.
98 Robson, 'Military Memoirs', p.60.
99 Patten, *History*, pp.104–105.

THE SECOND BATTLE OF PRESTON, 1715

Friargate. Looking towards the intersection of Fylde Road on the left and Moor Lane on the right. Scene of the dragoon attack on the afternoon of the first day. (Photograph by Charles Singleton, 2022)

being a Coward, by riding up to Mackintosh's barrier twice, in the very Face of the King's Troops: and when he was expos'd to the shot of those possessed of the Houses on both sides of the Street, when I heard him command the Brigadier to advance'.[100] A Lowlander also bemoaned the lack of offensive action, writing 'It was crav'd at first to be allowed to sally out upon them. If that had been done, we had made a very good Account of them, the most of their Dragoons being but new levied men'.[101]

There were also a number of other heroic acts on the part of the Jacobites. Captain Nicholas Wogan risked his life (and was wounded in the cheek) to save that of an enemy officer, Captain Preston, who later hoped that Wogan would be dealt with mercifully because of his kindness. As to Charles

---

100 Patten, *History*, p.98.
101 *Weekly Journal*, 10 March 1716.

Radcliffe, 'During the whole of the Action Mr Radcliffe was in the midst of the Fire, and Expos'd to so much Danger as the meanest soldier upon Duty'. Basil Hamilton, another Jacobite captain, 'behaved himself with a great deal of Courage in the Action'. It was not only the officers whose noble deeds were recorded, but an anonymous soldier who was the lowest of the low – a carrier of a gunpowder cask who also risked his life to supply the front line soldiers. He was shot dead.[102] Of the senior officers, Derwentwater stood out, 'No man of Distinction behaved better' by exposing himself to enemy fire, encouraging the men by gifts of money and helping throw up entrenchments for the artillery.[103] At the same time, their enemies' senior officers were leading from the front and presumably on horseback and so presenting

---

102 Patten, *History*, pp.39, 50, 102; Penrice Radcliffe, *Genuine and Impartial Memoirs of Charles Radcliffe* (London: Publisher Unknown, 1747), p.38.
103 *Political State*, XI (1716), p.165.

THE SECOND BATTLE OF PRESTON, 1715

Tithbarn Street. The edge of the town in 1715, where the bus station now stands, would have been open fields and barns. (Photograph by Charles Singleton, 2022)

an easier target; with brigadiers Honywood and Dormer, lieutenant colonel Forrester and Majors Preston, Lawson and Bland all being wounded by musketry; the latter's horse was also shot through the neck.[104]

Not all showed such valour, as a Lowlander complained of some of the Lancastrian recruits, 'of them that joined us, when we had use for them, few or none were seen'.[105] On the other hand, some Lancastrians were far from being faint hearted. One Edward Baines recalling that one of them 'bidd this informant farewell for he was going either to kill or be killed'. Furthermore, Manchester Jacobite, Edward Beswicke, 'encouraged his fellows, saying now my lads, now for it'.[106]

Another attack on Preston that day took place at the Windmill barricade on Friargate. Less is known about this because presumably none of the eyewitnesses were present; it is only known about at second hand. The dismounted dragoons there were in place at three in the afternoon, taking at least an hour to march and then form up after the initial attack on Churchgate Street. Clearly these attacks were not co-ordinated, though the Jacobites do not seem to have moved troops about the town to meet different threats. Patten made the following statement about this attack, made by the dismounted dragoons, and how it was resisted by Colonel Mackintosh's men:

… who, with his men, behaved very boldly, and made a dreadful fire upon the King's Forces, killing many on the spot, and obliging them to make a Retreat; which, however, they did very handsomely. This was owing to the Common Men, who were but new listed; though the Officers and old Soldiers behav'd themselves with great Bravery.[107]

There were also reports that the soldiers were reluctant to attack having seen their fellows killed and wounded, 'they never durst approach for the dragoons were all raw men and those that came within shot never returned'.[108] However, Horace Walpole later wrote of the behaviour of Captain Pelham of

---

104 Rae, *History*, pp.323–324.
105 *Weekly Journal*, 10 March 1716.
106 TNA: FEC1/1585, Towneley amd Tildesley.
107 Patten, *History*, p.88.
108 BC: 45/12/77, account of the Jacobite southern army to Preston.

Dormer's regiment, who 'gave proofs of personal courage' and Walpole was no admirer of Pelham.[109]

Rae was rather more succinct, writing, 'Brigadier Dormer, with the Troops under his Command; gain'd the end of the Town, but sustained a great fire in their Approaches'. Dormer led the attack and was wounded by a musket ball in his leg. Both agree that the attack on the barricades had been repulsed. In response to this, Dormer sent men from Stanhope's dragoons; Captain James Gardiner, sergeant Johnstoun and corporal John Marlow, together with a dozen troopers, to burn a number of properties in Friargate, as had occurred earlier at Churchgate. These included Edward Smith's house and barn, worth £140, Katherine Atherton's kilns worth £15, Astell Hodges' property worth £13 6s and others.[110] They did it so quickly that the properties burnt as far as the furthest barricade.[111] Gardiner's men were brave but their actions were hazardous, apparently he 'signalled himself very particularly: for he headed a little body of men … and set fire to a barricade of the rebels, in the face of their whole army while they were pouring in their shot, by which eight of the twelve that attended him fell'.[112] The Jacobites then fell back to the second barrier of Friargate.

The lack of Wills' manpower and the distance from Wills' starting point to the west end of Preston meant that there was never an attack on Fishergate Street, so Strathmore's battalion posted there was presumably idle.

Before the night's end, Wills viewed the results of the major attacks on the town. He then gave orders 'for making a Communication betwixt the two Attacks, in order to sustain each other, in Case they were push'd'. Lieutenant Robinson of Stanhope's had a trench drawn up to secure the attackers in case of a sally.[113]

There was certainly a suggestion among the Jacobites that such a counter attack should occur and this was advocated by Captain Murray and Derwentwater. According to a Jacobite, this 'could not have failed of success, for we were uppish and had lost six men, whereas many of the enemy were killed and wounded and were much fatigued, dispirited being mostly raw and new levied troops. But our generals positively refused'.[114]

By this time, however, night would have fallen. Darkness would have been fairly universal by about five o'clock. Men were tired, physically and mentally.

Apparently at 11 o'clock that night, Murray, finding his men short of ammunition, caused a deputation led by Robertson of Guy and another man to be sent to Forster's quarters to seek more ammunition, where they found him 'lying in his naked bed, with a sack posset, and some confections by him: which I humbly judge was not a very becoming posture at this time for a general … everyone is convinced that he failed in almost every point of his

---

109 Matthew Hodgart, ed., *Horace Walpole: Memoirs and Portraits* (London: Batsford, 1963). p.19.
110 TNA: FEC1/246–250, Original Claims.
111 Rae, *History*, p.320.
112 Phillip Doddridge, *Some Remarkable Passages in the life of the Hon. Colonel James Gardiner* (Hedley: Thomas Cornish, 1812), pp.95–96.
113 Rae, *History*, p.320.
114 TNA: SP54/9, 107, Jacobite prisoner's experiences in the rebellion.

prudentials if not worse'.[115] It must be assumed that Forster's responses to these enquiries was in the negative or at best unhelpful.

For the Jacobites, there was obvious cause for celebration, as Patten noted, 'the Rebels seem'd to have had some Advantage, having repulsed the King's forces in all their Attacks, and maintained all their Posts'.[116] The anonymous Jacobite wrote, 'In short the enemy was soundly beat … above 180 killed' and Clarke put that the British army had lost even more than that.[117] Mackintosh began to write a letter to Mar, informing him of the army's success (it is unfortunate that the exact contents of the letter are unknown).[118] Wills' forces had made but two small footholds into the town at great loss. The latter was especially among the veteran troops of Preston's regiment. Morale cannot have been high among his army. However, it had not been a complete failure. They had gained a foothold in the town by possessing the two mansions and had driven the Jacobites back from their outer barricades at Churchgate and Friargate. In a letter written that evening Charteris claimed, not wholly accurately, that Preston's foot had taken three of the Jacobites' cannons during their attack, that Derwentwater had been killed and that Wills 'has given orders not to give quarter'.[119]

Yet some Jacobites, those who had no stomach for actual fighting, took the opportunity to escape under the cover of darkness and because not all the exits to Preston were blocked by troops or militia such was possible. According to Rae, 'a great many made their Escape through the secret Passages and By-Lanes into the Country'.[120] Not all were successful, however, for the militia were 'very serviceable in guarding the Passes and several parties attempting to force their way through them, were either killed, taken or beat back'.[121] However, Clarke wrote that only 'severall of the Earl of Derwentwater's men made their escape'.[122] It is impossible to know how many escaped, but probably they numbered between 200–300 at most; possibly under 100 even, and were mostly Englishmen and probably mostly Lancastrians who knew the country well. At least three of Towneley's men did so. At least they are not listed on prisoner lists. Likewise several of Tyldesley's men escaped and those who appeared on the constables' listings as well (most of whom were Lancashire gentry and at least 25 were from Preston who had the necessary local knowledge of the best exits). Finally, some of the servants of some of the leading Jacobites were later arrested on suspicion. It is likely that few or none of the Scots tried to escape this way.

That night, British soldiers kept up their fire on the Jacobites from Hoghton's and Ayre's houses, killing a cornet Hume, a Mr Scattery and a gentleman from Nairn's battalion. Wills ordered that all the houses which his men had possession of should be illuminated, by candles being set up

---

115 *Weekly Journal*, 10 March 1716.
116 Patten, *History*, p.87.
117 TNA: SP54/9, 107, Jacobite prisoner's experiences in the rebellion.
118 Hibbert-Ware, 'Memorials', p.136.
119 Bl.Add.Mss. 47028, f.104v, Dering to Egmont, 15 November 1715.
120 Rae, *History*, p.324.
121 *Daily Courant*, 4391, 19 November 1715.
122 Paton, 'Journal', p.522.

THE BATTLE, 12–14 NOVEMBER 1715

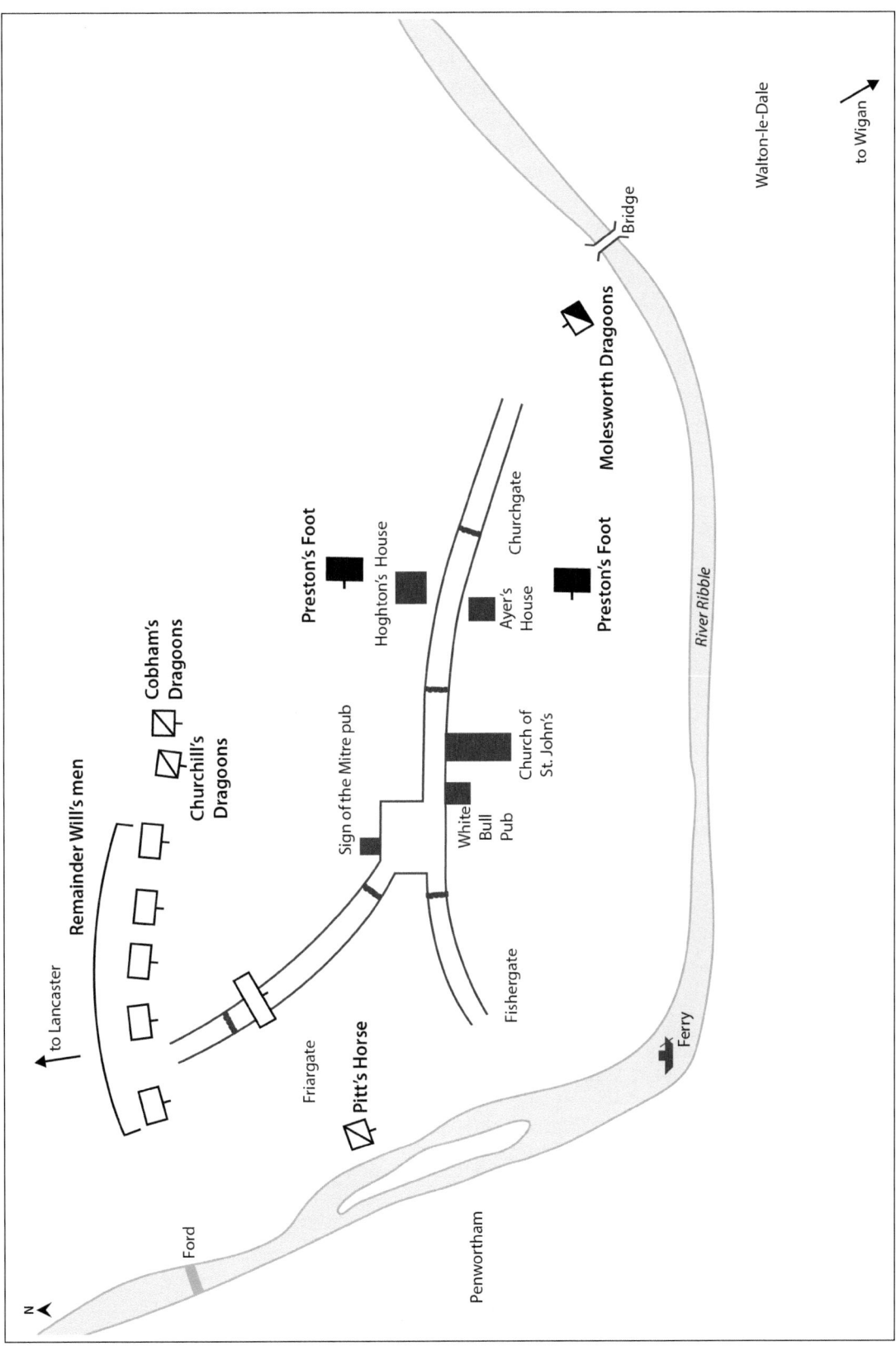

The Battle of Preston, Day 2

in their windows. This meant that Jacobites seen crossing the streets nearby could be seen and shot at, but it also meant the reverse to be true, so 'This was the Occasion of the Deaths of some, and Wounds of others, even on both sides', so an order was given to extinguish these lights, but the order was first mistook as to mean they should set out more lights.[123] Sniping continued throughout the night.[124] The cavalry stood to, however, 'The Horse and Dragoons continued at their Horses' heads all that night'.[125]

A number of the attackers had been taken prisoner, including Captain Preston and Captain Ogilby, both of Preston's battalion, presumably after having been wounded. There are diverse views as to how these men reacted in their captivity. According to Patten, though the Jacobites had believed that their enemies would join them, 'not one man offer'd to do so: for of several private Men made prisoners, being wounded, not one of them would listen to the offers made to Enlist, but chose rather to be shut up in Close Prison, than to foresake their King and Country's Cause'. Patten went to the White Bull and to the bed of a wounded private in his role as clergyman. He offered to pray with them and the soldier replied, 'If you be a Protestant, we desire your Prayers, but name not the Pretender as King'.[126] Preston told his rescuer, Nicholas Wogan, 'You will never be able to withstand the King's Troops'.[127]

Other prisoners assured Patten that not only would none of the prisoners join the Jacobites, but that their cause was doomed, as 'we could not be able to hold out, for that more Forces were also coming from all Quarters; they informed us of the Arrival of General Carpenter with three Regiments of Dragoons to surround us'.[128] A rather different impression is given by another Jacobite, who wrote 'their officers we took prisoner concluded the day was lost to them'.[129] Yet a few Jacobites were also taken prisoner, as Colville noted, and they were passed back to the dragoons in the rear.[130]

Although the Jacobites had many men with medical knowledge in their ranks, it seems that some were less than competent for the treatment of their wounded. Peter Farquharson, after being shot through the leg, 'endured a great deal of Torture in the Operation of the Surgeon'. Apparently he tried his best to be cheerful, 'taking a glass of brandy and urging his audience 'Come Lads, here is our Master's Health: tho' I can do no more. I wish you good success'. Then his leg was cut off by an 'unskilful Butcher, rather than Surgeon and he presently died'. Thomas Brereton's injuries were not discovered by the surgeons, otherwise he too, might have lived.[131]

Events elsewhere were less favourable to the Jacobites, had they but known it. Carpenter and his three regiments of dragoons had left Newcastle on 7 November. At Barnard Castle they had been joined by the Earls of Carlisle

---

123 Patten, *History*, pp.87–88.
124 Anon., *A Letter*, p.7.
125 *London Gazette*, 5382, 15–19 November 1715.
126 Patten, *History*, pp.88–89.
127 Anon., *Faithful Register*, p.284.
128 Patten, *History*, p.89.
129 TNA: SP54/9, 107, Jacobite prisoner's experiences in the rebellion.
130 Robson, 'Military Memoirs', p.60.
131 Patten, *History*, pp.85–86.

THE BATTLE, 12–14 NOVEMBER 1715

and Holderness, Viscount Lumley and Colonel Darcy, 'and a good many Country Gentlemen'. The latter may have been horse militia of Yorkshire together with mounted volunteers armed with swords and pistols, akin to the English Jacobites. Knowing that Wills was at Manchester, they first assumed that the Jacobite army in Lancashire would seek to avoid confrontation as they had previously and so march into the west of Yorkshire, via Skipton, not knowing that Jacobite intelligence of Wills' whereabouts was so poor until the last moment. On reaching Richmond they learnt that the Jacobite army was at Preston and so 'march's thither with all imaginable Resolution' and 'over high mountains and deep ways'.[132] On the evening of 12 November the force had reached Clitheroe, 12 miles from Preston. There, Carpenter found a letter from Hoghton, telling him of the imminent battle and so Wills 'made use of his wonted Vigilance to have the Horses taken care of, so that they might be early in the Morning be able to hasten towards Preston'.[133]

Sunday 13 November

On the next day, Wills clearly realised that a further assault with the troops he had, would be futile, even assuming the men could be persuaded to advance. He had, after all, fewer men at his command, given the numbers of dead, wounded and prisoners. So he wrote a letter to the Earl of Cholmondeley, Lord Lieutenant of Cheshire, but more importantly, governor of Chester Castle, the nearest garrison of British troops. He asked that Cholmondeley send him what artillery he could. Next day five cannons, presumably of small calibre, so easily moved by road, were sent from Chester castle.[134] However there was some additional fighting, for 'Some few men on both sides were killed this forenoone'.[135] Morale at the Jacobite front line seems still to have been high. Towneley was seen that morning 'marching amongst it … to oppose the King's forces' and John Gregson, a Preston shoemaker, was seen 'with a gun in his hand shooting at ye King's forces'.[136] As this was Sunday, some men may have attended a church service if one were held at the parish church.

More fighting was clearly envisaged as the Jacobites again looked for gunpowder. John Trafford of Croston went to Gradwell's warehouse, as Tunstall had earlier, 'and asked him if he had any gunpowder' but was told 'he had none'. Allen, a carpenter, went from house to house making similar enquiries, again fruitlessly.[137]

It is probable that the force under Carpenter began their march from Clitheroe at daybreak (as with Cromwell's army in 1648, he had marched to Preston via Skipton and Clitheroe). Their arrival to the north of Preston has been variously given as between nine and 10 in the morning, at 10 and

---

132 LRO: DDX 1788/1, Plan.
133 Patten, *History*, p.89.
134 *St. James' Post*, 75, 19–21 November 1715.
135 Paton, 'Journal', p.522.
136 TNA: FEC1/1585, Towneley and Tyldesley.
137 TNA: FEC1/1585, Towneley and Tyldesley.

THE SECOND BATTLE OF PRESTON, 1715

Preston Minster. Although altered since 1715, Jacobite troops were able to use the steeple to watch for movements of their enemies. (Photograph by Charles Singleton, 2022)

even as late as noon, though given that this force was entirely made up of horsemen, the earlier times are more likely.[138] As soon as he arrived, he was met by Wills, who told him what he had done, where he had placed his troops and offered to resign the army's command to Carpenter, who had the higher rank. Apparently, the latter approved of what had been done, which showed great tact, and refused the command, saying 'he had begun the Affair so well, that he ought to have the Glory of finishing it'. Given Carpenter's later comments about Wills, the latter might well have been sarcastic, especially as one account noted that he was told of the previous day's fighting and concluded that it had 'not [met] with the desired success'.[139]

However, after having refused command, Carpenter viewed the troops' dispositions and those he could see of the Jacobites and began to make alterations in those of the former. He thought that the situation of the British

---

138 Patten, *History*, p.89, LRO: DDX 1788/1, Plan; Rae, *History*, p.320.
139 Rae, *History*, p.320; LRO: DDX 1788/1, Plan.

THE BATTLE, 12–14 NOVEMBER 1715

troops was imbalanced, with most of the men on the east side of the town 'very incommodiously, on many Accounts, being crowded in a deep narrow Lane, near the End of the Town; and besides that, so inconvenient for the Service, that it was impossible to draw up above three or Four in the front, he brought them off in Parties to several other places'.[140]

He then viewed the west and south west of Preston, especially towards the river and again did not like what he saw there. No troops had been posted at the end of Fishergate Street to block up that part of the town. He could even see Jacobites riding away from the town using that route to do so before his very eyes. No attack had been made here, due to the lack of troops. However, his reinforcements were able to rectify this. Two squadrons of Pitt's horse, who had not taken part in the previous day's fighting, were despatched here from the north of Friargate and rode here.[141] In order to allow the scattered

---

140 Rae, *History*, pp.320–321.
141 Rae, *History*, pp.320–321.

forces to unite in case of a Jacobite sally, he had holes knocked in walls and hedges enclosing the fields around the town.[142] Molesworth's dragoons were marched to the south east of the town and Cobham's and Churchill's were placed to the north.[143]

It is worth stating that Carpenter's men and horses were probably not fit for immediate and effective combat. According to Patten, 'after his long, troublesome and dismal Marches after the Rebels, had very much weary'd his Men, but more the Horses'.[144] In the following year, Colonel Molesworth was reimbursed by the Treasury the sum of £600 on account of 'the losses sustained by his regiment by horses killed and disabled and other extraordinary expenses in the long and continued marches in a very rigorous season in pursuit of the rebels'.[145] It has been estimated that their combined strength was about 2,500 men, though this number may have included militia and volunteers.[146]

For some of the Jacobites, Carpenter's arrival was decisive. Patten noted, 'And now our People began to open their Eyes, and to see that there was nothing but present Death before them, if they held out longer; and that there was no Remedy, but, if possible, to make Terms, and get a Capitulation for Life, and lay down their Arms'. He then added, 'The Rebels being thus invested on all sides, so that they found themselves entirely block't up, and being sensible of their Condition, and also that they were short of Powder for an obstinate Resistance, began to consider what to do'.[147] Colville wrote that Carpenter's arrival 'might have added to their panic and confusion, which we afterwards learnt from themselves had seized them from the beginning'.[148] It is not known how many men made up each force at this time, but a Jacobite at Preston thought that they had 1,400 men and their enemies 2,500, which would have certainly worried his superiors, though the number of 1,400 was an under-estimate judging by listings of prisoners.[149]

Carpenter's men had been first seen from a look out on the church steeple. Carpenter later wrote, 'the chief prisoners assured me and others that as soon as they saw my detachment from the steeple, Lord Widdrington, who was in the churchyard and said very loud to their men that they were all undone, and upon that they consulted to ask termnes'.[150]

According to one author, what was decisive was that the Jacobites thought that their opponents were now 'without number'. What contributed to this

---

142 Patten, *History*, p.91.
143 LRO: DDX 1788/1, Plan.
144 Patten, *History*, p.89.
145 William Shaw and F.H. Slingsby (eds), *Calendar of Treasury Books*, XXXII (London: HMSO, 1958), p.18.
146 *Weekly Journal*, 10 March 1716.
147 Patten, *History*, pp.90–92.
148 Robson, 'Military Memoirs', p.60.
149 *Weekly Journal*, 10 March 1716.
150 *HMC Townshend*, pp.170–171.

belief was that they advanced towards Preston with large gaps between their formations and marching at a slow pace.[151]

There are differing accounts of the Jacobites' actions that morning. For some, despite the desertions of the previous night, morale was high and there was talk of taking the offensive to the enemy, following their successful defence of the previous day. Patten wrote, 'The Highlanders were for sallying out upon the King's Forces, and dying, as they call'd it, like Men of Honour, with their swords in their Hands'.[152] Yet they were not as fatalistic as Patten inferred. One anonymous Jacobite later claimed:

> Next morning many of the nobility and gentry assuredly solicited Forster that we might be allowed to march out and attack the enemy in what would not have faled of success, for we were uppish and had not had lost six men whereas many of the enemy were killed and wounded, were much more fatigued, dispirited, being mostly raw and new levied troops.[153]

A detailed suggestion was that the houses on Churchgate be burnt, the British troops lodged in Hoghton's house be attacked and the house retaken and then a general sally be made and it was inferred this would succeed because all Wills' men except Pitt's and Preston's were 'all recruits'.[154]

Oxburgh and Widdrington, neither of whom had been conspicuous in the previous day's fighting, sought a conference with Forster. A few others also attended this meeting. They, determined to surrender, persuaded Forster that this could be made on honourable terms and Oxburgh, who had served in the army two decades ago, stated that he had acquaintances there who would treat such a request, if made by him, favourably. This attitude may have been because they never expected to have to fight, having hoped for a peaceful restoration, and found the experience of warfare frightening and deadly and so wished to bring it to an immediate end. There had been an utter absence of fighting hitherto and what happened on the previous day must have been a terrible ordeal for these civilians. The rank and file were told that Wills had offered them decent terms if they submitted and this they believed. Patten wrote that if they had known it was otherwise, Oxburgh would have been shot dead before he could have left Preston.[155]

It was 2:00 p.m. when Oxburgh rode out and met Wills. The latter was adamant that 'They might expect no other Terms, than to lay down their Arms, and surrender at discretion'. Wills had no powers to parley and was merely following standard military procedure when dealing with insurgents who were not a recognised regular army. These were not the 'honourable terms' that had been confidently talked of in Preston, but merely meant that the Jacobites' lives would be spared in the short term only and that they

---

151 Anon., *A History of the Affairs of Europe from the Peace of Utrecht to the Quadruple Alliance* (London, Publisher Unknown, 1725), pp.35–36.
152 Patten, *History*, p.92.
153 TNA: SP54/9, 107, Jacobite prisoner's experiences in the rebellion.
154 BC: 45/12/77, account of the Jacobite southern army to Preston.
155 Patten, *History*, p.92.

The Harris Museum and Library. The Mitre Inn, where the surrender was agreed upon once stood in this location. (Photograph by Charles Singleton, 2022)

would go on to face trial as criminals and traitors, and face the death penalty if found guilty of rebellion and treason. There was no doubt that Oxburgh knew what Wills meant and so 'urg'd all the Arguments he could for better Terms' but was told that none other could be offered in the circumstances. He was given an hour to return with an answer.[156]

A disappointed man returned to Preston, but a more hopeful one departed on his arrival. This was Captain Dalziel, a former soldier. He arrived at Wills' headquarters and made a plea in regards to the Scots within the Jacobite army,

---

156 Patten, *History*, pp.92–93, Rae, *History*, p.322.

but received the same reply and then desired that the Jacobites would be given time to consider the offer that had been made to them; an hour was given.[157]

At three in the afternoon, no answer being forthcoming, Wills sent a staff officer, Lieutenant Colonel Stanhope Cotton, with a dragoon and a drummer beating a chamade, into Preston. They arrived in the market square and were shown to the Sign of the Mitre, the inn where the Jacobite leaders had made their headquarters. Jacobite troops left their barriers to enter the square, some believing that Wills was wanting to parley to seek terms from them. Yet Cotton wanted to know whether Wills' terms were accepted or not and was told that,

---

157 Patten, *History*, p.93.

due to dissension, they needed an extension to the cease fire until seven on the following morning. At that time they would submit, having hopefully resolved the divisions then existing between the English and Scots.[158]

Cotton clearly agreed to this and sent his drummer to beat a chamade before those houses occupied by the British troops to let them know of the cease fire. However, the drummer was allegedly shot dead and fell from his horse as he was beating his drum. It was assumed that this was not done by his comrades who would have known by his uniform that he was one of theirs, but rather by an angry Jacobite who was averse to any thought of surrender. However, pension records suggest otherwise; that the drummer was 28 year old Edward Blaber, 'shot in ye left side beating ye chamade' and further that Captain Pelham of Dormer's was also present. Blaber saw another 17 years of military service before receiving a pension in 1732. Cotton was asked by a Jacobite gentleman if they might have mercy and Cotton replied, 'Sir, that I cannot assure you of, but I know the King to be a very merciful Prince'.[159]

There were conditions attached to the cease fire. These were that no new entrenchments were thrown up, that none of the Jacobites attempted to escape and that two hostages be given. As a Jacobite later wrote, 'the first knowledge we had of it was when wee saw Colonel Cotton in the market place'. It was now known what some of the Jacobite leaders were working for and this provoked angry reactions. A number of Jacobite gentlemen approached Forster, 'calling him Rogue and Villain to his face and proposed shooting him as an Example'.[160] A Lowlander later wrote 'he failed in almost every point of his prudentials'.[161] Apparently 'all he could answer was, that he was sensible of the Incapacity he had for his office, cryed like a child, was sorry for what he had done'. Widdrington adopted a different position, when confronted with the results of his action, 'pretended by argument to defend the reasonableness of the capitulation'.[162] Apparently the rank and file were kept partly in the dark as to details, as the Merse trooper wrote, 'I know nothing of the Terms of Capitulation, only I heard them in the general said to be Necessary and Honourable by the Earl of Carnwath and Lord Wintoun and others'.[163]

Responses were varied. On the first news of such, Hamilton 'with tears declared clearly we were betrayed' and was in a rage. Lords Murray and Nairn, Major Nairn, Captains Lockhart and Straton and in particularly Derwentwater 'shew'd ane resentment against it', 'saying it was downright treachery'. On the other hand, Lords Carnwath and Nithsdale and Dalziel 'sy'd with Forrester and Witherington and brought the matter about'. Kenmure was of no use, 'he favoured altogether stupid matters doing in this deplorable condition'.[164] Nithsdale later claimed that his motives were humanitarian,

---

158 Patten, *History*, p.93; *Weekly Journal*, 10 March 1716.
159 Patten, *History*, p.96; TNA, WO116/2, Chelsea Out Pensioners, February 1732.
160 TNA: SP54/9, 107, Jacobite prisoner's experiences in the rebellion.
161 *Weekly Journal*, 10 March 1716.
162 BC: 45/12/77, account of the Jacobite southern army to Preston.
163 Anon., *A Letter*, p.8.
164 Anon., *A Letter*, p.8; BC: 45/12/77, account of the Jacobite southern army to Preston.

'willing to save the effusion of so much blood as might have been spilt if they had continued obstinate'.[165]

Those gentlemen who had been engaged in the previous day's fighting on foot now mounted their horses and met at the market place. Some were for retribution against Forster, 'bringing out Forrester as a publick sacrifice'. Indeed, Patten later wrote that 'had he appear'd on the streets, he would certainly have been cut to pieces'. One Murray aimed his pistol at Forster whilst inside the inn, but Patten knocked the weapon aside and the ball only damaged the wainscot of the wall.[166]

There was fighting between others over the surrender terms. According to Patten, 'their Madness was such, that nothing could quiet them for a good while; and it was astonishing to see the Confusion the Town was in, threatening one another, nay killing one another but for naming a Surrender, one was shot dead, and several wounded'.[167]

Although there were numerous options discussed outside, the conclusion was that Derwentwater and his brother Charles Radcliffe should join the other horsemen in their bid to escape the town and ride northwards towards Lancaster. Radcliffe declared 'he had rather die with his sword in his hand, like a man of honour, than be dragged like a felon to the scaffold'.[168] They marched to the barrier on Friargate and awaited Brigadier Mackintosh's arrival 'with the foote who promised upon honour to returne'. Forster and those nobility in favour of a surrender were to be left for the enemy.[169] The plan was for Mackintosh's infantry to flank the hedges on each side of the Lancaster Road, whilst the Scottish gentry led by Winton and Charles Radcliffe 'forced their way through the Enemy'.[170] Despite his comments on the previous day about the folly of a sally, Mackintosh agreed and the horsemen assembled at the barrier and waited for the infantry to join them. No one came.[171]

Captain Shaftoe was sent to the Brigadier.[172] On being found, Mackintosh 'told them, That it was too late to make such an Attempt'; apparently 'he was brock with the rest'.[173] In the meantime, Mackintosh had met Forster and the other lords and he was invited by them to join with them. He then failed to send any message nor any excuse to the men at the barricade. A Jacobite then noted 'And thus having been deprived of the Foot it was impossible for the horse to prosecute their design'.[174]

Patten was, in retrospect, opposed to such a plan and described its probable results in uncompromising terms:

---

165 Matthews, *Diary*, p.168.
166 BC: 45/12/77, account of the Jacobite southern army to Preston; Patten, *History*, p.97.
167 Patten, *History*, pp.96–97.
168 Radcliffe, *Genuine and Impartial Memoirs*, p.39.
169 TNA: SP54/9, 107, Jacobite prisoner's experiences in the rebellion.
170 Anon., *A Letter*, p.7.
171 Anon., *A Letter*, p.7.
172 Anon., *A Letter*, pp.7–8.
173 Anon., *A Letter*, pp.7–8; BC: 45/12/77, account of the Jacobite southern army to Preston.
174 TNA: SP54/9, 107, Jacobite prisoner's experiences in the rebellion.

It is true this might have been attempted, and perhaps many would have escap'd; but it could not have been performed without the Loss of a great deal of Blood, and that on both Sides; and it was told them it would be so, and that if they did get out, they would be cut off by the Country people.[175]

Resignation then reigned as morale collapsed. As a Jacobite wrote, 'After this all things went into confusion'. Later in the day one Jacobite suggested that the sentries be doubled 'as the practice of the army and our own safety'. Elsewhere, though, the majority were becoming resigned to their fate, 'so much surpass'd by grief they would take notice of nothing'. Instead of doubling the guards, most were withdrawn, except those led by Captain Lockhart, and so their enemy was able to advance safely. Apparently Carnwath discouraged any further act of resistance.[176] Another Jacobite later wrote, 'This was very choking to us all, but no helping of it, for no sooner had we left our posts than they made themselves masters of them, and of our cannon'.[177]

The options for the Jacobites were poor. Sitting tight and holding out was not even apparently considered; after so much shooting on the previous day, ammunition was running low ('they were short of powder for an obstinate resistance' according to Patten) and so this was ruled out. Yet if this was the case, then it also suggested that the effectiveness of infantry in making a dash for freedom was limited indeed. Some of the cavalry could probably have escaped, but the chances for the slower moving infantry were far less so. In fact, had the Jacobites stayed put, in a few days' time they would have been subject to a renewed attack, with the artillery from Chester having arrived, as well as Wills' two other battalions of infantry. The Jacobites in Preston were not to know this, of course.

The other issue is that the Jacobite leadership was as ever divided; it had been so on 27 October when the decision over facing Carpenter's men was discussed; it was so again four days later when the option of entering England was paramount. As always compromise and the path of least resistance was taken. The outlook was always short term. In the first two instances the consequences were not immediately obvious, but here it was a matter of life or death.

Early that evening, British soldiers set on watch gave word that there was an attempt by the Jacobites to break out of the town by the south west road. Carpenter ordered all the cavalry to mount and personally led a squadron of dragoons to the spot.[178] However, it was only a small body of Jacobites trying to escape and they were 'cut to pieces' by Pitt's horse, who had been positioned there for that very reason.[179] This force included cornet Richard Shuttleworth of Turnover Hall, of Edward Tyldesley's troop of horse, who was killed, and on him was found a green banner with a buff silk fringe and the sign of a pelican feeding her young and the motto 'Tantum Valet

---

175 Patten, *History*, p.96.
176 TNA: SP54/9, 107, Jacobite prisoner's experiences in the rebellion.
177 *Weekly Journal*, 10 March 1716.
178 LRO: DDX1788/1, Plan.
179 Patten, *History*, p.91.

amore Regis et Patria' (So prevalent is the love of our King and Country).[180] Yet some did escape; Anthony Barlow and one Bleasdale were seen with Cuthbert Hesketh this day but managed to flee successfully.[181]

Carpenter then sent Colonel Churchill into the town. The capitulation proceeded and because of the minor attempt at a break out, hostages demanded to avoid its repeat, Carpenter wanting one of the English lords and either Kenmure or Mackintosh.[182] Taking hostages was not an easy task and it was left to Carpenter to deal with. Derwentwater and Widdrington could not be found and Mackintosh was in bed. Dalziel said that Kenmure would not agree to it, and when Mackintosh was suggested, this was also refused. Carpenter later said, 'I was unwilling to make great difficulties, it growing towards Night'. He eventually settled on Colonel Mackintosh and Derwentwater and left at 8:00 p.m.[183]

Charles Owen later claimed that 'the surrender of the rebels was gained by General Wills's bullying and swearing rather than anything else'. When Derwentwater came out of the town as a hostage that evening, he suggested that Wills give them 12 days grace before they would surrender, providing they had no relief by then. Wills' reaction was furious:

> Upon this Wills swore a great oath and pulls his watch out of his pocket and swore that if they did not surrender within twelve hours' time he would cut every man of them to pieces and swore he would not give them a moment's time longer. This he confirmed by the most bitter oaths, curses and execrations in the world that Lord Derwentwater was perfectly terrified that his very lips trembled.

Derwentwater asked if he could remain with Wills during the latter's proposed attack, but Wills said no, for he wanted him in the town to 'spread terror among the rest of the rebels'. Derwentwater was sent back to Preston.[184]

Mackintosh then went out of the town. He was a sturdier fowl than the returning peer:

> … he being a man of passion and a terrible swearer as well as Wills they fell into a perfect passion together, and MacIntosh told him he had a thousand of his Scotch Highlanders that would every man of them fight two of his troops. Wills swore by all that was sacred that he, if he would bring out his thousand men, he would only set Pitt's horse against them, and if they did not cut them all to pieces he would be damned and promised he would not let any other soldiers assist them. In short, he swore so violently and with such a terrible air.[185]

By the end of the day, Pitt's regiment was divided into four, stationed at the west and south west of Preston. Wynn's was to the north east of the town,

---

180 *St. James' Post*, 131, 15–17 November 1715.
181 TNA, TS23/34, 3.
182 LRO: DDX1788/1, Plan.
183 Anon., *Life of General Carpenter* (London: T. Curll, 1734), p.23.
184 Matthews, *Diary,* pp.173–174.
185 Matthews, *Diary* p.174.

THE SECOND BATTLE OF PRESTON, 1715

Market Square. Location of surrender of Jacobite army. (Photograph by Charles Singleton, 2022)

with Preston's to the north and south of Churchgate. There was a patrol to the south of the town.[186]

Meanwhile, at 10 o'clock that evening, Wills was writing his own version of what had happened: 'I made such attempts as were necessary to convince the rebels of my being in a condition to reduce them by force … I imagine they will submit, being sufficiently convinced I have them entirely in my power'.[187]

Monday 14 November

Meanwhile, at the appointed hour of seven that morning, Forster arrived at Wills' camp to let him know that they were ready to surrender. Mackintosh was standing nearby when this occurred, and stated, 'He could not answer that the Scotch would surrender in that Manner, for that the Scots were People of desperate Fortunes, and that he had been a soldier himself and knew what it was to be a prisoner at Discretion'. Wills replied in the same determined manner as of the previous days, 'Go back to your People again, and I will attack the Town,

---

186 BL.Add.Mss. 33954, f.30r, Letters, papers and tracts relating to the Royal Family of Stuart, 1688–1788, Plan of the battle of Preston, 1715.
187 *HMC Manuscripts in Various Collections, II* (London: HMSO, 18), pp.409–410.

THE BATTLE, 12–14 NOVEMBER 1715

and the Consequences will be, I will not spare one Man of you'. Mackintosh went to Preston and quickly returned, telling Wills that Kenmure and the other noblemen agreed that they would surrender on the agreed terms.[188]

Before the actual surrender took place, British troops began to enter the town and into those parts that formerly had been held by the Jacobites. At six in the morning, Forrester moved troops into the churchyard to occupy it.[189] Elsewhere, they 'began to plunder, looking upon what they got their own, by Rule of War. But complaints being made, they were stopped for some time'. We shall return to this issue in the next chapter.[190] One Jacobite, however, presented this activity in stronger terms, claiming that the troops 'unprovoked butchered a great many in cold blood, abused, robbed and strippt at pleasure'. Apparently there was some last minute resistance, the same Jacobite claiming 'The Earl of Strathmore's men who behaved from the beginning to the end most consciously upon the first sight of the enemy in the streets, ran to their arms, drew up, refused to yield, fired and killed severall. But what could they do all alone. So they were forced to surrender also'.[191]

---

188 Patten, *History*, p.95.
189 Anon., *Faithful Register*, p.157.
190 Patten, *History*, p.100.
191 TNA: SP54/9, 107, Jacobite prisoner's experiences in the rebellion.

THE SECOND BATTLE OF PRESTON, 1715

Finally Wills and Carpenter, at the head of their troops, rode into Preston from the Lancaster road and Honywood rode in from the road leading to Manchester. However, when they were mounting up, dissension reigned as Carpenter later wrote:

> Mr Wills was taking on him great command, att which I used him very freely, and was going put him in arrest, butt my Lord Carlisle who was present, and Lord Lumley begged me nott to do itt, and indeed at that instant itt might have proved fatall to His Majesty's Service for the Rebells had yet possession of their armes and the town; and Wills was likely enough to have called the troopes that came with him to support him. So I did not do itt.[192]

They arrived to the music of trumpets and drums. Both parties met at the market place. The Highlanders were there drawn up in lines, with their arms. The nobility, gentry and officers were ushered into the inns nearby. All were then disarmed. Special care had to be taken of Forster, because, as with the previous day, some Jacobites were 'running about in quest of Forster to kill him', so a special guard had to be placed on him for his own safety. The rank and file were then taken into the parish church under guard. Carpenter's exhausted regiments were then marched off to Wigan, as there were insufficient quarters for them in Preston, leaving the care of the prisoners to Wills.[193] A disillusioned Jacobite later wrote, 'I believe this is the first instance of a victorious army after an action yielding themselves prisoners to the vanquished'.[194] Of Gabriel Hesketh, Patten 'heard him complain that he was made a prisoner without cause'.[195]

A Whig song, 'Loyalty or a Tale of Tory Rebellion' composed to mark the victory ran in part as follows:

> Soon Forster fled with all his coward crew
> Whilst Carpenter pursued them where soever the wretches flew
> By Wills were met and hard beset
> In Preston proud at last
> Thus they flee the field and then as basely yield
> At discretion, play submissive, rather than be killed
> Thence to London some o' the chiefs in triumph came
> Each with a sentry made his entry
> Here to meet his doom.[196]

The fighting was over and now it is time to turn to the consequences of that battle, for both victors and vanquished, as well as to consider how its outcome had a wider impact on the campaign.

---

192 *HMC Townshend*, p.171.
193 Patten, *History*, pp.100–101; TNA: SP54/9, 107, Jacobite prisoner's experiences in the rebellion.
194 TNA: SP54/9, 107, Jacobite prisoner's experiences in the rebellion.
195 TNA, TS23/34.
196 BL.Add.Mss.30381, f.25r, Anti-Jacobite Songs, 19th century, 30381.

6

The Consequences, 1715–1717

Counting the cost after a battle is often a controversial business, with commentators from both sides downplaying their own losses and exaggerating those of the enemy. No unbiased reporting of figures seems to exist. It would be expected that the victors usually have fewer casualties than the defeated, especially in the case of the defeated routing and being pursued (as at the bloody battles of Culloden and more so, Killiecrankie), but in the case of assaults on defended positions, the attacker can expect higher casualties as they lack the advantages of cover that the defender enjoyed. Contemporaries were always interested in the gentlemen and officers who were injured or killed but those lesser mortals likewise stricken were only of interest as numbers, not names. One of the first tasks after the battle was to bury the dead, though some of this seems to have taken place on the previous day or even on Saturday.[1]

To take the losses of the British army first. The most senior casualty was Honywood, who was hit on the shoulder by a musket ball and Dormer was wounded in his knee. Then there was Lord Forrester who received two or three wounds. Major Bland had a slight injury to his arm. Captain Preston was shot just above his breast and this quickened his death from consumption. Major Lawson was also wounded, but recovered and Captain Ogilby was hit in his side, though not fatally.[2]

Of the rank and file, Patten wrote, 'There were a great many private Men of his majesty's Forces kill'd; how many it is hard to determine, but the Number has been esteem'd above 200, tho' the publick Lists say not so many'.[3] Indeed, official lists were as follows:

---

1 TNA: SP54/10, 9, Cockburn–Pringle, 3 November 1715.
2 Patten, *History,* pp.101–102.
3 Patten, *History,* p.102.

Table 21. Fatal Casualties[4]

Unit	Field Officers	Captains	Lieuts.	Cornet/Ensigns	Others	Total
Pitt	0	0	0	0	0	0
Wynn	0	0	0	0	6	6
Honywood	0	0	0	0	0	0
Munden	0	0	0	0	0	0
Dormer	0	0	0	0	3	3
Stanhope	0	0	0	0	7	7
Preston	2	0	1	0	37	40
Total	2	0	1	0	53	56

Table 22. Wounded

Unit	Field Officers	Captains	Lieuts.	Cornet/Ensigns	Others	Total
Pitt	0	0	0	0	1	1
Wynn	0	1	1	1	21	24
Honywood	0	0	0	0	5	5
Munden	0	0	0	0	0	0
Dormer	0	1	0	0	4	5
Stanhope	0	0	0	0	3	3
Preston	2	2	1	4	43	52
Total	2	4	2	5	77	90

Table 23. Horses Killed and Wounded

Unit	Number
Pitt	0
Wynn	15
Honywood	12
Munden	12
Dormer	16
Stanhope	17
Total	72

---

4 *Flying Post*, 3734, 8–10 December 1715.

Table 24. Wounded Rank and File in Receipt of Pensions

Name	Unit	Wound
Edward Cavin	Wynn's	'shot in the head and left thigh'
Adam Cadwell	Wynn's	'shot through ye body'
Guy Cerlton	Wynn's	'his breast bone broke his right leg disabled by a sword'
Joseph Kellsall	Wynn's	'Cut on ye head'
Daniel MacCarthy	Wynn's	'wound on left cheek'
Henry Pawley	Stanhope's	'wholly disabled in his left thigh'
Henry Magnus	Stanhope's	'Bruised at attack'
Thomas Johnstone	Dormer's	'Shot in the left shoulder bruised in ye left side'
James Cowell	Dormer's	'wounded on forehead'
Edward Blaber	Dormer's	'Shot in ye side'
Robert Houghton	Dormer's	'cut over ye finger of ye left hand'.
Mark Mason	Dormer's	'his left knee dislocated'
Thomas Chatterton	Pitt's	Unknown
John Certs	Pitt's	'Shot through ye small of ye left leg … is now a running sore'
Edward Roe	Pitt's	'cut in his left cheek by stones thrown out of ye church'
William Hammer	Munden's	'forefinger of his right hand wrist cut'
Samuel Wallace	Preston's	'wounded in both legs'
Donald McKenzie	Preston's	'lost a piece of his right shoulder by a cannon ball'
David Rosse	Preston's	'shot in the left eye'
Alexander Russell	Preston's	'shot in the left eye'
John Dickson	Preston's	'Shot in the belly and left leg'
Duncan McDougal	Preston's	'shot through the left arm'
Donald McClean	Preston's	'shot through left hand … and cut on ye left arm'
William Lownes	Preston's	'shot on ye joint of the right arm, wounded in ye left leg'
John Cowper	Preston's	'Wounded in left thigh'
Robert Niscoll	Preston's	'a great rupture on ye right side got at Preston'
William Trew	Preston's	'Wounded by cannon shot'
William Ancrum	Preston's	'wounded'
John Christie	Preston's	'shot through ye upper arm of his left arm'.
Thomas Linton	Honywood's	'Cut over left hand by a broadsword'
John Wilkinson	Honywood's	'Wounded in right knee and thigh'
Thomas Watts	Honywood's	'a cut to the left side of his head'
Richard McCombe	Honywood's	'stabbed through jaw above mouth'.
John Grey	Unknown	'hurt by musket'
Valentine Swords	Unknown	'shot in right thigh and left leg'
Benjamin Walker	Unknown	'shot in ye left arm'
John Williams	Unknown	'shot'

THE SECOND BATTLE OF PRESTON, 1715

Edward Edwards	Unknown	'Wounded in leg'
Charles Whare	Unknown	'Scar in his head'
William Wallace	Molesworth's	'Stabbed in ye mouth'
Abraham Crowther	Unknown	'Wounded on forehead'
Matthew Matthews	Unknown	'Cut ye left side of head'
John MacCala	Unknown	'Shot in ye left arm by pistol'
William Hewitt	Unknown	'Shot in right thigh'
Daniel Clancy	Unknown	'stabbed by a bayonet'
Howell Phillips	Unknown	'Shot in right side of his belly by a ball'
William Jackson	Unknown	'Cut on left cheek'
Thomas Davison	Unknown	'shot in head'
George Alcock	Unknown	'Cut right side of head'
George Caine	Unknown	'Shot in right thigh'
Ralph Hamilton	Unknown	'Stabbed in left thigh by a dirk'
Thomas Labram	Unknown	'Shot in left leg'
Thomas Dyer	Unknown	'Wounded in left leg'
Daniel McAllister	Unknown	'cut in ye forehead'
Thomas Colt	Unknown	'Cuts on right wrist, fall from horse'
Joseph Scarborough	Unknown	'a cut at the right side of his head'
John Theobald	Unknown	'Right leg broke'
Robert Collins	Unknown	'rupture'
James Wilkinson	Unknown	'shot in ye right arm'
Joseph Cordingley	Unknown	'shot in right leg'
William Lewis	Unknown	'wounded in ye left leg'
Edward Cooper	Unknown	'right sight of the head hurt by a musket … which occasioned a deafness'
Henry Nailor	Unknown	'Shot in ye left arm'
John Jacobs	Unknown	'a bruise on ye left shoulder'
Richard Burke	Unknown	'stabbed by a sword'
George Brown	Unknown	'stabbed in his left thigh'
Peter McClinton	Unknown	'cut on ye right arm a little elbow ye elbow'
Peter Jennings	Unknown	'his left shoulder hurt'
William MacAllister	Unknown	'cut in ye forehead and near left eye'
John Eberell	Unknown	'wounded above his forehead by a musket'
William Clements	Unknown	'cut down left side of face'
John Wilson	Unknown	'shot through both thighs'
Elias Pearce	Unknown	'slight cut on right knee'
Finlay MacKenzie	Unknown	'disabled in left hand'
James Jackson	Unknown	'shot in both thighs and lost little finger'

Roger Hyde	Unknown	'shot left elbow'
Alexander Pezee	Unknown	'cut on right shoulder badly'
David Jones	Unknown	'left leg broke from a horse'
Charles Schlatter	Unknown	'cut over his left eye … a scar in his left leg'
Robert Bally	Unknown	'shot outside of left leg'
John Farrell	Unknown	'disabled in his left leg by a shot'
James Mekenzy	Unknown	'sore right shin by a shot also lost a finger'
Samuel Goddard	Unknown	'complains of aches which have been growing on him since'
William Wisdom	Unknown	'large rupture by a fall from his horse'
John Hans	Unknown	'cut by a broadsword across his breast'
Robert Hamilton	Unknown	'stabbed left thigh by dirk'
James Churchill	Unknown	'bruised in ye right hip by fall from his horse'
James Killingsley	Unknown	'his right leg broke by his horse falling on him'
George Johnston	Unknown	'ye left thigh broke in ye middle'
John Bavington	Unknown	'shot in small of ye right leg'
Thomas Rubbery	Unknown	'disabled right arm'
William Wilson	Unknown	'wounded back part of head by a blow'

Of those 92 wounded who we know about from pension records, 31 (33 percent) were shot and 16.5 (17 percent) injured by unspecified cutting weapons. Three (three percent) were wounded by unspecified stabbing weapons, three (three percent) explicitly by swords, two (two percent) by dirks and one (one percent) by a bayonet. Finally, two (two percent) were injured by a cannonballs, three (three percent) by muskets, 4.5 (five percent) by horses, one (one percent) by stones and the reason for the remaining 26 injuries are unknown (30 percent). It was common for the bulk of those injured in battle in the eighteenth century to have been wounded by cannon, musket or pistol shot, but in the majority of the Jacobite battles, melee weapons usually caused most injuries. In this battle about half of the known injuries were caused by distance weapons, which fits witness descriptions concerning the amount of shooting. Injuries were inflicted on the following parts of the body: head, 23.5 (25 percent); arms and hands, 19.5 (22 percent); 32 (33 percent) legs; six (seven percent) to the torso; and 11 (13 percent) are unknown.[5]

Caveats must be made here. These figures are based on the men claiming pensions only; others who were wounded may have died or deserted or may not have received pensions due to disciplinary problems, so this is not a complete list of injuries. We should also recall that it is not known which weapons caused the fatalities; quite possibly more shooting wounds than cutting wounds as the latter are usually less deep and so less deadly than a musket or pistol shot which by contrast penetrates deep. Again, it is probable

---

[5] TNA: WO116/1–3, Chelsea Out Pensions registers.

THE SECOND BATTLE OF PRESTON, 1715

Market Street West and the Sun Hotel. Location of a mass grave of those buried during the fighting. (Photograph by Charles Singleton, 2022)

that the location of wounds for fatalities would be more likely to have been torso wounds rather than the more survivable arm and leg injuries.

Rae wrote that four officers and 53 other ranks had been killed and 92 men of all ranks had been wounded.[6] Wills stated that 60–70 men were killed and 130 were wounded.[7] Jacobites gave far higher figures: Clarke writing that either 320 or 270 had been killed and the Merse trooper estimated that it had been 335 killed and wounded.[8] A Lowlander plumps for 300 British casualties.[9] Lionel Walden wrote that 'Wills lost near 300 men'.[10]

---

6 Rae, *History*, pp.323–324.
7 Patten, *History*, p.95.
8 Paton, 'Journal', p.521–522; Anon., *A Letter*, p.7.
9 *Weekly Journal*, 10 March 1716.
10 Rannie, 'Hearne's Collections', VI, p.88.

THE CONSEQUENCES, 1715–1717

Yet it was not only Jacobites who made such high estimates. A newspaper gave a casualty figure of 150 for Preston's battalion alone.[11] Carpenter wrote that Wills had 'made a rash attack, highly blameable, by loosing so many men to no purpose (of which you will hear more) except to serve his own ambition by ending it before I came up'.[12] Carpenter was unfriendly towards Wills, so whilst such a remark may be expected, perhaps that of Forrester, whose sympathies are unknown, should be given more credit. He wrote in a letter on 16 November:

> We have had our share of it, all the officers that wee along with me were either kill'd or wounded save two, with very near 100 of our best men, soe you may

---

11 *St. James' Evening Post*, 73, 15–17 November 1715.
12 *HMC Townshend*, p.170.

believe the loss of soe many brave gentlemen, takes off a good dale of the joy I should have had, in gaining so considerable ane affair ... I escaped myself having only received two slight wounds, one in the face and the other in the hand.[13]

The official figures also underplay the deaths of a number of officers: Captains William Sinclair and Robert Preston, lieutenant William Ferguson and ensign William Elphinstone, all of Preston's battalion, were killed. Sinclair and Preston presumably died of wounds and so were listed as wounded in the tables above (Preston was buried on 27 November at Preston). A Captain William Westerdean whose unit is unidentifiable was also killed and buried with Captain Preston.[14]

Forrester was asked how many soldiers were killed or wounded and he replied, 'I cannot exactly tell: a good many', recalling that 30 were shot dead on the spot.[15] It is thus impossible to come up with a definitive figure, except to reason that the official figures may be too low, though many of those wounded may have died of those wounds due to relatively primitive medical techniques and facilities being available. Wounds whilst not initially fatal may have become infected by gangrene as the musket ball pushed the man's clothing into the wound and thus infecting it. As noted with those receiving pensions in the years after the battle, some of those wounded did survive, and the officers injured mostly did, too. The figures for casualties broken down by unit do reinforce the fact that Preston's suffered the most and that Pitt's, held in reserve, suffered hardly at all. Forrester's remark that most of the officers in his battalion were killed and wounded also casts doubt on the official figures, which list only a dozen, out of the 23 who are known about.

Jacobite losses were deemed far lower, unsurprisingly so, given the fact that they were able to shoot at their enemies whilst under cover. As Patten wrote, 'Of the Rebels, there were 17 kill'd and 25 wounded, and no more, for they were every where under Cover'.[16] Rae accepted these figures, and Clarke's of 18 or 19 dead is similar.[17] The Merse trooper gives a total of 35 killed and wounded.[18] A Lowlander gave the fewest figures: eight to nine dead and five to six wounded.[19] It is possible that most of these fatalities were inflicted during escape attempts on 13 November, for one Jacobite alleged that in the fighting on the previous day, only six Jacobites had been killed.[20]

Those killed among the Jacobites included Peter Farquharson of Rochaley, shot through the leg and then died after a botched leg amputation, a Mr Clifton who died hours after been shot through his knee, Thomas Brereton, who died of blood loss after many wounds and a younger Shuttleworth was killed on the next day. Mr Hume, Mr Scattery and a Scottish gentleman of Nairn's battalion were also among the Jacobite dead. All were gentlemen and

---

13 NRS: GD220/5/601, Montrose Papers, Forrester–Montrose, 16 November 1715.
14 *St. James' Evening Post*, 83, 15–17 November 1715; LRO: PR 1435, Preston parish registers.
15 Anon., *Faithful Register*, p.157.
16 Patten, *History*, p.102.
17 Rae, *History*, p.324; Paton, 'Journal', p.522.
18 Anon., *A Letter*, p.7.
19 *Weekly Journal*, 10 March 1716.
20 TNA: SP54/9, 107, Jacobite prisoner's experiences in the rebellion.

so recorded by name. An anonymous common man who was shot dead was 'a lame man, and had the care of the Gunpowder', 'tho a person of no Note, yet he is not to be forgotten, seeing the Bravery of Mean Persons ought not be buried'.[21] John Hunter was shot through the leg.[22] John and Edmund Ord from Westwood, Northumberland, were also reported among the Jacobite dead.[23] Andrew Hogg was reported by his father as 'being shot through his Body at Preston' was among those wounded and as noted Nicholas Wogan was shot in the cheek.[24] It is probable that some of these wounded later died in captivity. As late as 4 May 1716 it was noted that two prisoners still bore the wounds from the battle, one having being shot in the leg and the other in the arm.[25]

Most of the dead were probably buried not far from where they were killed, in mass graves, as had occurred in the aftermath of the battles of the civil wars of the previous century. Only a few were interred elsewhere. There was a report in a nineteenth century newspaper of skeletons being found in the district of Friargate during excavations for new buildings and it is likely that such may exist near Churchgate.[26] Only four men (all from the British army) were buried in the churchyard: Captains Preston and Westerdean, and two unnamed lieutenants.[27]

To the victor the spoils is a common military maxim and the aftermath of this battle was no exception. There are numerous reports of the conquering soldiers benefitting from their victory and these were indignantly reported by civilians sympathetic to the Jacobite cause. Clarke wrote:

> … they with force and armes broke open doers and locks of chambers and clossetts, and the moneys, plate, goods and chattles of most of the inhabitants of that towne (who were and still are good subjects to His Majesties King Georges government), contrary to the will of the owners of the said goods, feloniously did steal, take, and carry away contrary to his said Majestie's peace, crowne and dignity, and also contrary to the laws of the nation in that case made and provided.[28]

There were other references to the like behaviour. Timothy Craggs wrote of 'They then plundered several Papists' houses and then there was some little quietness'.[29] On 22 November, troopers Judd and Daniell of Cobham's dragoons went to Mr Steel's, a Catholic at Thwaite Gate 'and plundered the house inhumanely and villainously destroying what they could not carry

---

21 Patten, *History*, pp.85–86, 102; Rae, *History*, p.324.
22 Patten, *History*, p.118.
23 Gooch, *Desperate Faction*, p.183.
24 TNA: SP54/10, 118, Hogg-Pringle, 10 December 1715.
25 TNA: SP35/5, f.136r, Rapin to unknown, 4 May 1716.
26 Baynes, *Jacobite Rising*, p.127.
27 LRO: PR 1435.
28 Paton, 'Journal', pp.520–521.
29 Jonathan Oates and Katherine Navickas (eds), Jacobites and Jacobins', RSLC, 3rd series, 25 (2006), p.55.

off'. They were arrested and brought before the York Assizes, condemned to death but pardoned.[30]

Robert Dormer had pleaded their case to Townshend, stating:

> … they were heated with Liquor under a Transport of Joy for the late success of His Majesty's Arms at Preston, to which they had contributed … [and he had had] a very good character of the prisoners from many worthy officers of the army … both of their merit in His Majesty's service and their former inoffensive behaviour towards all His Majesty's subjects.[31]

From the vantage point of Manchester, Harrold wrote, 'From confusion and military government, good God deliver'.[32]

The town of Preston undoubtedly suffered as a result of the battle fought within it, though was considerably less damaged than Dunkeld had been in 1689 because the wind did not blow the flames into it. Robert Cotesworth wrote to his father in the following year, 'Preston is not so much damaged as to ye outward appearance of the houses as one might have Reasonably expected'.[33] Defoe wrote 'not that the battle hurt many of the inhabitants, but so many families there and thereabout, have been touched by the consequences of it, that it will not be recovered in a few years'.[34] Four civilians 'were killed accidentally in the fight in ye town': Robert Sergeant, Thomas Seed, Robert Green and the widow Cowell.[35]

Nor were the captured Jacobite prisoners immune from such thefts and had to be protected by some of the officers. Forrester wrote 'it has been lucky for them that I was here, else they would have been very ill used by our people'.[36] The horses belonging to the Jacobites were sold and the proceeds shared among the soldiers, but each man did not receive much. Those taken by the Jacobites along their march were, however, returned to their rightful owners.[37] In conventional warfare, captured officers, as La Roone noted in Spain, could expect to have to surrender their arms and horse/s but to retain other personal possessions.[38]

The number of prisoners taken was sizable and was an unprecedented number since the battles of the civil wars of the previous century. Almost an entire army had been taken; the first and last time this ever happened throughout the Jacobite campaigns. The numbers taken have been disputed. One published list of prisoners was that there were 75 English noblemen and gentlemen, 83 servants, and 305 other Englishmen, 143 Scottish noblemen, gentry and officers, with 862 other Scots and 21 men who had

---

30 Oates (ed.), 'Memorandum Book of John Lucas, 1712–1750', *Thoresby Society* (2006), pp.52–53.
31 TNS, SP35/5, f.132r, Dormer to Townshend, 15 May 1716.
32 Horner, *Diary*, p.352.5, 627.
33 TWAS: CP3/22, Robert–William Cotesworth, 2 June 1716.
34 Rogers, *Defoe's Tour*, p.549.
35 Henry Fishwick, *History of the Parish of Preston* (Rochdale: James Clegg, 1900), p.420.
36 NRS: GD220/5/601, Forrester–Montrose, 16 November 1715.
37 Colville, 'Military Memoirs', p.60.
38 Smith, *Nollekens*, II, p.268.

been recaptured, totalling 1489.[39] The actual numbers, as noted in chapter four were higher: 1,641.

The prisoners were divided into officers and men. The former, which included gentry and nobility, were divided into three groups and housed in The Sign of the Mitre, the White Bull and the Windmill, being 'the most commodious Houses and Inns'. Some of the Northumberland and Lancashire gentry were sent to Mr Wingleby's house in Preston. Most of these men were sent to Wigan on 21 November and were followed two days later by the Lancashire gentry. On 25 November about 300 of them were divided into four groups and sent under guard to Warrington. These were the nobility, and most of the gentry, officers and their servants.[40]

It was important that the prisoners were secure and Forrester wrote of the arrangements made, 'under closer confinement than the general intended'.[41] There was also a zeal to confine prisoners, for 'several of the country people were in the disorder and confusion hurried into the church with the rebels'.[42]

Lord Carlisle, who had accompanied Carpenter to Preston, took the opportunity to question some of the captured lords and gentry. Naturally he found them to 'being at this time under great dejection of mind'. He suggested that mercy would be shown to them if they could provide useful information about other Jacobites, especially those from Durham and Sir William Blackett. He concluded that they did not know very much at all and that they had been under Forster's orders.[43] A list of men were questioned after the battle, numbering 229, and of these about a quarter had been in the battle. The others were mostly from Lancashire and mostly Catholic and presumably had been taken up because they had allegedly helped the Jacobite army in some way or had been making remarks sympathetic to the cause.[44]

A number of men escaped just before the surrender. Littleton, a priest, disguised himself as an apothecary and so slipped through the net.[45] Mrs Whitehead concealed one.[46] One Mr Dickenson escaped.[47] Simon Fraser, having been wounded in the leg in the day's fighting, evaded capture, too.[48] Thornburrow escaped in women's clothes, Hilton, Gartside and an anonymous joiner also escaped.[49] Not all were so lucky, as though Sydall initially escaped, he was later rounded up by dragoons on 15 November, 'who were with great Difficulty, dissuaded from hanging him by the way' and was returned to Preston with a halter around his neck.[50]

---

39 Patten, *History*, p.123.
40 Patten, *History*, pp.103–104.
41 NRS: GD220/5/601, Forrester–Montrose, 16 November 1715.
42 *HMC Townshend*, p.169.
43 *HMC Townshend*, p.169.
44 TNA: KB8/66, Baga de Secretis.
45 Patten, *History*, p.103.
46 Frances Legh (ed.), *Lyme Letters, 1660–1760* (London William Heinemann, 1936), p.307.
47 Addy and McNiven, 'Diary', II, p.476.
48 *HMC Stuart Papers, II*, p.138.
49 EUL, La III, 257, ff.3v, 5r, Clarke's Journal.
50 *Flying Post*, 3578, 24 February 1716.

At Wigan, Widdrington took Mackintosh to task about why he made alleged mistakes in the battle of Preston (withdrawal of troops from the bridge, not defending the extremes of the town and not following up the town's defence) and he defended himself. Neither was reconciled to the other. The rank and file, housed in the parish church, were fed by the townspeople with bread and water. The prisoners ripped the lining from the pews and seats to make them into breeches and hose 'to defend themselves from the Extremitys of the Weather'.[51] On 23 November, some were sent to Wigan, then to Chester, with some marched to Lancaster.

The first six Jacobite prisoners to be dealt with were those six who held commissions in the British army and so could be tried by courts martial, which were summary and immediate, compared to the longer drawn out nature of the civil criminal law. Wills initially claimed that he did not have the power to hold courts martial so wrote to Pulteney who replied that he did and that he should proceed without further delays, 'It is a little unfortunate that any delay should have happened in the trying of ye prisoners'.[52] Those tried were guilty of desertion which was punishable by death. Lord Charles Murray, third son of the Duke of Atholl, realised his peril and on 16 November wrote to his father, who was a government supporter, 'I have the misfortune to be taken prisoner' and noted that along with the other men who held commissions, were 'under much stricker confinement than the other prisoners who have not serv'd'. Unlike them, they had two guards permanently stationed in their room. They knew what awaited them, 'We doe not doubt that we will be treated as deserters and I will certainly suffer such if your Grace does not make use of your interest at court to save me'. Wills allowed him to write this latter and to have it sent to Atholl.[53]

Orders were sent to Wills on 17 November to have the six tried by court martial. A Deputy Judge Advocate with a commission to hold such a trial was sent from London and on 28 November the trial took place. Major Nairn and Philip Lockhart pleaded not guilty. John Shaftoe and ensign Erskine admitted their guilt. Ensign Dalziel, who had resigned his commission prior to the beginning of the campaign, was no longer a commissioned officer in the army and so was not liable to such a charge of desertion and so was acquitted. The others were found guilty. They were sentenced to death by firing squad.[54]

Meanwhile, the Earl of Orkney noted that Atholl had 'a great deale of merite to His majesty and all your behaviour since the beginnings of these troubles'. George I was 'sory for your son, and did not know how to distinguish him from the others, who were of good quality also, that were guilty of the same, that he inclined much for mercy, but it was thought necessary that officers who deserted should be made examples of'. Atholl told the Earl of Nottingham, one of the few Tories still in government, that

---

51 Patten, *History,* p.103.
52 TNA: WO4/17, p.291, Pulteney–Wills, 25 November 1715.
53 James, Duke of Atholl, ed., *Chronicles of the Atholl and Tullibardine Families* (Edinburgh, published privately, 1908), II, p.212.
54 Rae, *History*, p.326.

his son would repent and make amends if reprieved. As it was, the court martial unanimously recommended him for mercy, to the great anger of the government. He was given a month's reprieve, which became permanent, but died of illness in 1720 in London.[55]

No such successful interventions were made for those other four found guilty. On 2 December they were shot dead. According to Patten, of Shaftoe, 'He died very Penitent'.[56] Another commentator stated, they 'seem'd to die with Courage and Resolution, and as became Men in their Condition'.[57] Similarly 'They died all very resolutely, like soldiers and gentlemen, but very penitent, as to their Guilt, and profess'd themselves all to be Protestants to the last'.[58]

On 16 November, Stanhope had written to Carpenter to tell him to send 'all the noblemen, gentlemen, clergy and others of any note' to London'.[59] The prisoners, about 312 in number, who were taken to London were guarded by Stanhope's dragoons. They were marching over a heath and a Highlander, seeing some country people, cried out, 'Where are all your High Church Tories? If they would not fight with us, why do they not come and rescue us?' The commanding officer had the man dismount and then walk, his hands tied. As the procession progressed southward, the guards were changed, and a squadron of Lumley's horse replaced Stanhope's and the commander was now Brigadier Thomas Panton, lieutenant colonel of Lumley's horse.[60] At Warrington, where there had been a Jacobite riot earlier in the year, the prisoners were given ale and bread by sympathisers (mostly women); Sydall was given a pint of beer by a Tory curate (however he, as with two others, were sent back to the northern gaols on account of their being too ill to travel).[61]

At Daventry, Forster and Patten were segregated from the others, with none being allowed to speak to them and being confined in a guard room all night. Forster caught a cold by lying on the ground, which made him very ill, and so by the time they arrived at St Albans he was no longer able to ride so was carried on in a coach. Lieutenant Benjamin Bishop of Lumley's horse was in personal charge of the two men. From Daventry to London, Patten and Forster were distinguished by having halters on their horses' necks and being led by two troopers, 'which gave the People, as we passed along, an Opportunity to compliment us with Encomiums upon a warming pan'.[62] This was a satirical reference to the birth of James Stuart; not really his mother's child but a baby smuggled into the confinement room by means of a warming pan.

At Barnet all the prisoners were pinioned and at Highgate they were met by detachments of horse guards and foot guards, so each prisoner's horse was led by a soldier. From this time on, crowds of people came to watch

---

55 James, *Chronicles of Atholl*, II, pp.212–213, 216–217.
56 Rae, *History*, p.326; Patten, *History*, p.113.
57 Anon., *Faithful Register*, p.22.
58 Anon., *Annals*, II, pp.143–144.
59 TNA: SP44/117, p.331, Secretaries of State: State Papers, Entry Books, 1714–1716, Stanhope-Carpenter, 16 November 1715.
60 Patten, *History*, p.105.
61 *Flying Post*, 3730, 28 November–1 December 1715.
62 Patten, *History*, p.106.

the prisoners, 'we were met by such Numbers of People, that it is scarce conceivable to express, who with Long Live King GEORGE! and down with the Pretender! Ushered us throughout to our several Appartments'. When a Quaker insulted Patten, his guard, a grenadier, pushed him with the butt end of his musket and the man fell into a ditch, cursing the soldier.[63] Some of the prisoners 'returned with Spirit' some of these insults.[64] According to Ryder's cousin, they 'deserve hanging for their cowardice as well as their rebellion' and believed it was morally wrong to desert a cause once engaged on it.[65]

Forster had hoped that there might have been a rescue attempt 'by a Tory Mob' and told Patten that a gentleman had assured him of such when they were at Highgate. He was disappointed in this 'those Bravaders will not hazard themselves, tho' they speak Great things'. He was further troubled when he learnt that he would be sent to Newgate, he a member of Parliament, and furthermore, that he saw the remains of three Jacobites who had been hanged on the previous day.[66] Although, as Ryder observed, 'The rebels looked very much dejected', it was Forster who was the target of most animus, 'they were very much insulted by the mob, who reproached them, especially Forster, in a very provoking manner'.[67] Yet according to Lady Cowper, Baron Bernstorff, one of the King's Hanoverian advisers, had made an offer to her, via Mademoiselle Schutz 'which was to let Tom Forster escape, if I had a mind to it'.[68]

The prisoners were then separated into a number of prisons. The noblemen and a few others were sent to the Tower of London, as befitted their social status. Forster, Mackintosh and about 70 others were sent to Newgate. Sixty were sent to Marshalsea. The remainder, mostly nobles' and gentlemen's servants, were sent to the Fleet Prison.[69] At Newgate, 'their daily Practice was profane Swearing, Drunkenness, Gluttony, Gaming and Whoring, especially on Sundays, when they had most of their Female Visitors'. Forster won games of shuttlecock, 'he triumphed with his Feathers in the Prison, tho' he could not do it in the Field'.[70]

On 10 January 1716 the seven Jacobite lords captured at Preston were impeached of high treason at the House of Lords. They were allowed nine days to put together their replies. On 19 January all except Winton pleaded that they were guilty of the charges laid. The six 'laid themselves at the King's mercy and desired that the Lords would intercede for them'. Winton requested a lawyer to prepare his defence on a not guilty plea.[71] They heard their sentence on 9 February and made pleas as to why they should receive mercy. Lady Cowper wrote 'They all pretend to know Nothing and would have People believe this Affair was never concerted, and Nobody knows how he came into this Rebellion. God help them! Tis a wrong way to mercy

---

63 Patten, *History*, p.106.
64 Cowper, *Diary*, p.62.
65 Matthews, *Diary*, p.147.
66 Patten, *History*, p.107.
67 Matthews, *Diary*, p.147.
68 Cowper, *Diary*, p.62.
69 Rae, *History*, p.327.
70 Anon., *Secret History of the Rebels in Newgate* (London: J. Roberts, 1718), pp.49, 7.
71 Matthews, *Dairy*, pp.168–169.

THE CONSEQUENCES, 1715–1717

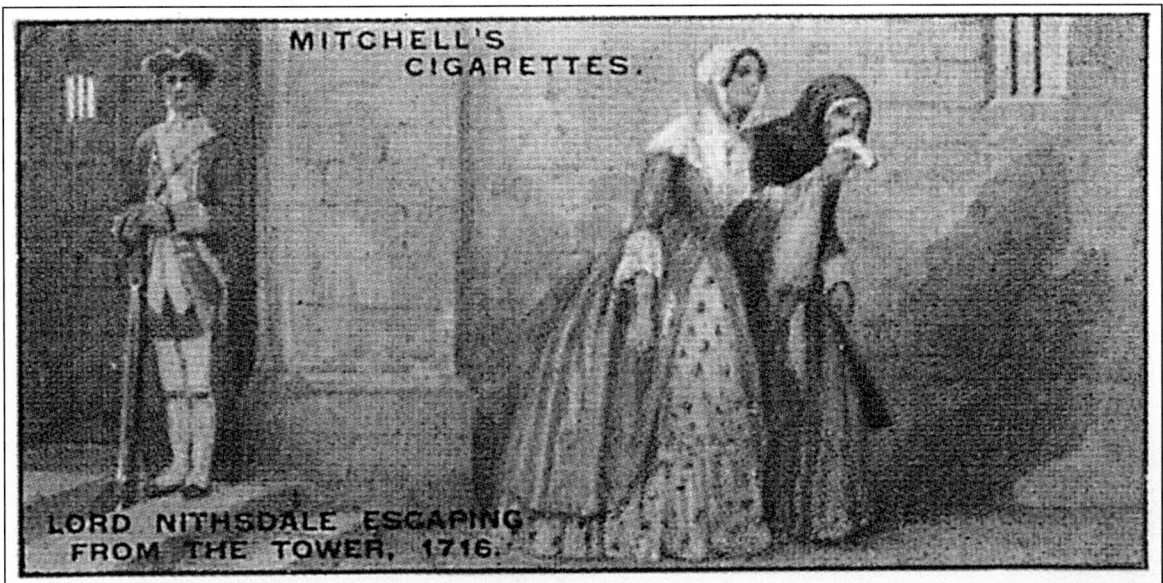

Lord Nithsdale escaping from the Tower, 1715. Nithsdale was one of several high-profile Jacobite escapes from captivity in London in 1716. (Mitchell's Cigarettes, c.1960. Author's collection)

to come with a lie in their Mouth'.[72] They were all sentenced to death, but time was given for lobbying on their behalf. Derwentwater, Kenmure and Nithsdale, were, however, given dates for their execution on 23 February, but the others received reprieves until 7 March. Nithsdale managed to escape with the aid of his wife and her servants, by exchanging clothes with one of the latter and so escaping from the Tower. Derwentwater and Kenmure were beheaded on Tower Hill on 24 February.[73]

The double execution was a significant affair. Ryder wrote, 'the whole hill was full of people that I never saw so large a collection of people in my life'.[74] Derwentwater made a speech justifying his loyalty to James Stuart, but Kenmure made none, but equally died 'with great Courage and Intrepidity'. Lady Cowper wrote 'Fatal necessity that it should be necessary for the well being of the Community that our Fellow-creature should suffer'.[75] Ryder, though moved by the sight of the two men's deaths, justified them, writing:

> I was very well pleased to see that the King had resolution enough to execute these lords. I think he has given in this a greater proof than ever of his fitness to govern this nation and I am persuaded it will have a good effect both at home to make the Tories partly despair and partly to come over to the King, and abroad to raise his character in foreign nations, and convince them that it is not the clamour and noise of rebels or the mob that shall interrupt the course of justice or shake his resolute mind.[76]

---

72 Cowper, *Diary*, p.79.
73 Rae, *History*, pp.375–377.
74 Matthews, *Diary*, p.187.
75 Cowper, *Diary*, pp.86–87.
76 Matthews, *Diary*, p.188.

Castle Gateway, Lancaster. Many Jacobite prisoners were incarcerated here after the battle, awaiting trial or disposal. (Lawson's series, c.1900. Author's collection)

Winton's trial took place on 15 and 16 March, with various witnesses brought against him, such as Patten, Wills, Munden, Carpenter and Forrester. There were no witnesses brought on his behalf and nothing further was said in his defence except what was in his initial plea, that is to say, Wills offered him mercy if he surrendered, and this had been refuted. He was found guilty and sentenced to death, but as with Nithsdale, made his escape successfully (several months later, on 15 August).[77] Some approved of these escapes, Lady Cowper writing about Nithsdale's, 'It is confirmed that Lord Nithsdale is escaped. I hope he'll get clear off. I never was better pleased at Anything in my Life, and I believe Everybody is the same'.[78] Other prisoners were viewed sympathetically, too. Alexander Menzies wrote that on his way to his trial, 'All the ladyes and mob cryed and weeped, and cryed that the Almighty would preserve us against our eneimies'.[79]

Meanwhile, Stanhope had told Carpenter on 16 November that regarding the majority of the prisoners, he was to 'dispose of them in the castles and prisons of Lancaster, York, Chester and Hull'.[80] About 530 men were despatched to Chester, arriving on 27 November. Prescott wrote that this was 'a melancholy and shocking triumph, a scene of human infelicity and mortifiaction', but a newspaper reported that 'There seemed to be a prodigious number of spectators who seemed well pleased with the sight'. Another 200

---

77 Rae, *History*, p.377; Matthews, *Diary*, pp.197–199.
78 Cowper, *Diary*, p.87
79 *HMC 5, 6th Report*, p.703.
80 TNA: SP44/118, p.331, Stanhope–Carpenter, 16 November 1715.

prisoners arrived there by the years' end.[81] At some point in November, there were 162 prisoners in Wigan, 222 in Lancaster, 446 in Preston and 467 in Chester (1297 in total).[82]

It was not the intention that all the prisoners be tried and thus face the death penalty. It would take too long and be too expensive. An order in council of 13 December merely noted that 'the publick peace of the kingdom' decreed 'that a speedy example be made of some of them'. The focus would be on 'gentlemen or men of estates, or such as shall appear to have distinguished themselves by any extraordinary degree of guilt'.[83] As a contemporary historian stated, 'some few who were noted for being idle and turbulent persons, and were therefore looked upon, as have fittest example to deter the rabble.'[84] After a month or more of time was spent in gathering evidence, it was noted that at the beginning of January 1716 there were 1,259 Jacobite prisoners in Lancaster, Wigan, Chester and Preston combined (presumably 38 had either died or escaped; at least 17 fell into the latter camp). It was decided to try all 40 gentlemen prisoners, 55 others who were deemed particularly notorious such as Thomas Sydall, 'colonel of the mob at Manchester and being a notorious offender & of great esteem there amongst the disaffected the gentlemen of the shire desire he may be executed there for example's sake'. Of the other 383 against whom there was evidence, they were lotted with every twentieth man standing trial.[85] Joseph Porter wrote, 'When I was prisoner at Chester Castle I and many others were ordered by Colonel Vincent to draw lots in order as we were told by him to subject us to trial, to save us from a tryall. That I drew a blank lott (which I was told free me from a trial)'.[86]

The bulk of the prisoners resided in Preston, Lancaster, Wigan and Chester since late November, whilst evidence and witnesses against them were gathered together. Instead of trial at the regular assizes, the bulk of the prisoners meant that as in 1685, a special commission of Oyer and Terminer was used, and on 4 January 1716 the judges appointed for the trial left London. They were Mr Baron Thomas Bury, Mr Justice Robert Eyre and Mr Baron James Montague. They arrived at Liverpool on 11 January, the place designated for the trials. Their commission was opened on 12 January and a Grand Jury sworn. Bills of indictment were read against 48 prisoners and these men were then given copies and were allowed eight days in which to prepare their defence. The court then adjourned for this period.[87]

In this interval, other prisoners were brought from Lancaster and Chester to Liverpool and the court delivered another 113 bills against them. As before, copies of the indictments were given to the prisoners in question, 40 of whom were Scottish. The court sat again on 20 January as planned. The hearings took place on 20–21, 23–28 of January, and on 1–8 February. In all 73 men were

---

81 Addy and McNiven, 'Diary', II, pp.476, 418; *The Daily Courant*, 4401, 1 December 1715.
82 TNA: KB8/66, Baga de Secretis.
83 TNA: SP44/118, pp.155–156, Privy Council, 13 December 1715.
84 *A History of the Affairs of Europe*, p.61.
85 TNA: KB33/1/5/54, 65, Court of King's Bench, Crown Side: Precedents and Miscellanea, 1715–1716; BL. Stowe Mss 750, f157r, Boothe–Parker, 29 January 1716.
86 TNA: KB8/66, f121r, Baga de Secretis.
87 Rae, *History*, pp.377–378.

tried. Of these, 66 were found guilty (63 after a trial, three others confessed their guilt) and seven were reprieved, some of the latter because it could be proved that they were forced into the Jacobite army and were unable to escape thereafter. Executions then began to take place in the last week of January and carried on until late February.[88] According to Lady Cowper, 'they would not believe the King durst hang any of them till the day of Execution came'.[89]

Additional trials took place in London of the gentry and officers. Parliament had to pass an Act that they be tried in London, rather than have the cost and inconvenience of them being tried in Lancashire. Some took placed at Westminster. On 7 March the first indictments were read out: against Forster, Mackintosh, Oxburgh and eight others, and they were given time for their defence. In the meantime, Forster managed to make his guards drunk and escaped from Newgate Prison with his valet, Thomas Lee, on 10 March. Despite a reward on his head for £1000, he and his valet escaped to Calais within a few days, leading some to believe that he had help from the government to do so.[90]

Many of the prisoners charged pleaded not guilty, which bought them time. As with Forster, some used this to break out of prison, and on the night of 4 May, Mackintosh and 15 others broke out of Newgate by force, knocking the keepers down and fleeing into the streets. Some were retaken, not knowing the streets, but Mackintosh and seven others escaped, with rewards of £1000 on the brigadier and £500 for the others. On 7 May another 14 prisoners were served indictments and all pleaded not guilty. Trials began on those indicted in March and all were found guilty. The execution of Oxburgh took place at Tyburn on 14 May; his head was placed on Temple Bar. There were other trials, but whilst all were found guilty, many were given reprieves, except for Richard Gascoigne, who was hanged at Tyburn on 25 May.[91] Hall and Paul were hanged together on 13 July. According to Ryder, 'there was a vast crowd of people stood all along Holborn to see them go by that it was difficult to see them in the sledge. The women were all in tears and were mightily concerned for the clergyman'. One Mr Jackson later told Ryder that 'He is mightily pleased as well as myself that the parson is hanged for an example and warning to other priests that they might not fancy their cloth will be protection them against the justice of the law'.[92]

Some of those who faced execution used the opportunity to justify themselves and their cause. Paul 'talked in the cart at Tyburn very insolently and traitorously so as to acknowledge the Pretender and deny King George's title'.[93]

There were also trials of the prisoners at Marshalsea prison at Southwark. The court first sat on 10 April and continued until early July. Most pleaded not guilty but were tried and were found guilty, but some were acquitted, such as Innes and Farquharson; Towneley's and Tyldesley's acquittals led to accusations that the juries there had been corrupted. Some of these men's

---

88 Rae, *History*, pp.378–379.
89 Cowper, *Diary*, p.78.
90 Rae, *History*, pp.382–383.
91 Rae, *History*, pp.383–384.
92 Matthews, *Diary*, p.274.
93 Matthews, *Diary*, p.274.

followers had been hanged in Lancashire, and the evidence against both were strong, witnesses having seen both in Preston, armed and at the head of armed men. Some others withdrew their not guilty pleas and begged for mercy.[94] The final trials at Westminster began on 4 July and there were another 30 trials.

Most of the executions took place in Lancashire, after the majority tried were found guilty. A graphic description was given of the first batch of executions in Lancashire and their aftermaths:

> … on the 28th [they] were carried to Sandy Hill (about half a mile north from Preston, near the road to Lancaster) in a sledge about half a yard high with ropes about their necks their arms & legs tied. Mr Moncaster who was a Protestant was very penitent, the rest being all Papists were pensive but showed no signs of repentance.
>
> When they had hung so long that they were concluded to be dead, they were cut down, then stripped, laid on their backs, and their privy members being cut off were thrown into a great fire made there for the purpose, then they were turned upon their faces and their heads being chopped off, they were turned over again and their bellies ripped open to their hearts, their bowels, their livers, and lastly their hearts, thrown into the fire, then their arms, legs & thighs were chopped off, which, with the trunks of their bodies and heads were putt into coffins, except Mr Shuttleworth's head, which was set on the town hall of Preston for terrible example to all passengers.[95]

Apart from the Special Commission in the north west in January and February, another 84 men were listed in constables' returns in 1716 as having been at the battle and further 21 were tried at the autumn assizes in 1716, on 21 and 23 September. There was clearly less appetite for condemning men to death now, 'the Juries were grown stiff; and notwithstanding they had been Eye Witnesses of, and even felt the dismal effects of the late unnatural rebellion, yet they acted like the Jurors of Surrey, thought fit to break up the Assizes'. There were another five executions, on 2 October; and these were the last.[96]

Table 25. Summary of Executions of Jacobite Prisoners, 1715–1716[97]

Name	Place	Date
Richard Shuttleworth	Preston	28 January 1716
Roger Muncaster	Preston	28 January 1716
Thomas Coupe	Preston	28 January 1716
William Butler	Preston	28 January 1716
William Arkwright	Preston	28 January 1716
Richard Chorley	Preston	9 February 1716
James Drummond	Preston	9 February 1716

---

94 Rae, *History*, p.384.
95 Oates, 'Memorandum Book', p.69.
96 *Weekly Journal*, 29 September,1716, 13 October 1716, 16 March 1717.
97 Anon., *Faithful Register*, pp.398–400.

THE SECOND BATTLE OF PRESTON, 1715

Name	Place	Date
William Black	Preston	9 February 1716
Donald MacDonald	Preston	9 February 1716
Rorie Kennedy	Preston	9 February 1716
John Ord	Preston	9 February 1716
John Rowbotham	Preston	9 February 1716
James Burn	Wigan	10 February 1716
John McGillivray	Wigan	10 February 1716
William Whalley	Wigan	10 February 1716
James Blundell	Wigan	10 February 1716
James Finch	Wigan	10 February 1716
Thomas Sydall	Manchester	11 February 1716
William Harris	Manchester	11 February 1716
Stephen Seagar	Manchester	11 February 1716
Joseph Finch	Manchester	11 February 1716
John Porter	Manchester	11 February 1716
Thomas Goose	Garstang	14 February 1716
Thomas Cartmell	Garstang	14 February 1716
James Wadsworth	Garstang	14 February 1716
Allan Sanderson	Garstang	14 February 1716
Robert Crowe	Lancaster	18 February 1716
Donald Robertson	Lancaster	18 February 1716
Hercules Durham	Lancaster	18 February 1716
George Mackintosh	Lancaster	18 February 1716
Earl of Derwentwater	London	24 February 1716
Viscount Kenmure	London	24 February 1716
Archibald Burnett	Liverpool	25 February 1716
George Collingwood	Liverpool	25 February 1716
John Hunter	Liverpool	25 February 1716
Alexander Drummond	Liverpool	25 February 1716
Richard Gascoigne	London	25 May 1716
Henry Oxburgh	London	14 May 1716
William Paul	London	13 July 1716
William Charnley	Preston	2 October 1716
Thomas Shuttleworth	Preston	2 October 1716
John Bruce	Preston	2 October 1716
George Hodgson	Preston	2 October 1716
John Winckley	Preston	2 October 1716

In total, 48 of the men taken at Preston were executed (including the four officers in the previous year). The remains of some of them were displayed in public as a bloody warning to passersby. Richard Shuttleworth's head in Preston town hall, Sydall's on the market place at Manchester and others at Garstang and Lancaster. As a tourist in 1716 noted, 'There was Gallawayes [sic] and heads put up at every Town we came at'.[98]

Some of those about to be executed made final speeches to the crowds assembled. Unusually, Muncaster was penitent, announcing 'I am brought here to be a miserable and dismal spectacle to you all. The Crime I am accus'd of, Condemn'd and brought hither to be executed, bears no meaner nor less infamous title, than Rebellion, a Crime prohibited by the laws of God and Man'. He begged God's forgiveness. Yet he was much the exception, as he wrote, most were not so. Captain Straiton, a Jacobite, wrote that 'all of them, save one, died justifying what he had done'. Alexander Drummond underwent his ordeal, 'with a becoming Courage and Resolution and drew a Great deal of Compassion from his spectators'.[99]

At least one man spoke about the battle of Preston in his final speech. According to Hall:

> ... the surrender not only ruined many of His majesty's brave and faithful subjects, but gave up their King and Country into the bargain: For it was then in their power to have restor'd the King with Triumph to his throne; and hereby to have made us a happy and free people. We had repulsed our Enemies at every attack, and were ready and willing to have attacked them. On our side, even our common men were brave, courageous and resolute. On the other hand theirs were directly the contrary: in so much, that after they had run away from our first fire, they could never be brought so much as to endeavour to stand a second ... The truth is, after we had conquered them our superiors thought fit to capitulate and ruin us.[100]

Only a small minority were executed, therefore. This had always been the intention. As early as 22 November, Stanhope had told Wills, 'You may easily imagine the King's clemency will incline him to pardon the greater part of the meaner sort'. The prisoners would petition the King for clemency and in return for their lives would submit to seven years labour in the new world.[101] Most did so, but about 206 refused.[102]

The majority of the prisoners in the northern gaols, 638 in all and almost entirely Scottish, were transported to the American colonies and the West Indies from Liverpool in a number of ships in the summer of 1716.

These were as follows:

---

98 TWAS: CP3/22, Robert–William Cotesworth, 2 June 1716.
99 Weekly Journal, 329, 11 February 1716; Rae, *History*, p.380n, *HMC Stuart Papers*, II, p.9; Anon., *Faithful Register*, p.31.
100 Hibbert-Ware, 'Memorials', p.352.
101 TNA: SP44/117, p.339; 118, p.186, Stanhope–Wills, 22 November 1715.
102 TNA: KB33/1/5/14–15.

Table 26. Summary of Jacobite Prisoners Transported, 1716[103]

Date Sailed	Ship	Destination	Number of Men
30 March 1716	*Scipio*	Virginia	95
21 April 1716	*Wakefield*	South Carolina	81
26 April 1716	*Two Brothers*	Jamaica	47
7 May 1716	*Susannah*	South Carolina	104
24 May 1716	*Friendship*	Virginia	80
25 June 1716	*Hockenhill*	St Christopher's	30
29 June 1716	*Elizabeth and Anne*	Virginia	126
28 July 1716	*Goodspeed*	Virginia	56
15 July 1716	*Africa*	Barbados	1
31 July 1716	*Anne*	Virginia	18

Treatment aboard ship was grim, as a Jacobite later noted:

> You can't imagine the bad treatment we had from the master while he had us in his power, having all been kept in irons except one and myself, who had bought our freedom. However, as to everything else, we all fared alike, our meat being a salt hough of beef for five, and a biscuit to everyone once a day, and an allowance of stinking water as red as blood, being kept in claret casks. Our beds were in everyway answerable to our diet. This and the insults we suffered every hour from the master and the crew, added to the unspeakable misfortunes we suffered from a long imprisonment.[104]

Some prisoners escaped by taking over the *Hockenhill* and sailing to France, for example. Others escaped from Chester castle, a total of 35, in January and February 1716, with 22 escaping when the prisoners were at Wigan. Various methods were used, including bribing guards.[105]

Numerous men died in prison: at least 41 died in Lancaster castle; 15 died in Liverpool. Likewise in Chester, as Lady Otway recorded, 'so much sickness now in our castle that they die in droves like rotten sheep and be 4 or 5 a night throne into the castle ditch for graves'.[106] At least a dozen men died in Newgate, some by fever.[107] Two men on trial in Liverpool died before sentence could be carried out.[108]

---

103 *Calendar of State Papers: Colonial America and the West Indies, 1716–1717*, 29 (London, 1930), pp.167–173.
104 *HMC, Stuart Papers*, III, p.305.
105 Addy and McNiven, 'Diary', II, p.489; *Weekly Journal*, 309, 21 January 1719; *Flying Post*, 3769, 28 February–1 March 1716; TNA, SP35/5, f.209r.
106 Anon., *Faithful Register*, pp.399–400; Liverpool Record Office: 283, PET1/1, St Peter's parish registers; HMC Xth Rep. App. IV, p.352.
107 Anon., *Secret History*, pp.8, 12, 18, 22-23, 29–30; Patten, *History*, pp.114, 119.
108 Rae, *History*, pp.378–379.

These deaths were partly caused by poor sanitation but also because the winter of 1715/1716 was one of the worst on record. Even the Thames froze. Prescott wrote in February of the conditions, 'Contagious and fatal distempers, fever Flux & small pox spread among the prisoners in the Castle'. John Rutherford, a prisoner, claimed, 'A fever raged amongst us while few hath escaped, and hath brought several to their graves'.[109] Captain Straiton wrote, that the men were 'crowded like beasts in a fold, having a raging fever amongst them, and daily dying with ill usage and want of necessities, little or no distinction being made between gentlemen and the meaner sort'.[110] As many as 165 men were ill in January.[111] However, the gaolers were not wholly inhumane, as money was recorded as being spent on medicines for the prisoners.[112]

Prisoners were allowed four pence of food per day by the prison: beer, cheese and bread. In addition to this, many were helped by Jacobite sympathisers in Chester. Stout, one of the food contractors, also wrote, 'Besides the King's allowance, they had supplys privtely from the Papists and disaffected, so as to live very plentyfully'.[113] Robert Cotesworth told his father in 1716 that 'We saw a great number of ye gentlemen Rebells at liver[pool] they have money in abundance are not at all daunted and are Drunk every Night'.[114]

Those who survived up to the summer of 1717 were set free by an Act of Grace of July. From the north western gaols, this number amounted to 194, though one source states 200 were released from Chester and others from Lancaster. Prescott wrote in his diary about seeing, on 29 August 1717, 'Wee pass in the road, on this side of Frodsham, thoro a considerable number of the prisoners this morning discharged by virtue of the Act of Pardon, cheerfully returning to their Country, Scotland & Northumberland'.[115] The numbers of prisoners in the northern gaols who were executed, transported, released, died or escaped do not add up to the number who were recorded there in January 1716. The fates of these men is not known; clearly they were not executed or transported, so it must be presumed that some were discharged, died or escaped and were not recorded.

Apart from this, the government instituted the Forfeited Estates Commission in 1716 to seize the estates of Jacobites taken in rebellion. This especially hit the Lancastrian and Northumberland gentry: 25 of the former had their estates taken. Furthermore, all Catholics had to register their lands with the county quarter sessions. Most of the Scottish Jacobites evaded the efforts of the commission, often with help from former enemies.[116]

---

[109] Addy and McNiven, 'Diary', II, p.491; J.C. Bridge (ed.), 'Diary of Nehemiah Griffiths', *Journal of the Chester and North Wales Archaeological and History Society* (1909), p.49.
[110] *HMC, Stuart Papers*, II, p.9.
[111] TNA: KB33/1/5/8, Court of King's Bench, 1715.
[112] Shaw and Slingsby, *Calendar*, XXXI, p.315, 372–373.
[113] Marshall, 'Autobiography', p.176.
[114] TWAS: CP3/22, Robert–William Cotesworth, 2 June 1716.
[115] Addy and McNiven, 'Diary', II, p.588; Anon., *Annals*, III, pp.260–261.
[116] Sankey, *Punishing Treason*, pp.138–149.

THE SECOND BATTLE OF PRESTON, 1715

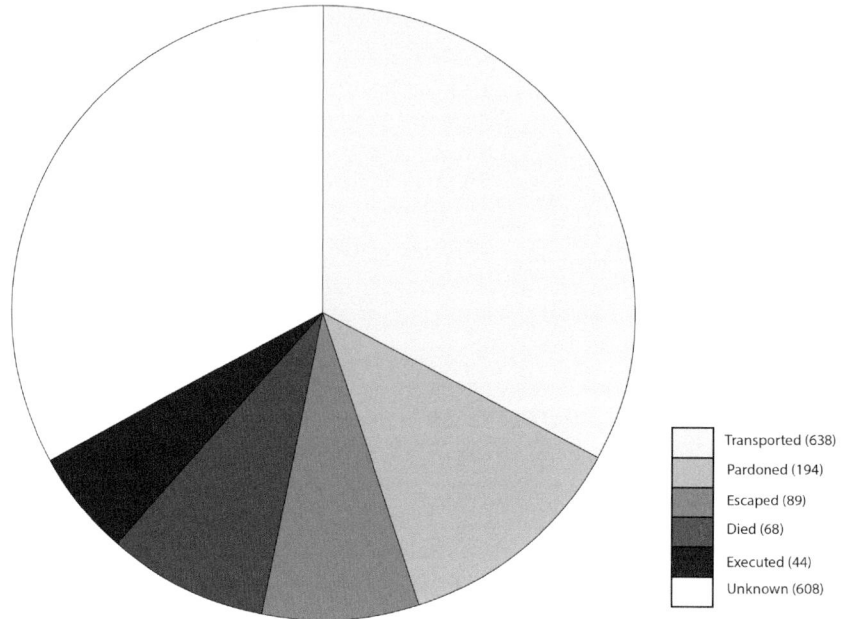

The Fates of Jacobite Prisoners

Transported (638)
Pardoned (194)
Escaped (89)
Died (68)
Executed (44)
Unknown (608)

Thomas Forster was blamed for the Jacobite defeat. Some Jacobites went as far as to deem him a traitor. Patten wrote 'Another Scandal upon Mr Forster, is, That he betray'd them to the King's Troops'. Patten defended Forster's reputation, which he argued was by a faction who wished to 'blast the Reputation of the Commanding officers of his Majesty's Troops, and of the Troops himself' as well as to slander Forster.[117] As we have seen, some of the Scottish participants placed the blame for the defeat on their leaders, and Forster in particular. Prescott wrote ''tis from probable reasons suspected that gen. Forster betray's his own party'.[118]

The question was whether Forster was a traitor or not. Thomas Hearne (1678–1734), an Oxford Jacobite, after some conversation with Scottish Jacobite officers who had been at Preston, wrote:

> … there was no treachery in General Forster or any of the rest, but Cowardice, Forster being a timorous Man, and unwilling to fight, or shew the least part of a General, and so surrendered his men, whereas had he been at all courageous, the Business had been certainly done for the King.[119]

When Forster met James Stuart in Avignon at the Jacobite court in 1716, the latter attached no blame to Forster and even appointed him steward of the exiled court's household.[120] Furthermore, Forster as well as Mackintosh

---

117 Patten, *History*, pp.98–99.
118 Addy and McNiven, 'Diary', II, p.475.
119 John Buchannan-Brown (ed.) *The Remains of Thomas Hearne* (London: Centaur Press Ltd, 1966), p.240.
120 *ODNB*, 20, pp.426–427.

THE CONSEQUENCES, 1715–1717

were explicitly excluded from the government's general pardon of 1717.[121] There was also much discussion about the blame not falling on Forster but on Mackintosh. As noted, Patten was quick to latch onto this and it was a view shared by Widdrington.[122] In 1717, Dr Patrick Abercomby informed Mar:

> The avarice, roguery, insufficiency and cowardice of the commanders and others of our people at Preston are perpetually talked of, and asserted with great oaths by not a few here and at St. Germains. The persons they chiefly exclaim against are the Brigadier Mackintosh, his two brothers and bastard son. Capt. Dalziel etc. The particulars related of them are so infamous that one cannot prevail with oneself to believe them.[123]

Lionel Walden, after he had been released from the Fleet prison in 1717, met Thomas Hearne in Oxford and gave an account of what happened:

> General Wills' men were repulsed at every attack, and were cowardly and timerous, whilst King James' men were brave and resolute, is literally true. He says that Mr Forster, Lord Widdrington and one Mackentosh, were the three traytors that surrendered them up, otherwise they had got a complete victory, & that there was no doubt but that they should have restored the King.[124]

George Home, however, attributed the defeat due to lack of manpower, writing to Mar in 1717 thus, 'The scarcity of hands contributed as much, if not more to our ruin than the ignorance of our leaders'. He claimed this could have been rectified if James had arrived in England.[125] Walden, the day after his meeting with Hearne, added the following statement, concurring with Home, 'the Tories (as they are called), & others proved worse than their words, they having promised to joyn them. But this failure must be attributed in good measure to the treacherous surrendering. Had this not happened, they had certainly been joyn'd by thousands'.[126]

To move to the victors. Wills sent Colonel Maurice Nassau of Grant's foot to relay the news to London and he arrived at the capital on 15 November. He was given £500 as a reward for his information.[127] Lady Cowper wrote in her diary of this information, 'The Surrender of these prisoners filled the Town with Joy'.[128] Liddell wrote to Cotesworth, 'You see a joy throughout the City which can't be parallel'd and the court shew no less satisfaction. This noble action has nipp'd the designs of our enemys in the budd so they can't expect a plentifull crop'.[129]

---

121 *HMC Stuart Papers*, IV, p.229.
122 Patten, *History*, pp.98–99.
123 *HMC, Stuart Papers*, III, pp.456–457.
124 Rannie, 'Hearne's Recollections', VI, p.88.
125 *HMC Stuart Papers*, V, p.214.
126 Rannie, 'Hearne's Recollections', VI, p.88.
127 Shaw and Slingsby, *Calendar* (1716), p.18.
128 Cowper, *Diary*, p.57.
129 Ellis, 'Liddell–Cotesworth Letters', p.200.

THE SECOND BATTLE OF PRESTON, 1715

Some saw the battle as important because the Jacobites were potentially on the verge of great success, as Craggs informed Townshend on 22 November, 'I find this expedition was as fortunate for the conjuncture as any other circumstance because the rebels in two or three days time would certainly have been joined by many thousands well armed and well mounted'.[130] Pulteney wrote on 16 November to Carpenter:

> I write this letter with a very good deal of pleasure because it gives me an occasion to express to you the Joy which I have upon you and Mr Wills success against the King's enemys. I never did question but His Majesty's Forces would be victorious under such commands, and there is not a person in the world takes a greater share in your success than myself.[131]

George Bubb, British ambassador in Madrid, did not hear of the news of the battle until the following month and then, on 23 December, he wrote, 'It is with the greatest satisfaction I congratulate His Majesty &c upon the defeat of the English rebels'.[132]

It also meant that the Dutch battalions which had been to march to Lancashire, could be diverted towards Hull and thence to Scotland. Other troops, such as Stanhope's dragoons, were also be sent to Scotland. Confidence in the regime rose with victory over the Jacobites at Preston and Sheriffmuir, too. On 2 November, with undefeated Jacobite forces in both countries, South Sea stock stood at 90 5/8 to 89 and Bank Stock at 118 ¾ to 119. By 19 November, with the government looking far more secure, these figures stood at 94 ½ to ¾ and 124 ¼ to 124 ½.[133]

John Macky noted about the battle:

> And the Last Action was visibly the Hand of God, by the Action of Dunblain's happening on the same Day, at above 200 Miles Distance; and that whole Rebellion, however spread, quashed without any Resistance here, notwithstanding the Advantage of Ground and Numbers against new raised Troops.[134]

The extent of the victory should not be exaggerated, as Argyle, never optimistic, wrote to Townshend on 19 November:

> I received last night a letter from Mr Carpenter with the good news of the Rebells at Preston being all Prisoners but he makes a Reflection at the end of his letter wch is a very wrong one, he imagines those at Perth may upon this news desire to capitulate. I hope His Majesty's ministers have not been of this opinion, because it would literally very greatly endanger the whole.[135]

---

130 *HMC Townshend*, p.170.
131 TNA: WO4/17, p.276, Pulteney–Carpenter, 16 November 1715.
132 TNA: SP94/84, Secretaries of State: State Papers Foreign, Spain, Bubb–Stanhope, 23 December 1715.
133 *The Daily Courant*, 4376, 2 November 1715; 4391, 19 November 1715.
134 John Macky, *A Journey around England*, II (London. J. Pemberton, 1722), p.154.
135 TNA: SP54/10, 64, Argyle–Townshend, 19 November 1715.

THE CONSEQUENCES, 1715–1717

More moderately, the Lord Justice Clerk wrote, 'this will putt ane end I hope to the rebellion in England, and must have good consequences as to us'.[136]

Carpenter was unhappy with Wills' role in the victory, writing 'I find the prints give him all the power and applause, I suppose by his own or his friends' direction, and I fear His Majesty may be under that mistake also'.[137] Wills became a lieutenant general later that year. Both men disputed who had been the victor. On 6 February 1716 it was announced that Wills, who had recently arrived in London, was to fight a duel with Carpenter. This was a great surprise to all and a shock to loyalists. Carpenter issued the challenge. Colonel Churchill was his second and Brigadier Honywood was Wills' second. The Duke of Montagu prevented the duel by sending a guard to the place where it was to have occurred and Marlborough also interposed. The grudge between the two men had begun in Spain and 'bled afresh at Preston, upon the Competition of Command' but the two decided to postpone their quarrel until they met again in London. Carpenter was unhappy because Wills got his version of the battle in first and this was widely published in late 1715; Carpenter's not appearing until the following year.[138] However, Carpenter's contribution to the victory was noted and he was made commander in chief in Scotland in 1716 and was given the honorary post of governor of Minorca:

> In consideration, among other things of his good serving in subduing the rebels at Preston; so that the Action at Preston is publickly ascrib'd to his conduct, not to that of Geeneral Wills, which seems to confirm what some have said, viz., that if General Carpenter had not come seasonably into the Action, General Wills and his troops had been repulsed, but that General Carpenter, by altering the disposition which the other had made, cut off entirely the escape of the Rebels and their receiving any supplies; upon which Alteration they immediately capitulated; whereas before they had evidently the Advantage.[139]

Preston was also known about in the Jacobite camp at Perth. On 13 November, the major battle in Scotland had been fought at Sheriffmuir between Mar's army and that of Argyle, with the latter being heavily outnumbered. Neither side scored a tactical victory and both returned to their respective bases, making this a strategic victory for Argyle, for he had prevented the Jacobite army from marching south as was its intent. In the days following this battle, news of Preston arrived and initially the reporting was untruthful.

News came of it as having been a Jacobite victory and it was celebrated in the Jacobite held Perth by bells being rung, cannons firing, 'the whole city was lit up and 'no demonstration of joy omitted'. Sinclair found General Hamilton in a pensive mood and he soon suspected the worst. Mar tried to portray it was a victory and ordered public celebrations, which took place. He wrote to Strowan thus, 'The government gives out that our Friends in

---
136 TNA: SP54/10, 60, Cockburn–unknown, 17 November 1715.
137 *HMC Townshend*, p.171.
138 *Political State*, XI, pp.177–178.
139 Anon., *Annals*, II, p.340.

England have been defeated but I am sure their accounts are not true, tho' it is very likely there has been some action there: Lord Nairn disbelieved it'.[140]

The reality was soon widely known. A day or two after the celebrations for the imagined Jacobite victory at Preston had been made, 'the melancholie account was conformed from all hands' that it was quite the reverse. Sinclair owned that he was not surprised:

> I never expected better: it was not to be imagin'd that a handfull of raw, undisciplines men, without armes, care or thought, could marche so far into a country, without anie man of authoritie nor knowledge at their head, without falling into a snare. Mr Douglas had told me enough of them to judge what should hapne, tho' I must say, had they been armed, and any man of authoritie and service at their head, with a few officers, they might have given such troupes as they had to deal with worke enough.[141]

Sinclair put the defeat down to poor leadership, stating that apart from Derwentwater, Winton and Lord Nairn 'their mock Generals … being not good for much, no more than our oun'. There was dissension among the leaders, 'Their politick, as some of themselves have told me, was much the same with ours, which consisted in lying, no order and making them believe to the last there was no fighting'.[142]

James Keith, a junior Jacobite officer, recalled the demoralising effects of the result of the news of the surrender at Preston. Several leading Jacobites at Perth, 'seeing that the English, which we always looked on as our principal strength, were quelled … began to think of making terms for themselves'.[143] Sinclair added, 'One might imagine that all this storm threatening to break upon us, at a time when we were abandoned by the whole world.'[144] Eventually Mar wrote to James of the surrender at Preston, 'I'm afraid will putt a stop to any more riseings in that country at this time'.[145] Bolingbroke later commented that when 'the business at Preston was over, there remained not the least room to expect any commotion in his [James'] favour among the English'.[146]

In Scotland desertions blunted the Jacobite offensive edge and prevented another attempt at an advance to the south. Although James arrived in Scotland on 22 December, reinforcements from England and the Dutch Republic tipped the numerical balance in Argyle's favour and by the end of January 1716, despite the snow, his army was able to advance against the Jacobites at Perth. There was no final stand and the army retreated northwards. Mar, James and others took ship to France, never to see Scotland again. Few of their army suffered, however. In England, as seen, it was different, and

---

140 National Library of Scotland, Advocates' Library, ADV MS 13.1.8.43, Mar to Strowan, November 1715.
141 Scott, *Memoir*, pp.251–252.
142 Scott, *Memoir*, p.252.
143 Keith, *Fragment of a Memoir* p.23.
144 Scott, *Memoir*, p.256.
145 *Report on the Manuscripts of the Earls of Mar and Kellie* (London: HMSO, 1904), p.514.
146 Bolingbroke, *Works*, I, p.153.

many of those landed Jacobites there saw their estates confiscated and sold. It was a hard lesson, but one most of their descendants heeded for the response to the initially more successful Jacobite campaign in 1745 was to do nothing and thus preserve their lives, liberty and properties.

As to some of the winners, Carpenter oversaw the defeat of the next Jacobite incursion and Spanish invasion in Scotland in 1719 as commander in chief in Scotland following Argyle's dismissal. Wills became a lieutenant general. Bland rose to become a major general and noted military theorist, playing a prominent part in the Jacobite defeat in 1746. Gardiner became a colonel of dragoons and was killed at Prestonpans in 1745. Pelham left the army shortly after the campaign and entered politics: becoming George II's leading minister in 1743 until his death in 1754. Cobham, now a general, led the British raid on Spain 1719. Patten was rewarded and became a naval chaplain, dying in 1733. Molesworth's, Stanhope's and Churchill's dragoons were disbanded in 1718, though the officers went on half pay. One of these was La Roone and he joined Kerr's dragoons in 1724 and retired in 1732 as a major. Some of the rank and file received pensions on their discharge; from 1716 until as late as 1742, with infantry privates receiving five pence a day, corporals and drummers seven and sergeants eleven pence. Dragoons received sixpence a day and corporals of dragoons eight pence.[147]

The losers had various fates. Some retained their Jacobite loyalties: the Master of Nairn joined the Jacobite insurrection in 1745, the Wogan brothers remained in the Stuarts' service for decades and in 1719 Charles rescued Clementina Sobieska, so she could marry James Stuart and became mother to Charles Edward Stuart. Mackintosh was involved in the 1719 expedition but was later gaoled for life in Edinburgh castle. Forster died in exile abroad. Lionel Walden was murdered in 1719. Younger relations of some of the Jacobites of 1715 took part in the Forty Five: Francis Towneley, Richard's nephew, led the Jacobite Manchester Regiment and one of Thomas Sydall's sons was one of his junior officers; both were executed for treason. Charles Radcliffe was involved in the Forty Five but was captured and the sentence of death passed in 1716 was carried out 30 years later, so was the last Englishman to be executed for Jacobitism. Most of the vanquished and their descendants prudently kept their heads down in 1745, however.

---

147 Cormack, 'These Meritorious Objects', p.44.

Conclusion

Preston was a small battle, not just by Continental standards (a little over 100,000 men had fought at Blenheim in 1704), but even by British standards, with almost 14,000 combatants being at Sheriffmuir. Yet for all its size, it was more decisive than either. It is rare for an army to be completely defeated and destroyed as a fighting force. Neither of those two better-known battles put an end to the conflict that they were part of. Armies had been mauled and objectives thwarted in both cases, but the campaign continued. At Preston the Jacobite army in England ceased to exist and so the military campaign was over at a stroke.

This was important because both sides saw the campaign in England as being the crucial one. There were more British troops in England than there ever were in Scotland, much to the chagrin of the commander there. As in the Civil Wars, England was the key to holding the British Isles. Once it was secure, then any enemies elsewhere were in a very weak strategic position. England was after all the centre in regards to population, financial and commercial power. The fear induced by the Jacobite army's march through the north western counties virtually unopposed was elegant testimony to that.

Its immediate impact was that the Dutch and Swiss troops brought over to England could all be despatched towards Scotland, where Mar, despite the Jacobite setback at Sheriffmuir and subsequent desertions, still had several thousand men in arms at Perth. It also allowed two dragoon regiments to be sent to Scotland, thus providing Argyle with a substantial reinforcement and making his military position far stronger than that of his opponent, for the first time in the campaign.

Yet the outcome of the battle was far from inevitable. On 12 November, the numbers on each side were comparable, and the Jacobites quite possibly had the edge. Furthermore, they were defending relatively strong positions for an enemy lacking artillery and where the British cavalry could not be utilised to any major degree. The rank and file of part of the Jacobite army at least showed itself resolute in the defence and capable of inflicting serious casualties whilst receiving few in return. Tactically they had won the first day's fighting.

Yet the Jacobite army had at least two weaknesses. They had a lack of ammunition which meant that a successful defence could only be temporary. They could probably have not fought another day's battle with what few musket balls and powder they possessed. Secondly, and perhaps more important, was the state of their mostly inexperienced leadership, which had never been good and was perpetually divided or cautious at best. The very success of the rank and file and junior officers on 12 November combined with the arrival of Carpenter's cavalry on the next day was a fatal combination for them, and as it transpired, their men. Forster and Widdrington were not soldiers but civilians. They had emerged as leaders for their political, religious (in Forster's case) and social standing, not for any military knowledge or experience, and their adviser, Oxburgh, was little better. Their morale collapsed on the morning of 13 November on sighting their new foes coming just after the bloody fighting of the previous day.

Could the battle have had another outcome? There could have been a counter attack after the repulse of the attackers on day one. This might well have led to the mounted cavalry slaughtering the Jacobite infantry as they sallied out into the open. Or it might have led to a Jacobite victory. The other opportunity was on the second day when it was advocated among some to fight their way out. This would not have led to a victory but could have led to some of the army escaping, though they might well have been rounded up later on unless they had been able to keep together. Since neither option was attempted the answers cannot be known. The former might have led to a major Jacobite victory and more recruits joining, the taking of Liverpool or a march on London, which would have led to further fighting against the troops located in the capital under Cadogan.

To return to reality: Preston was a tactical victory for the Jacobites on 12 November. It became a defeat on the next day when their leaders decided to try and negotiate. In this they failed and so took what was in the short term, the easiest way out: to surrender unconditionally. In doing so they played a major part in the defeat of the Stuart cause. For the British army, a tactical victory was unlikely on day one, but there was no talk of retreat. When reinforcements arrived, the situation changed, though a renewed offensive was probably not on the cards until the artillery from Chester arrived. When it did, the Jacobite position would have been hopeless.

News of the Jacobite surrender also impacted on the larger Jacobite army in Scotland, which had already experienced the setback at Sheriffmuir and was beginning to haemorrhage. It was yet another nail in the coffin of the overall Jacobite campaign throughout Britain as well as signalling its end in England. It can also the argued that the Jacobite defeat at Preston and subsequent punishments meant that support for the Jacobites in 1745 in England was even lower than it had been in 1715.

Preston then, was not only the last battle in England, it was also one of the most decisive in the Jacobite campaigns; alongside the little known Glenshiel of 1719 and the better known Culloden of 1746. Arguably it was more so; at these two battles which finished the campaigns in question, many of the Jacobites escaped and in the latter there was even talk of continuing the struggle. No such option was available after Preston in 1715. It was an utter defeat, or from the British army's perspective, a complete victory, won not so much by fighting but from the morale of the respective leaders.

THE SECOND BATTLE OF PRESTON, 1715

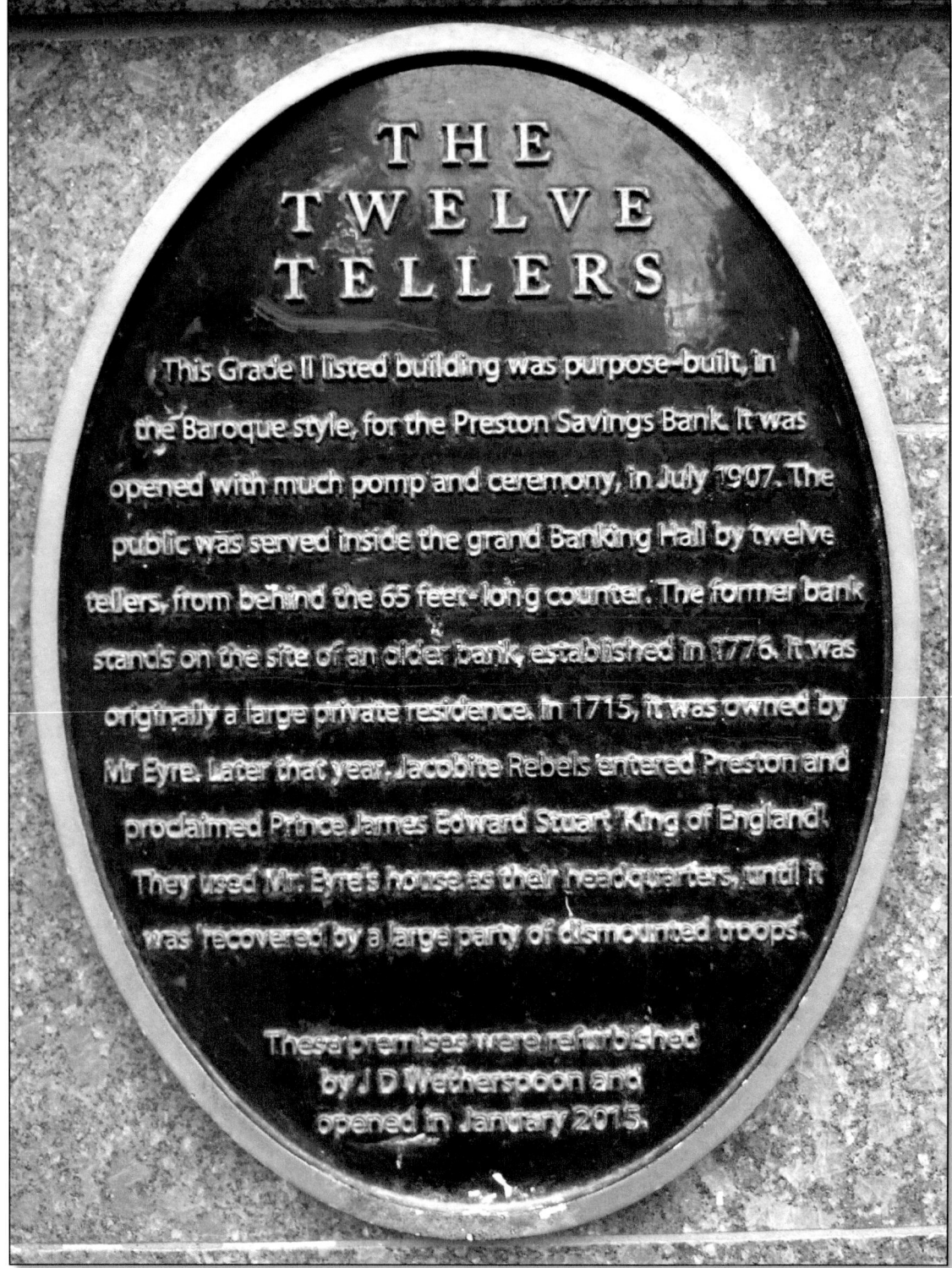

Plaque on The Twelve Tellers pub, Preston. This is the only explicit public reference to the battle outside the museum. (Author's photo, 2019)

Appendix I

The Jacobite Army

1. The Scottish Infantry

The Earl of Strathmore's Battalion

Many men from this battalion had not even made it across the Forth on 10–11 October. These included its two commanding officers: Strathmore as Colonel and Lieutenant Colonel Walkinshaw of Barrowfield. According to Patten, 'This Regiment was not in Highland dress, as the others were'. It was probably a lowland battalion, therefore. It was made up of four companies, judging by the officers listed below and by the prisoner lists, though it is not known who was in overall command, presumably the senior captain, whoever he was. Unlike other units, all four companies remained more or less intact as recognisable forces at the time of the battle. This was only one of the few Jacobite units in which there were any attempts made at training and discipling the men.[1]

Table 27. Strathmore's Officers

Rank	Name	Parish of Origin
Captain	William Douglas	
Captain	William Miller	
Captain	John Screnger/Scrimson	
Captain	James Balfour	
Lieutenant	William Lyon	Glamis, Angus
Lieutenant	Alexander Murray	Thurso, Caithness
Lieutenant	Alexander Orrack	Burntisland, Fife
Lieutenant	John Barnes	Glamis, Angus
Ensign	Patrick Douglas	
Ensign	Hugh Ker	Perth
Ensign	Alexander MacGiven	

---

1 Scott, *Memoir*, p.51.

THE SECOND BATTLE OF PRESTON, 1715

Rank	Name	Parish of Origin
Ensign	Andrew Ramsey	Abbotshall, Fife
Ensign	Henry Ogilby	Forgan, Perth
Quartermaster	William Henderson	Dundee, Angus

Patten referred to William Miller as Major and thus infers he was in charge of the battalion. A summary of the rank and file:

Captain Douglas' Company (34 men)

Table 28. Parish/County of Origin

Name	Number
Aberdalgie, Perthshire	1
Airlie, Angus	5
Ardclach, Angus	1
Athlon, Angus	1
Brechin, Angus	3
Crail, Fife	1
Curs, Perth	1
Essich, Angus	1
Edinburgh, Midlothian	1
Fettercairn, Nairn	1
Forfar, Angus	1
Glamis, Angus	6
Kerriemuir, Angus	1
Kilmuir, Angus	3
Kinnaird, Angus	1
Montrose, Angus	1
Ollinder, Perth	1
South Queensferry, Midlothian	1
Strathallan, Angus	1
Tannadice, Angus	1
Trannent, Midlothian	1

Table 29. Occupations

Name	Number
Butcher	1
Gentleman	2
Labourer	18
Oilmaker	1

Name	Number
Pedlar	1
Sailor	1
Servant	1
Shoemaker	2
Smith	1
Tailor	3
Thatcher	1
Weaver	1
Yeoman	1

Captain Miller's Company (34 men)

Table 30. Parish/County of Origin

Name	Number
Aberdeen, Angus	1
Cawford, Angus	1
Duns, Angus	1
Essich, Angus	1
Fern, Angus	4
Forfar, Angus	11
Forford, Aberdeen	1
Forgan, Perth	1
Glamis, Angus	3
Kilmuir, Angus	2
Kilsyth, Edinburgh	1
Kinnaird, Angus	1
Kinnettles, Angus	2
Rescobie, Angus	1
Seleaig, Ferris	1
St Andrew's, Aberdeen	1
Thurso, Caithness	1

Table 31. Occupations

Name	Number
Dyester	1
Gentleman	2
Labourer	12
Maltman	1
Servant	1

THE SECOND BATTLE OF PRESTON, 1715

Name	Number
Shoemaker	3
Smith	1
Tailor	3
Weaver	8
Yeoman	2

Captain Balfour's Company (35 men)

Table 32. Parish/County of Origin

Name	Number
Baronnie, Angus	1
Airlie, Angus	2
Brechin, Angus	1
Comrie, Fife	1
Essich, Angus	1
Eleck, Angus	1
Falkland, Fife	1
Farnell, Angus	1
Fern, Angus	1
Forfar, Angus	1
Glamis, Angus	20
Glasgow, Lanark	1
Kilmuir, Angus	2
Kinnaird, Angus	1

Table 33. Occupations

Name	Number
Dyester	1
Joiner	1
Labourer	19
Linner	1
Quarryman	1
Servant	1
Tailor	3
Weaver	8

Captain Scrimson/Scrimshaw's Company (33 men)

Table 34. Parish/County of Origin

Name	Number
Airlie, Angus	4
Atholl, Angus	1
Brechin, Angus	1
Cupar, Angus	1
Essich, Angus	1
Fernell, Perthshire	1
Glamis, Angus	8
Kerrimuir, Angus	1
Kilmuir, Angus	11
Kilsyth, Angus	1
Kingoldrum, Angus	1
Tannadice, Angus	2

Table 35. Occupations

Name	Number
Brewer	1
Joiner	5
Labourer	13
Merchant	1
Miller	2
Shoemaker	2
Slater	1
Smith	1
Tailor	2
Weaver	5

Company Unspecified (2)

Table 36. Parish/County of Origin

Name	Number
Gentlemen	1
Servant	1

Table 37. Occupations

Name	Number
Dalkeith, Midlothian	1
Canongate, Edinburgh	1

The regiment was mostly recruited from Angus (especially from Glamis) and Perthshire to a lesser extent and the majority of rank and file had been labourers prior to being involved in the campaign as foot soldiers.

Total strength: 14 officers and 138 men (total 152). Source: TNA: KB8/66, Baga de Secretis.

Earl of Mar's Battalion

Again, only part of the unit successfully crossed the Forth and only one company was recognisable as a formed unit by the time of the battle (down from four). Major Nathaniel Forbes was in command and Patten described him thus: 'a Man singularly brave, of pleasant discourse, mixing the Thread thereof with a great many Scots Proverbs, which were very well apply'd and gave great Entertainment to those that were acquainted with that Dialect. He was very strong'. The officers at Preston were as follows:

Table 38. Mar's Officers. Source: Patten, *History*, pp.43, 122.

Rank	Name
Major	Nathaniel Forbes
Captain	John James
Captain	Donald Ferguson of Tullich, Aberdeen
Captain	John Gordon of Migvie, Aberdeen
Lieutenant	John Cattanach
Lieutenant	Henry Lamsden
Lieutenant	Robert Gordon

Forbes' Company (31 men)

Table 39. Parish/County of Origin

Name	Number
Achundoir, Aberdeen	1
Benverough, Aberdeen	1
Coldstone, Aberdeen	1
Glenbuchet, Aberdeen	2
Kalkirk, Caithness	1
Kildrummy, Aberdeen	10
Logie, Aberdeen	2
Migvie, Aberdeen	1
Strathdon, Aberdeen	8
Towie, Aberdeen	4

THE JACOBITE ARMY

Table 40. Occupations

Name	Number
Barber	1
Farmer	1
Labourer	27
Miller	1
Yeoman	1

Innes' Company (3 men)

Table 41. Parish of Origin

Parish	Number
Tenvey, Aberdeen	1
Strathdon, Aberdeen	2

Table 42. Occupations

Occupation	Number
Labourer	1
Servant	2

The majority of the rank and file were from Aberdeenshire, especially from Kildrummie, and had been labourers in civil life.

Total strength: 7 officers and 34 men (41).[2]

Logie Drummond's Battalion

Logie Drummond's regiment seems to have been reduced to a handful by 12 November, presumably most deserted prior to the march into Cumberland, and were composed of the following officers:

Table 43. Drummond's Officers

Rank	Name
Captain	David Drummond
Captain	John Carnagy
Captain	Alexander MacGrudder
Lieutenant/Captain	James Drummond
Captain	Alexander Drummond

---

2 TNA: KB8/66, Baga de Secretis.

Rank	Name
Lieutenant	Archbald MacLachlan
Lieutenant	William Grudder

As noted, MacGrudder had transferred to Nairn's battalion. And there were two men, a gentleman and a labourer, both from Perthshire.

Total strength: 7 officers and 2 men (9).

Lord Nairn's Regiment

Nairn was a brother of the Duke of Atholl, but on marrying a Scottish heiress, changed his title to hers. According to Patten, 'He is a gentleman well belov'd in his country, and by all that had the advantage to be acquainted with him: He had been formerly at Sea and gave signal Instances of his Bravery: He was a mighty Stickler against the Union'. Another commentator noted that he was 'no souldier [but] was very honest'.[3] Sinclair wrote that Major Nairn was 'ane alerte young fellow, who had been ane officer of the armie' and had been appointed because he was a friend of the colonel.[4] At his trial it was noted that he had had considerable military experience and there was a reference to his 'disciplining the rebels on their march', so this regiment had some rudimentary training at least.[5]

It may have begun with eight companies, judging by the eight company officers, but there were only three remaining by the time of the battle. The officers were as follows:

Table 44. Nairn's Officers

Rank	Name	Parish of Origin
Colonel	Lord Nairn	
Lieutenant Colonel	John Stuart	Fortingall, Perth
Major	John Blair	
Captain	Alexander Robertson	Logierait, Perth
Captain	James Stuart	Blair, Perth
Captain	James Robertson	
Captain	John Stuart	Logierait, Perth
Captain	Robert Stuart	Commor, Perth
Captain	John Nairn	
Lieutenant/Captain	Archibald Butler	
Lieutenant	James Ramsay	

---

3 BC: 45/12/77, account of the Jacobite southern army to Preston.
4 Scott, *Memoirs*, p.129.
5 Anon., *Faithful Register*, p.22.

Rank	Name	Parish of Origin
Lieutenant	Malcolm Stewart	
Lieutenant	Alexander Ferguson	
Lieutenant	John Stewart	
Lieutenant	Donald Robertson	
Lieutenant	John Stewart	
Lieutenant	Robert Menzies	
Lieutenant	John Cunison	
Lieutenant	James Robertson	
Lieutenant	Gilbert Reid	
Ensign	John MacDonald	Fortingall, Perth
Ensign?	Finlay Ferguson	
Ensign?	Robert Ferguson	
Ensign?	Robert Robertson	
Ensign?	James Ferguson	Moulin, Perth
Ensign?	Alexander Stewart	Moulin, Perth
Ensign?	Archibald Menzies	Dull, Perth (Gruther's)
Ensign?	Robert Stewart	Perth (Stewart's)
Ensign?	John Stewart	

The rank and file were as follows:

Captain Robertson's Company (38 men)
It is not known whether this was Captain James Robertson or Captain Alexander Robertson.

Table 45. Parish/County of Origin

Name	Number
Blair, Perth	19
Fortingall, Perth	3
Kennoway, Fife	1
Logierait, Perth	5
Moulin, Perth	10

Table 46. Occupations

Name	Number
Gentleman	4
Labourer	32
Servant	2

Captain Stuart's Company (70 men)

It is not known if this is Captain Robert Stuart, Captain John Stuart or Captain James Stuart; it may well have been Lieutenant Colonel John Stuart's company.

Table 47. Parish/County of Origin

Name	Number
Belnwither, Perth	8
Blair, Perth	1
Comrie, Perth	1
Dores, Perth	1
Dull, Perth	32
Fortingall, Perth	1
Logierait, Perth	23
Moulin, Perth	1
New Church, Edinburgh	1
Unknown, Perth	1

Table 48. Occupations

Name	Number
Gentleman	4
Labourer	62
Servant	3
Writer	1

Captain MacGruther (10 men)

This officer does not appear on Patten's list of Nairn's battalion's officers, but there was a Captain Alexander McGrudder in Logie Drummond's battalion, so perhaps this company had been transferred to Nairn's battalion.

Table 49. Parish/County of Origin

Parish	Number
Comrie, Perthshire	10

Table 50. Occupations

Name	Number
Labourer	10

Company Unspecified (31 men)

Table 51. Parish/County of Origin

Name	Number
Labourer	10

Table 52. Occupations

Name	Number
Butcher	1
Gentleman	3
Labourer	7
Servant	8
Surgeon	12

Total strength: 29 officers and 149 men (178). Almost all the men were from Perthshire, especially from Dull, Logierait and Blair. The majority were labourers.[6]

Charles Murray's Regiment

Lord Murray was the younger son of the Duke of Atholl and a neighbour of Lord Nairn. Unlike many Jacobite officers, he had served in the British army as a cavalry cornet. According to Patten, he:

> … had gained a mighty good character for his Bravery, even Temper and graceful deportment. Upon all the marches, he could never be prevailed with to ride, but kept at the head of his Regiment on Foot, in his Highland dress without Breeches, He would scarce accept of a Horse to cross a River, which his men in the Season of the Year forded above mid-thigh deep in water. This powerfully gained him the Affection of his Men … he was singularly brave.[7]

The officers were:[8]

Table 53. Murray's Officers

Rank	Name	Parish of Origin
Colonel	Lord Charles Murray	Falkland, Fife
Lieutenant Colonel	Master of Nairn	
Major	James Stuart	

---

6 TNA: KB8/66, Baga de Secretis.
7 Patten, *History*, p.44.
8 Patten, *History*, p.122.

Rank	Name	Parish of Origin
Captain	James Mineries/Menzies	
Captain	Alexander Mineries/Menzies	
Captain	Donald Robertson	Blair, Perth
Captain	John Robertson	Little Dunkeld, Perth
Captain	Patrick Robertson	Logierait, Perth
Lieutenant	Alexander Mineries/Menzies	
Lieutenant	Adam Reid	
Lieutenant	John McKevan	
Lieutenant	John Cameron	Dull, Perth
Lieutenant	John Robertson	Little Dunkeld, Perth (Robertson's)
Lieutenant	Duncan Campbell	Weemyss, Perth
Lieutenant	John Stuart	Logierait, Perth
Lieutenant	John Ratson	Dunkeld, Perth
Lieutenant	Alexander Stuart	
Lieutenant	John Robson	
Lieutenant	James Ratson	
Lieutenant	John Stuart	
Ensign?	John Stuart	
Ensign?	James Stuart	
Ensign?	John Cummings	
Ensign?	John Robertson	
Ensign	James Robertson	
Ensign?	Donald MacDonald	Fortingall, Perth (Menzies')

The men may have been organised into eight companies, but only three existed in any number by 12 November.

A summary of the rank and file:

Captain Stewart's Company (9 men)
This individual was probably Major James Stuart.

Table 54. Parish/County of Origin

Name	Number
Balquhidder, Perth	1
Comrie, Perth	2
Logierait, Perth	4
Moulin, Perth	2

Table 55. Occupation

Name	Number
Labourer	9

Captain Robertson's Company (25 men)

This man could have been Captain Donald Robertson, Captain John Robertson or Captain Patrick Robertson.

Table 56. Parish/County of Origin

Name	Number
Blair Atholl, Perth	1
Denby, Perth	1
Denleigh, Perth	7
Dull, Perth	1
Little Dunkeld, Perth	6
Logierait, Perth	9

Table 57. Occupations

Name	Number
Labourer	25

Captain Menzies' Company (37 men)

This could have been the command of either Captain James Menzies or Captain Alexander Menzies but is probably two companies which cannot be differentiated.

Table 58. Parish/County of Origin

Name	Number
Alvie, Inverness	1
Avendow, Perth	1
Fortingall, Perth	34
Madderty, Perth	1

Table 59. Occupation

Name	Number
Gentleman	1
Labourer	34
Servant	1
Yeoman	1

Company Unspecified (8 men)

Table 60. Parish/County of Origin

Name	Number
Dull, Perth	1
Dunkeld, Perth	1
Edinburgh, Midlothian	1
Logierait, Perth	2
Unknown	3

Table 61. Occupations

Name	Number
Gentleman	3
Farmer	1
Servant	4

Total strength: 22 officers and 79 men (101). As with Nairn's battalion, the majority of the men were from Perthshire and from the parishes of Fortingall and Logierait. As with the others in the army labourers made up most of the rank and file.[9]

Mackintosh's Battalion

The clan Mackintosh was the only clan regiment to cross the Forth and it did so almost intact. The clan included many followers, including the MacPhersons, the Farquharsons, the MacGillivrays, Shaws, MacBeans and MacQueans.

Its lieutenant colonel, according to Patten, was 'a Gentleman that few People expected in the Rebellion, having always appeared on the other side; but the persuasions of the Brigadier prevailed with him. He is a handsome brave young Gentleman, of a very considerable Interest in his own Country; for he can bring into the Field upon any occasion 1000 stout, hardy, and well-armed Men'.

In theory there were 13 companies, but at the time of the battle this was reduced to 12.[10]

Table 62. Mackintosh's Officers (52 men)

Rank	Name	Parish of Origin
Colonel	William Mackintosh	
Lieutenant Col.	Ferguson of Invercall	
Major	John Mackintosh	

---

9 TNA: KB8/66, Baga de Secretis.
10 Patten, *History*, pp.45–46, 120–121.

Rank	Name	Parish of Origin
Senior Captain	Lachlan Mackintosh	
Captain	Farquhar McGillivray	
Captain	Angus MacBean	Dores, Inverness
Captain	Robert Shaw	
Captain	Duncomb Mackintosh	
Captain	William Mackintosh	Dunlichity, Inverness
Captain	Angus Mackintosh	
Captain	Lachlan Mackintosh, junior	
Captain	Francis Farquharson of Whithouse	
Captain	Laughlan MacLean	
Captain	Fergus MacBean	
Captain	Fergus Mackintosh	
Captain	John Casseron	
Captain	William MacGillivray	Alvie, Inverness
Lieutenant	William MacGillivray	Dunlichity, Inverness
Lieutenant?	John Farquharson of Kirktoun	
Lieutenant	John Mackintosh	Inverness, Inverness
Lieutenant	Farquhar MacGillivray	
Lieutenant	John MacBean	Ormiston, Inverness
Lieutenant	Angus Shaw	
Lieutenant	Benjamin Mackintosh	
Lieutenant	James Mackintosh	
Lieutenant	William Maquin	Petty, Inverness
Lieutenant	John Mackintosh	
Lieutenant	Duncan Mackintosh	
Lieutenant	John Abercromby	
Lieutenant and ADC	Skeen	
Lieutenant	David Stuart	Forress, Murray
Lieutenant	William Mackintosh	
Lieutenant	Donald Mackintosh	Damarry, Inverness
Lieutenant	Fergus Shaw	
Ensign	Patrick Mackintosh	
Ensign	Duncan Mackintosh	Dunlichity, Inverness
Ensign	Allen MacLean	
Ensign	James Mackintosh	

Rank	Name	Parish of Origin
Ensign	William McGillivray	
Ensign	Hugh Fraser	
Ensign	Daniel Shaw	
Ensign	John Mackintosh	
Ensign	Duncan MacQueen	
Ensign	Lachlan Mackintosh	Inverness
Ensign	Paul MacShaile	
Ensign	William Nail	
Ensign	John Dunbar	
Ensign	Colin Falmouth	
ADC	John Mackintosh	
Adjutant	Daniel Grant	
Paymaster	David MacQuean	
Quartermaster	William Shaw	Dunlichity, Inverness

Clearly Skeen and David Stuart had transferred from the Gentlemen Volunteers to Mackintosh's battalion between Kelso and Preston. Of the 13 companies existing in October, 11 still existed the next month but two did not (Francis Farquhar and one of the Lachlan MacKintosh's) and another had been created: Colonel Mackintosh's.

Colonel Mackintosh's Company (23 men)

Table 63. Parish/County of Origin

Name	Number
Alvie, Inverness	5
Argrave, Argyllshire	1
Croy, Inverness	2
Dores, Inverness	1
Dunlichty, Inverness	1
Glengarry, Inverness	1
Inverness	7
Killean, Argyllshire	1
Laggan, Inverness	2
Owhurst, Inverness	1
Royeld, Inverness	1

Table 64. Occupation

Name	Number
Gentleman	3
Labourer	17
Miller	1
Shoemaker	2

Lieutenant Colonel Farquharson's Company (11 men)

Table 65. Parish/County of Origin

Name	Number
Coldstone, Aberdeen	6
Craithie, Aberdeen	2
Glengairn, Aberdeen	2
Tullich, Aberdeen	1

Table 66. Occupations

Name	Number
Gentleman	1
Yeoman	9
Weaver	1

Major Mackintosh's Company (14 men)

Table 67. Parish/County of Origin

Name	Number
Alvie, Inverness	4
Ardclach, Inverness	1
Cromdale, Inverness	1
Croy, Inverness	1
Daviot, Inverness	1
Dunlichity, Inverness	1
Inverness	1
Kingussie, Inverness	1
Moy, Inverness	3

Table 68. Occupations

Name	Number
Gentleman	1
Labourer	1

Name	Number
Servant	1
Yeoman	11

Lachlan Mackintosh's Company (18 men)

Table 69. Parish/County of Origin

Name	Number
Alvie, Inverness	4
Damarry, Inverness	1
Dunlichity, Inverness	1
Insch, Inverness	1
Laggan, Inverness	11
Petty, Inverness	1

Table 70. Occupations

Name	Number
Gentleman	8
Miller	1
Yeoman	10

Fergus MacGillivray's Company (40 men)

Table 71. Parish/County of Origin

Name	Number
Daviot, Inverness	4
Duirinish, Inverness	6
Dores, Inverness	1
Dunlichity, Inverness	27
Inverness, Inverness	1
Tullich, Aberdeen	1

Table 72. Occupations

Name	Number
Gentleman	4
Labourer	4
Tailor	1
Yeoman	31

Captain Angus MacBean's Company (15 men)

Table 73. Parish/County of Origin

Name	Number
Croy, Inverness	1
Daviot, Inverness	2
Dores, Inverness	10
Kingussie, Inverness	1
Moy, Inverness	1

Table 74. Occupations

Name	Number
Gentleman	3
Labourer	1
Yeoman	11

Robert Shaw's Company (23 men)

Table 75. Parish/County of Origin

Name	Number
Alvie, Inverness	6
Croy, Inverness	3
Daviot, Inverness	1
Dores, Inverness	1
Dunlichity, Inverness	8
Insch, Inverness	1
Inverness	2
Moy, Inverness	1

Table 76. Occupations

Name	Number
Gentleman	3
Miller	1
Tailor	2
Volunteer	1
Yeoman	16

Duncomb Mackintosh's Company (13 men)

Table 77. Parish/County of Origin

Name	Number
Alvie, Inverness	6
Croy, Inverness	1
Dores, Inverness	1
Inverness	1
Inverrain, Inverness	1
Kingussie, Inverness	3

Table 78. Occupations

Name	Number
Gentleman	1
Volunteer	3
Yeoman	9

Captain William Mackintosh (13 men)

Table 79. Parish/County of Origin

Name	Number
Gentleman	8
Miller	1
Yeoman	10

Table 80. Occupations

Name	Number
Volunteer	1
Yeoman	12

Angus Mackintosh's Company (43 men)

Table 81. Parish/County of Origin

Name	Number
Alvie, Inverness	1
Duirinish, Inverness	28
Dunlichity, Inverness	3
Inverness, Inverness	5
Kingussie, Inverness	1
Moy, Inverness	5

Table 82. Occupations

Name	Number
Gentleman	2
Tailor	1
Wright	1
Yeoman	39

James MacQueen's Company (10 men)

Table 83. Parish/County of Origin

Name	Number
Alvie, Inverness	1
Dalrossie, Inverness	1
Dalamoy, Inverness	1
Moy, Inverness	4
Petty, Inverness	2
Nairn, Inverness	1

Table 84. Occupations

Name	Number
Farmer	2
Labourer	2
Gentleman	5
Servant	1

Captain Lachlan MacLean (7 men)

Table 85. Parish/County of Origin

Name	Number
Chapel of Garioch, Aberdeen	1
Dalkeith, Midlothian	1
Dunfermline, Fife	1
Dunkeld, Perth	1
Fores, Inverness	1
Tarbat, Ross	1
Wick, Caithness	1

Table 86. Occupations

Name	Number
Gentleman	3
Goldsmith	1
Labourer	1
Pedlar	1
Tailor	1

Company Unspecified (18 men)

Table 87. Parish/County of Origin

Name	Number
Alury, Inverness	1
Croy, Inverness	2
Dores, Inverness	1
Dunlichity, Inverness	1
Edinburgh, Midlothian	1
Inverness	1
Moy, Inverness	7
Mussleburgh, Lothian	1
Petty, Inverness	1
Unknown, Inverness	2

Table 88. Occupations

Occupation	Number
Farmer	1
Fiddler	1
Gentleman	2
Labourer	1
Painter	1
Servant	4
Surgeon	1
Tailor	1
Yeoman	6

Total strength: 52 officers and 249 men (301). The majority of the men were from a few parishes in Inverness-shire: Moy, Duirinish and Dunlichity. Most were farming men: yeoman and labourers.[11]

---

11 TNA: KB8/66, Baga de Secretis.

2. Cavalry

There were numerous small troops of horsemen, mostly from the Lowlands and the north of England.

English Cavalry

There were five troops of English cavalry at Kelso, but these were subsequently added to.

Derwentwater's Troop

John Shaftoe, gentleman, was captain and he was joint commander with Charles Radcliffe, Derwentwater's younger brother. Richard Stokoe, a Protestant from Northumberland, was the quartermaster. He had served in Portmore's dragoons during Anne's reign.[12]

Table 89. Parish/County of Origin

Name	Number
Allingham, Northumberland	1
Chollerton, Northumberland	1
Corbridge, Northumberland	2
Holy Island, Northumberland	3
Kirkham, Lancashire	1
Kirkwhelpington, Northumberland	1
Leeds, Yorkshire	1
Marske, Yorkshire	1
Newcastle, Northumberland	1
Ryton, Durham	1
Unknown	1
Wetheral, Cumberland	1
Whittingham, Northumberland	5
Unknown, Northumberland	2

Table 90. Occupations[13]

Name	Number
Cobbler	1
Gentlemen	3
Groom	1
Innkeeper	1

---

12 Patten, *History*, pp. 47, 114.
13 TNA: KB8/66, Baga de Secretis.

THE SECOND BATTLE OF PRESTON, 1715

Name	Number
Labourer	2
Servant	10
Shoemaker	2
Smith	1
Whitener	1

Total strength: 22.

Widdrington's Troop

These men were commanded by Thomas Errington, 'a gentleman of a very ancient family in Northumberland' and 'formerly an officer in the French service, where he had got the reputation of a good Soldier'. Henry Widdrington, labelled as 'quartermaster', was probably another officer.[14]

Table 91. Parish/County of Origin

Name	Number
Beaufront, Northumberland	1
Hartburn, Northumberland	3
Holy Island, Northumberland	1
Northumberland other	1
Wetheral, Cumberland	2
Woodhorn, Northumberland	11
St John's, Northumberland	1

Table 92. Occupations

Name	Number
Carpenter	1
Coachman	1
Gentleman	2
Servant	15
Weaver	1

Total strength: one officer and 19 men; mostly servants from Northumberland (20 total).[15]

Hunter's Troop

John Hunter, a gentleman born in North Tyne in Northumberland, was captain. Although he had been commissioned at the end of Queen Anne's reign to raise a company, apparently he had never received any pay nor had he enlisted any men. According to Patten, 'He was famous for running

---

14　Patten, *History*, p.48.
15　TNA: KB8/66, *Baga de Secretis*.

uncustomed goods out of Scotland into England. He behav'd with great vigour and obstinacy'.[16]

Table 93. Parish/County of Origin

Name	Number
All Saints, Durham	1
Bellingham, Northumberland	1
Bowle, Northumberland	1
Bywell, Northumberland	1
Chester le Street, Durham	1
Hartburn, Northumberland	6
Hexham, Northumberland	3
Kirkandrew, Cumberland	1
Kirkwhelpington, Northumberland	1
Newburn, Northumberland	2
St Giles, London	1
Tinford, Waterford	1
Whittingham, Northumberland	1
Witham, Durham	1

Table 94. Occupations

Name	Number
Carpenter	1
Chandler	1
Cooper	1
Distiller	1
Farmer	2
Gentleman	4
Mason	2
Servant	7
Smith	2
Weaver	2

Total strength: 23; mostly servants from Northumberland.[17]

---

16 Patten, *History*, p.49.
17 TNA: KB8/66, Baga de Secretis.

Douglas' Troop

Robert Douglas, brother to the Scottish laird of Finland, was captain. According to Patten, 'He was indefatigable in Searching for Arms and Horses, a trade, some were pleased to say, he had follow'd out of the Rebellion as well as in it. He was also very Vigorous in the Action'.[18]

Table 95. Parish/County of Origin

Name	Number
Aberlady, East Lothian	1
Airth, Stirling	1
Alnwick, Northumberland	1
All Saints, Northumberland	1
Hexhamshire, Durham	1
Bellingham, Northumberland	1
Bolam, Northumberland	2
Cumbernaud, Dumbarton	1
Elvet, Durham	1
Fromgate, Durham	1
Gretna, Annandale	1
Haddington, East Lothian	1
Hartburn, Northumberland	1
Hexham, Northumberland	1
Liberton, Midlothian	1
Morpeth, Northumberland	1
Newcastle, Northumberland	2
Ryton, Durham	1
Selkirk, Ferris	1
Shields, Northumberland	1
St Corbells, Cumberland	1
Wetherkirk, Ashdale	1
Unknown, Durham	1
Unknown	1

Table 96. Occupations

Name	Number
Brazier	1
Farmer	2
Gentleman	2

---

18   Patten, *History*, p.49.

Name	Number
Glover	1
Innkeeper	1
Labourer	3
Merchant	1
Servant	5
Shoemaker	1
Skinner	3
Unknown	1
Waterman	1
Weaver	3
Wigmaker	1

Total strength: one officer (Douglas) and 25 men (26). The majority of the men were from Northumberland and the Scottish borders; unlike the Scottish units, the men came from a more diverse range of professions, with servants predominating.

Wogan's Troop

Nicholas Wogan was an Irish gentleman, though his family had its roots in Wales. According to Patten, 'He a Gentleman of a most generous Mind, and a great deal of Bravery, unwearied to forward the good of his Cause'. He was one of the first to support the Jacobite cause in Northumberland.[19]

Table 97. Parish/County of Origin

Name	Number
Alingston, Northumberland	1
Allingham, Northumberland	1
Ancroft, Northumberland	1
Ayton, Berwick	1
Durham	1
Hartburn, Northumberland	2
Hexham, Northumberland	3
Holy Island, Northumberland	5
Norham, Northumberland	1
Stadhouse, Yorkshire	1
Stanfordham, Northumberland	1
Ireland	1
Wetheral, Cumberland	3
Whetham, Cumberland	1

---

19 Patten, *History*, p.50.

Name	Number
Whittingham, Northumberland	4
Woodhorn, Northumberland	3

Table 98. Occupations

Name	Number
Butcher	1
Carpenter	2
Farmer	1
Gardener	1
Gentleman	2
Labourer	4
Mason	2
Quartermaster	1
Servant	12
Smith	1
Tailor	1
Weaver	1
Unknown	1

Total strength: two officers (including Wogan) and 28 men (30).[20]

Lowland Cavalry

Kenmure's Troop

This was the designated the first troop of Scottish Jacobite cavalry and Basil Hamilton was troop commander.

Table 99. Parish/County of Origin

Name	Number
Abbotshall, Fife	1
Baldoon	1
Colwen, Kirkcudbright	1
Edinburgh, Midlothian	2
Eleth, Perthshire	1
Garvock, Kinneran	1
Gretna, Annandale	1
Lonmay, Aberdeen	1

---

20 TNA: KB8/66, Baga de Secretis.

Name	Number
Rothwell, Annandale	1
Roxburgh, Tinedill	1
Unstated	6

Table 100. Occupations

Name	Number
Gentleman	4
Groom	1
Merchant	1
Servant	7
Surgeon	1
Weaver	1
Writer	2

Total strength: 17.

Hume's Troop

This was the Merse Troop, led by the Hon. James Hume, the Earl of Hume's brother, 'This Youth is of a good Temper, but not very Capable of having the Command of a Troop, as well on account of his Age, as other Incapacities.'[21]

Table 101. Parish/County of Origin

Parish	Number
Ayton, Berwickshire	6
Braile, Berwickshire	1
Chirnside, Berwickshire	1
Coldingham, Berwickshire	2
Coldstream, Berwickshire	1
Duns, Berwickshire	3
Eccles, Berwickshire	1
Edram, Berwickshire	1
Fouga, Merse	1
Hollam, Tinedale	1
Landell, Berwickshire	2
Unknown	2

---

21 Patten, *History*, p.39.

Table 102. Occupations

Occupation	Number
Gentleman	12
Labourer	1
Servant	9

Total: 22.[22]

Winton's Troop

This was the third troop and was led by Winton personally.

Table 103. Parish/County of Origin

Name	Number
Aberlemno, East Lothian	1
Airth, Stirling	1
Alloa, Stirling	1
Bothkennar, Stirling	1
Corrin, Linlithgow	1
Cupar, Fife	1
Edinburgh, Midlothian	4
Falkirk, Stirling	1
Gladsmuir, East Lothian	2
Glanton	1
Hoddom, Annandale	1
Pencaitland, East Lothian	1
Raveltig	1
Tranent, East Lothian	5
Uphall, Linlithgow	1
Unknown	11

Table 104. Occupations

Name	Number
Baker	1
Farmer	4
Gentleman/nobility	8
Innkeeper	2
Labourer	2
Mason	1

---

22 TNA: KB8/66, Baga de Secretis.

THE JACOBITE ARMY

Name	Number
Merchant	1
Servant	13
Shoemaker	1
Surgeon	1

Total strength: 34.[23]

Carnwath's Troop

Led by Carnwath's uncle, James Dalziel, 'This Gentleman has a very good Character, and gave sufficient Demonstrations of his Affections to the Pretender's Interest, by his Courage and Conduct'.[24] It comprised three commands, one led by James Dalziel, one by Captain Basil Hamilton and another by a Captain Askin.

Table 105. Parish/County of Origin

Name	Number
Artheret, Cumberland	1
Falkirk, Stirlingshire	1
Hoddom, Annandale	1
Kirkpatrick, Annandale	1
Lauder, Berwickshire	1
Morpeth, Annandale	1
St. Mungo's, Annandale	1
Wamphray, Annandale	2
Whickham, Cumberland	1
Unknown	6

Table 106. Occupations

Name	Number
Gentleman	11
Servant	5

Total strength: two officers (Hamilton and Dalziel) and 14 men (16).[25]

Lockhart's Troop

Captain Philip Lockhart was a half pay officer of Lord Mark Kerr's regiment and brother to Lord Carnwath. This troop was raised by Lockhart's brother's interest and included some of Carnwath's servants. One Mr Lamb was quartermaster and a Mr Auxton, an Edinburgh merchant, paid the men.

---

23 TNA: KB8/66, Baga de Secretis.
24 Patten, *History*, p.41.
25 TNA, KB8/66, Baga de Secretis.

According to Patten, 'He was a Young Gentleman of a comely Appearance, and very handsome. He gave several Instances of his Bravery'.[26]

Table 107. Parish/County of Origin

Parish	Number
Chidgehall, Dumfries	1
Coldstream, Berwick	1
College Church, Midlothian	1
Crail, Fife	1
Durse, Chidgehall	1
Edinburgh, Midlothian	1
Inverness	1
Lasswade, Midlothian	1
Liberton, Midlothian	1
Nether Canshire, Nairn	1
Trowchurch, Midlothian	2
Unknown	2
Westwood, Midlothian	2

Table 108. Occupations

Occupation	Number
Farmer	1
Gentleman	3
Mason	1
Merchant	1
Servant	6
Smith	1
Tailor	1
Wigmaker	1
Writer	1

Strength: 16.[27]

Gentlemen Volunteers (39 men)

Patten wrote 'there were a great many Gentlemen Volunteers who were not formed into any Troop'.[28] These were led by Captains MacLean and Skeen, Lieutenant David Stuart and Ensign John Stuart, once an exciseman, were this company's officers in October but as noted above, by November, Skeen and David Stuart had joined Mackintosh's battalion as ADC and Lieutenant.

---

26 Patten, *History*, p.41.
27 TNA: KB8/66, Baga de Secretis.
28 Patten, *History*, p.42.

It is presumed that these men had their own horses.

Table 109. Parish/County of Origin

Parish	Number
Unknown parish, Northumberland	1
Airth, Stirling	1
Ancrum, Roxburgh	4
Biggar, Lanark	1
Davich, Roxburgh	1
Edinburgh, Midlothian	9
Fogo, Berwick	2
Fyvie, Aberdeen	1
Hawick, Roxburgh	3
Hinton, Roxburgh	1
Holnain, Roxburgh	1
Jedburgh, Roxburgh	1
Kirkpatrick, Annandale	2
Lendell, Roxburgh	1
Linton, Roxburgh	1
Migvie, Aberdeen	1
Moneburgh, Aberdeen	1
Peterhead, Aberdeen	2
Salaman, Stirling	1
Stepelgorton, Roxburgh	1
Torpichen	1
Unknown	2

Table 110. Occupations

Occupation	Number
Burgess	1
Freeholder	1
Gentleman	33
Merchant	2
Writer	1
Exciseman	1

Strength: two officers and 37 men.

However, apart from these Lowland and English troops, there were a number of others which went unmentioned by Patten, but which can be reconstructed using manuscript lists of prisoners.

Other Troops

Talbot's Troop (25 men)

Richard Talbot was listed as an 'Irish papist' by Patten and is probably the Robert Talbot from Ireland mentioned elsewhere, but his troop is not listed as being at Kelso by Patten. Yet another source lists that it was in existence at Morpeth before riding to Kelso and was composed of 25 men, who were disciplined by Talbot. James Talbot may have been the second officer.[29]

Table 111. Parish/County of Origin

Parish	Number
Corbridge, Northumberland	2
Garston, Lancashire	2
Hexham, Northumberland	2
Hoghton le Spring, Durham	1
Kirkalow, Clare	1
Newburgh, Northumberland	1
Ovingham, Northumberland	3
Ovington, Northumberland	1
Ryton, Durham	1
Simonburn, Northumberland	2
Stannington, Northumberland	3
Warden, Northumberland	1
Wemworth, Northumberland	1
Wetheral, Cumberland	2
Whetham, Cumberland	2

Table 112. Occupation

Occupation	Number
Butcher	1
Carpenter	1
Farmer	2
Feltmaker	1
Gardener	1
Gentleman	1
Labourer	1
Mason	1
Seaman	1
Servant	11

---

29 Anon., *Faithful Register*, p.259.

THE JACOBITE ARMY

Occupation	Number
Smith	3
Surgeon	1
Weaver	1

Strength: two officers and 24 men (26).[30]

Sawhill's Troop (18 men)

This troop was founded after the rendezvous at Kelso on 22 October. Their captain has not been identified.

Table 113. Parish/County of Origin

Parish	Number
Aldington, Northumberland	1
Aleneth, Northumberland	1
Allingham, Northumberland	1
Arbune, Northumberland	1
Bywell, Northumberland	1
Gutsford, Northumberland	1
Hartburn, Northumberland	3
Holy Island, Northumberland	2
Kirkwhelpington, Northumberland	1
Morpeth, Northumberland	2
Rotterdam	1
Ryton, Durham	2
Wetheral, Cumberland	1

Table 114. Occupations

Occupation	Number
Barber	1
Butcher	1
Carpenter	1
Farmer	2
Labourer	1
Mason	2
Servant	7
Skinner	1
Tailor	1
Weaver	1

---

30 TNA: KB8/66, Baga de Secretis.

Tindale Troop

This troop of Lowland horse was commanded by Captain Walter Scott of Wooler.

Table 115. Parish/County of Origin

Name	Number
Baronnie, Tindale	1
Gladsburgh, Tindale	2
Hige, Tindale	1
Linton, Tindale	1
Onernon, Tindale	1
Roxburgh, Tindale	3
Wooller, Tindale	1

Table 116. Occupations

Name	Number
Gentleman	2
Servant	8

Strength: 10.

Richard Towneley's Troop

There are various eyewitness statements about the numbers and arms borne by this troop. On Saturday 12 November 1715 he was 'with about 10 or 15 rebels most well armed who seemd to follow him and be commanded by him'. On the previous day he had 12 men 'with swords and guns, 4 of which the witness knew to be the prisoner's servants' and 'they were all well armed with sword and pistols and some of them had guns'. The men were on horseback: six on Towneley's coach horses.[31]

Table 117. Parish/County of Origin

Parish	Number
Burnley, Lancashire	13
Claughton, Lancashire	1
Padiham, Lancashire	1

Table 118. Occupations

Occupation	Number
Gentleman	2
Jersey comber	1

---

31 TNA, TS23/34, 1.

THE JACOBITE ARMY

Occupation	Number
Joiner	1
Labourer	2
Servant	4
Shoemaker	1
Smith	1
Weaver	3

Total Strength: 14 (plus Towneley), 15.[32]

John Dalton's Troop

All the troop, numbering about 20, were on horseback, 'which each man a sword, a musket and a case of pistols'. Dalton headed them, 'with a drawn sword in his hand, waving it about'.[33] They were presumably all from Lancashire. Nothing is known about the individual members.

Edward Tyldesley's Troop

According to Patten, Edward Tyldesley of the Lodge 'had a Troop and entered Preston at the Head of it' and Colonel Rapin later wrote 'he marched in that town att ye head of about 60 men, swords drawn, flying colours, for he had a standard (viz.) green damask with gold coloured fringe round with his crest on, being a pelican'.[34] However, Rapin was probably exaggerating; he was not there, after all. An eyewitness noted that the troop was armed 'In the like manner' to Dalton's, numbering 20 men.[35] As with Towneley there were a number of eyewitness statements about them, with various numbers: 20, 30 or 40, or 'about 60'. It was reported that 'Each man had a sword and musket or case of pistols'. All were on horseback and 'marched in ranks'.[36]

Some of those were as follows:

Table 119. Parish/County of Origin

Parish	Number
Broughton, Lancashire	2
Heversham, Westmorland	1
Lancaster	1

---

32 TNA: FEC1/1585, Towneley and Tyldesley.
33 TNA: FEC1/1585, Towneley and Tyldesley.
34 Patten, *History*, p.116; TNA: SP35/5, f.156v, Rapin–unknown, 13 June 1716.
35 TNA: FEC1/1585, Towneley and Tyldesley.
36 TNA, TS23/34, 1,2.

Table 120. Occupations

Occupation	Number
Farmer	1
Gentleman	2
Labourer	1

Total known strength, including Tyldesley: four, but numbers given in total were between 20 and 60; clearly most escaped before the surrender.[37]

Ingleby Thorp's Troop

Nothing is known about this troop except that one man was a tailor from Kirkham, Lancashire. Thorp was a Preston gentleman who escaped after the battle.

John Langdale's Troop

Nothing is known about this troop, except that one man was a gentleman from Lancaster.

One of the difficulties here is that not all men are designated as being part of a company or troop, but this does not mean to say that they were not part of one; of Towneley's men that we know about from an eyewitness before the battle, 11 were taken prisoner but for none is the name of their unit stated. Quite why this is, is another question, for presumably the men themselves would have known.

Then there are the men, whose regiment, company or troop, if they were ever assigned one, is unknown.

English Gentlemen

Surgeons are usually included with gentry, as are professionals.

Table 121. Parish/County of Origin

Name	Number
Aldborough, Yorkshire	1
Alwinton, Northumberland	3
Ashton, Lancashire	1
Alnwick, Northumberland	1
Bambrough, Northumberland	1
Bavington, Northumberland	1
Beetham, Westmorland	1
Bishopric, Durham	2
Bilbarrow, Lancashire	1

---

37 TNA, KB8/66, Baga de Secretis; FEC1/1585, Towneley and Tildesley.

Name	Number
Burn in Thornton, Lancashire	1
Bywell, Northumberland	2
Barton, Lancashire	1
Brockhall, Lancashire	2
Burnley, Lancashire	1
Doddington, Cambridgeshire	1
Caphalton, Northumberland	2
Chorleyhill, Yorkshire	1
Claughton, Lancashire	5
Croxteth, Lancashire	2
Cockrington, Northumberland	1
Corkram, Lancashire	1
Croston, Lancashire	2
Chorley, Lancashire	1
Congleton, Lancashire	1
Eccleston, Lancashire	1
Elsdon, Northumberland	1
Embleton, Northumberland	1
Felton, Northumberland	2
Framlington, Northumberland	1
Garstang, Lancashire	2
Gedding, Huntingdonshire	1
Glanton, Northumberland	1
Gray, Lancashire	1
Halton, Lancashire	6
Hexham, Northumberland	4
High Lee, Northumberland	1
Holy Island, Northumberland	1
Hothersall, Lancashire	1
Ireland	4
Kendal, Westmorland	1
Kirkwhelpington, Northumberland	1
Lancaster, Lancashire	2
Latham, Lancashire	3
Leighton, Lancashire	1
London	6
Lostock, Lancashire	2
Lyme, Cheshire	1

THE SECOND BATTLE OF PRESTON, 1715

Name	Number
Lugg	2
Littlewood, Lancashire	1
Leighton, Lancashire	1
Morland, Westmorland	1
Myhills, Lancashire	1
Myerscough, Lancashire	2
Nateby, Lancashire	4
Netherwitton, Northumberland	1
Newcastle, Northumberland	2
Norham, Durham	1
Otterburn, Northumberland	1
Ousby, Cumberland	1
Padiham, Lancashire	1
Pilling, Lancashire	1
Preston, Lancashire	22
Rawcliffe, Lancashire	3
Ribbleton, Lancashire	3
Rothbury, Northumberland	1
Samlesbury, Lancashire	1
Sandow, Northumberland	1
Scarisbrick, Lancashire	1
Shewley, Lancashire	2
Simonburn, Northumberland	2
Singleton, Lancashire	2
St. John's, Yorkshire	1
Standish, Lancashire	1
Sunderland, Durham	1
Stonecraft, Northumberland	1
Swinburn, Northumberland	1
Thurnham, Lancashire	2
Tone	1
Walton, Lancashire	2
Warden, Northumberland	1
Warkworth, Northumberland	2
Westby, Lancashire	1
Whitehaven, Cumberland	1
Whittingham, Northumberland	3`
Whitworth, Northumberland	1

Name	Number
Wigan, Lancashire	1
Whitton, Lancashire	1
Whitehill, Lancashire	2
Winder	1
Wooler, Northumberland	1
Unstated	13
Unstated Northumberland	5

Table 122. Occupations

Name	Number
Cornet	1
Esquire	11
Gentleman	163
Surgeon	4
Student	1
Upholsterer	1
Former officer	1

Total number: 181.

Other English Servants and Followers

Table 123. Parish/County of Origin

Name	Number
Aighton, Lancashire	1
Aldingham, Northumberland	4
Allingham, Northumberland	1
Alston Moor, Northumberland	1
Alston, Lancashire	3
Alwinton, Northumberland	1
Arenton, Derbyshire	1
Arkholme, Lancashire	1
Ashton, Lancashire	4
Barrow, Derbyshire	1
Barton, Lancashire	1
Bedale, Yorkshire	1
Bellingham, Northumberland	2
Biddlestone, Northumberland	2
Bilbarrow, Lancashire	4

THE SECOND BATTLE OF PRESTON, 1715

Name	Number
Blackburn, Lancashire	8
Bleasdale, Lancashire	3
Bralo, Lancashire	1
Brindle, Lancashire	5
Brockhall, Lancashire	2
Broughton, Lancashire	5
Burn in Thornton, Lancashire	2
Burnley, Lancashire	17
Bury, Lancashire	1
Cartmell, Lancashire	4
Cartmell, Northumberland	1
Catterall, Lancashire	2
Charwick, Lancashire	1
Chester le Street, Durham	1
Chippock, Lancashire	1
Chollerton, Northumberland	1
Chorley, Lancashire	2
Claughton, Lancashire	5
Clayton, Lancashire	1
Clifton, Yorkshire	1
Cold Park, Northumberland	2
Corbridge, Northumberland	8
Corkram, Lancashire	3
Corsenside, Northumberland	1
Croston, Lancashire	8
Cuerdale, Lancashire	4
Castle, Lancaster	1
Carleton, Yorkshire	1
Deane, Lancashire	1
Denton, Cumberland	1
Derby	2
Dornington, Northumberland	1
Ellingham, Northumberland	1
Elsdon, Northumberland	1
Elsham, Lancashire	1
Elston, Lancashire	2
Fishwick, Lancashire	3
Firfar	1

Name	Number
Fulwood, Lancashire	1
Garstang, Lancashire	1
Grimsargh, Lancashire	5
Habergham, Lancashire	1
Hartburn, Northumberland	3
Hexham, Northumberland	6
Holy Island, Northumberland	1
Ingell	1
Kirkby Lonsdale, Westmorland	1
Kirkham, Lancashire	4
Kirkwhelpington, Northumberland	1
Lancaster, Lancashire	9
Latham, Lancashire	2
Leigh, Cheshire	1
London	3
Lostock, Lancashire	1
Manchester, Lancashire	5
Maseo, Lancashire	1
St. Michael's on the Wyre, Lancashire	1
Middlewich, Cheshire	1
Mitton, Lancashire	1
Morpeth, Northumberland	1
Myerscough, Lancashire	12
Nateby, Lancashire	1
Nether Wyresdale, Lancashire	1
Newburgh, Northumberland	1
Newcastle, Northumberland	6
Newlett, Durham	1
Oakson, Cambridgeshire	1
Ollingston, Northumberland	1
Ormskirk, Lancashire	2
Ovingham, Northumberland	2
Pagaine, Lancaster	1
Pennington, Cumberland	1
Pleasington, Lancashire	1
Plumpton, Lancashire	1
Prestbury, Cheshire	1
Preston, Lancashire	23

THE SECOND BATTLE OF PRESTON, 1715

Name	Number
Ribbleton, Lancashire	5
Ribchester, Lancashire	2
Rothbury, Northumberland	6
Ryton, Durham	1
Salwick, Lancashire	1
Samlesbury, Lancashire	1
Scalford, Leicestershire	1
Scotforth, Lancashire	1
Sheffield, Yorkshire	1
Simonburn, Northumberland	3
Singleton, Lancashire	10
Sippon, Staffordshire	1
St John Lee, Northumberland	2
Standish, Lancashire	6
Stockport, Cheshire	1
Stonyhurst, Lancashire	3
Thornley, Lancashire	1
Thornbrush, Lancashire	1
Townley, Lancashire	1
Tweedmouth, Durham	1
Upper Wyresdale, Lancashire	1
Walton, Lancashire	39
Weeton, Lancashire	2
Westham, Lancashire	2
Wetheral, Cumberland	2
Whalley, Lancashire	1
Whicham, Durham	2
Whittingham, Lancashire	3
Whittingham, Northumberland	4
Widdrrington, Northumberland	1
Wigan, Lancashire	6
Winwick, Lancashire	1
Witherslack, Westmorland	1
Wooler, Northumberland	1
Woodhorn, Northumberland	4
Woodplumpton, Lancashire	1
Wyresdale, Lancashire	1
Unstated Northumberland	3

Name	Number
Unstated, Yorkshire	1
Unstated	64

Table 124. Occupations

Name	Number
Apothecary	1
Barber	2
Bricklayer	2
Blacksmith	1
Butcher	2
Carpenter	6
Carrier	1
Chapman	3
Collier	1
Collarmaker	1
Engraver	1
Farmer	9
Frazier	1
Glover	2
Groom	1
Hatter	2
Husbandman	80
Innholder	3
Ironmonger	1
Invalid	1
Jersey comber	2
Joiner	6
Labourer	11
Mason	1
Miller	2
Perriwigmaker	1
Piper	2
Saddler	1
Sailor	2
Servant	147
Ship builder	1
Shoemaker	6
Silk dyer	1

THE SECOND BATTLE OF PRESTON, 1715

Name	Number
Silversmith	1
Skinner	1
Smith	4
Storeman	1
Tailor	5
Waterman	1
Webster	8
Weaver	26
Whitener	2
Yeoman	26
Unstated	54

Total number: 434.

There were also two Irishmen, a yeoman from Sligo and a silk weaver from Carrindale, Tyrone.

Other Scottish Nobility and Gentry

Although the majority of Scots were members of a battalion or troop, a minority were not and they were differentiated by contemporary by social rank, as were the unregimented Englishmen.

Table 125. Parish/County of Origin

Name	Number
Airth, Stirling	1
Ayton, Berwick	2
Bedrule, Roxburgh	1
Bridge, Linlithgow	1
Carnwath, Lanark	1
Clackmannan, Clackmannan	1
Dumfries	1
Dundee	1
Dunlichity, Inverness	1
Edinburgh, Midlothian	13
Eyemouth, Berwick	2
Falkirk	1
Hawick, Roxburgh	1
Jedburgh, Roxburgh	3
Keith, Banffshire	1
Kincaird	1

Name	Number
Kirkmichael, Nithsdale	1
Rescobie, Angus	1
Rothes, Moray	1
Straiton, Ayshire	1
Strathnaver, Kirkcudbright	1
Wedderburn	2
Whitburn, West Lothian	1
Whitfield	2
Wooler	1
Winder	1
Unstated	47

Table 126. Occupations

Name	Number
Doctor	10
Gentleman	67
Excise officer	2
Innholder	1
Writer	2
Ex-Officer	1
Lieutenant	1
Merchant	4
Medical Student	1
Unstated	1

Total number: 90.

Other Scottish Servants and Followers

Table 127. Parish/County of Origin

Name	Number
Abercorn, Linlithgow	1
Airth, Stirling	1
Alvie, Inverness	3
Applegarth, Annandale	1
Ashkirk, Roxburgh	1
Athelstane, East Lothian	2
Berwick, East Lothian	1

THE SECOND BATTLE OF PRESTON, 1715

Name	Number
Canongate, Midlothian	1
Coldstream, Merse	1
College Church, Midlothian	1
Comrie, Perth	1
Conay, East Lothian	1
Craghton, Midlothian	1
Crichton, Midlothian	1
Cupar, Angus	1
Cupar, Stirling	1
Daton, Annandale	1
Dull, Perth	1
Dunlichity, Inverness	1
Dunstaffnage, Argyll	1
Eccles, Berwick	1
Edinburgh, Midlothian	3
Enstone, Perth	1
Fogo, Berwick	1
Glamis, Angus	1
Glasgow, Lanark	1
Greyfriars, Midlothian	1
Humbie, East Lothian	1
Kilsyth, Stirling	1
Kirkham, Tindill	1
Kirkmichael, Nithsdale	2
Lasswade, Midlothian	2
Longford, Tindill	1
Monteith, Stirling	1
Muswell, Northdill	1
Ormiston, East Lothian	1
Petty, Inverness	1
Simontown, Ayr/Lanark	1
Tenvey	2
Tindell, Nithsdale	1
Tranent, East Lothian	6
Truthware, Twidell	1
Ratho, Midlothian	2
Unstated	18

Table 128. Occupations

Name	Number
Apprentice	1
Goldsmith	1
Servant	68
Wigmaker	1
Yeoman	2
Unstated	3

Total number: 76.

Most of the Lancastrians were not regimented: only 11 in all, whereas 17 of the men from Cumberland were and this probably was because the former joined first and thus were allocated units, and there was no time for most of the former having just joined.

Patten also refers to there being 'a great many Gentlemen Volunteers that were not formed into any Troop'. There is a reference in the battle to these troops and these were probably the Northumbrian and Durham gentlemen who were with the army at Kelso. These were added to by the Lancashire, Cumberland and Westmorland gentlemen by the time of the battle. The former numbered at least 31, the latter perhaps up to 58, and that excludes those gentry from other counties and the fact that at least some of the gentlemen's servants were armed and may well have ridden into battle with their masters.[38]

A complete listing of the men in the Jacobite army, with their names, parish/county of origin, rank, unit and fate where known can be found in this author's forthcoming volume of the *Record Society of Lancashire and Cheshire*.

How some of the Jacobites were armed were described by witnesses as follows:[39]

Table 129. Eyewitness Descriptions of Arms Borne by Jacobite Soldiers

Name	Arms
Albert Hodgson	Sword and pistols (horseman)
Christopher Eccleston	None (horseman)
Richard Butler	Musket and sword
Hugh Anderton	Musket and sword
Standish's servant	Sword (horseman)
Edward Tyldesley and servant	Sword and pistols (horsemen)
Richard Shuttleworth	Sword
Nathan Allan	Sword
Ingleby Thorp	Sword and pistols (horseman)

---

38 Patten, *History*, p.50.
39 TNA: KB8/66, Baga de Secretis; TS23/34, 1–3.

THE SECOND BATTLE OF PRESTON, 1715

Name	Arms
James Bleasdale	Sword (horseman)
Anthony Barlow	Sword (horseman)
Luke Hodgkinson	Sword (horseman)
Richard Cowper	None
James Gregson	None
Thomas Bryers	Sword
Henry Cowper	Musket
James Gerrard	None (horseman)
William Arkwright	Sword and pistols (horseman)
Hugh Anderton	Sword and pistols (horseman)
William Hardwick	Sword (horseman)
George Collingwood	None
John Stewart	Sword and dagger
John Ryley	Sword and musket
Matthew Jenkinson	Sword (horseman)
James Murray	Bayonet
Kenneth Mackenzie	Musket (horseman)
John Dalziel	None (horseman)
Henry Wilson	None
Miles Begg	None
Donald Robertson sr	Musket
James Stewart	Sword and target
Finlay Mackay	Musket
Kenneth Mackenzie	Sword (horseman)
William Craster	Sword (horseman)
Archibald MacLachlan	Sword and target
Archibald Menzie	Sword and target
John Stewart	Sword
John MacGregor	Sword and target
Duncan Campbell	Sword and pistols
Donald Robertson junior	Sword and target
James Robertson	None
James Mackenzie	Sword
Robert Stewart	None
Donald Robertson	Sword
Archibald Lachlan	Sword
Alexander Drummond	Musket
Hercules Durham	Musket

Name	Arms
Alexander Stuart	Sword
Malcom Stewart	Sword and target
John Porteus	Sword and pistols (horseman)
Henry Nicholson	Sword and pistols (horseman)
Caine Liddell	Sword (horseman)
Charles King	(horseman)
Leonard Hunter	Sword and pistols (horseman)
James Kennedy	None
Foster	Sword (horseman)
Finlow Ferguson	Sword and target
John MacCallum	Musket
Donald Smith	Sword
George Mackintosh	Musket
John MacGillivray	Musket
James Blackwood	None (horseman)
Alexander Binnie	Musket
Andrew Dull	Musket
Andrew Davidson	Musket
William Ferguson	Drum
Patrick Smith	Musket

Table 130. Eyewitness Descriptions of Arms Borne by English Jacobites

Name	Arms etc.
Richard Towneley	Sword by his side, blunderbuss across his arms, pistols, cockade and hats, wearing boots
Edward Tyldesley	Sword and pistols, cockade in hat
John Leybourne	Sword and pistols
Gabriel Hesketh	Sword and pistol, cockade in hat
Cuthbert Hesketh	Sword and pistol, cockade in hat
Thomas Walton	Blunderbuss
Albert Hodgson	Sword and pistols
William Tunstall	Sword and gun

The above numbers in the Jacobite army are derived from a variety of manuscript sources at the National Archives and from several printed contemporary lists. However, despite numerous counting, recounting and cross referencing, some of the above totals do not tally; principally between tables 4 and 6–7, and between 121–126 the former totals have a mismatch of 5, the latter between 1 and 3. It is hoped that these discrepancies will be resolved in the forthcoming volume solely devoted to the Jacobite army in England of 1715. These figures do not include unnamed Jacobites and so the figures in tables 4 and 6–7 do not tally with those of the total strength of the army as listed in Chapter 4.

Appendix II

The British Army

Major Charles Wills' Command

William Stanhope's Dragoons
One of the regiments raised in July 1715 to deal with the Jacobites.

Table 131. Officers[1]

Captain	Lieutenant	Cornet
Colonel William Stanhope	Marcellus La Roone	Henry Durrell
Lieutenant Colonel R. Nansan	Richard Gregson	Paul Stephen Hewson
Major R. Manning	Matthew Swiney	George Bernard
David Martell	John Leighton	Tristram Stafford
James Deleazor	Alexander Le Grande	Robinson
James Gardner	Robert Bransby	Wheats

Table 132. Rank and File

Age at Battle	Number
21	1
30	2
34	1
40	1
42	1
47	2
49	1
52	1
56	1

---

1   *London Gazette*, 5353, 6–8 August 1715.

Table 133. Rank and File[2]

Years of Experience	Number
0	3
7	1
11	1
14	1
16	1
18	2
23	2
29	1

Richard Munden's Dragoons
Raised in July 1715.

Table 134. Officers[3]

Captain	Lieutenant	Cornet
Colonel Richard Munden (1702)	Henry de Grangues (1707)	Gerald Fitzgerald
Lieutenant Colonel T. Strickland	Philip Bridgeman	Charles Greenwood
Major J. Orleur	Thomas Mason	William Freeman
John Pierson	Francis Hall	William Williamson
Giles Stevens	Henry Dawson	John Watson
John Prideaux	John Molyneux	Martin O'Bryan

One of the men below was born in Newport, Shropshire.

Table 135. Rank and File[4]

Age at Battle	Number
32	1
40	1
49	1
53	1

---

2 TNA, WO116/1–3, Chelsea Out Pensions, 1715–1733.
3 *London Gazette*, 5353, 6–8 August 1715.
4 TNA: WO116/1–3, Chelsea Out Pensions, 1715–1733.

Table 136. Rank and File

Years of Experience	Number
0	1
3	1
6	1
19	1

James Dormer's Dragoons

Raised in July 1715.

Table 137. Officers[5]

Captain	Lieutenant	Cornet
Colonel James Dormer	James Stevens	Edward Stroode
Lt. Col. Henry Killigrew (1702)	Henry La Sale	Thomas Ellis
Major Solomon Rapin (1689)	Peter Davenport	Thomas Delahaye
Henry Pelham	Jonathan Pirke	William Hamilton
William Boyle	Cuthbert Smith	Rigley Molyneaux
Beverley Newcommin	James Fleming	Andrew Forrester
Adjutant	Thomas Stevens	First commissioned 1710
Chaplain	Francis Duret	First commissioned 1708

Some of Dormer's officers were thus experienced soldiers; as well as their colonel, both Killigrew and Rapin had had over a decade of soldiering. This was not the case with all the regiment's officers, however. One of these new officers, Pelham (1694–1754), was the son of wealthy parents. He had been to Westminster School and recently attended Hart Hall, Oxford and was about 21 in 1715. His slightly older half brother, Thomas Holles-Pelham was a zealous young Whig politician in London and perhaps Pelham was equally zealous for the cause of George I. He had, though, no experience of warfare.

Table 138. Rank and File[6]

Age at Battle	Number
19	1
25	1
28	1
34	1
39	1
41	1

---

5   *London Gazette*, 5353, 6–8 August 1715.
6   TNA: WO116/1-3, Chelsea Out Pensions, 1715–1733.

THE SECOND BATTLE OF PRESTON, 1715

Age at Battle	Number
44	2
48	1
57	1

Table 139. Rank and File

Years of Experience	Number
0	2
1	1
3	0
17	1
19	2
24	1
28	2

Owen Wynn's Dragoons
Raised in July 1715.

Table 140. Officers[7]

Captain	Lieutenant	Cornet
Colonel Owen Wynn (1689)	Crawford	Owen Wynn
Lt Col. H. Pearson (1705)	William Witherington	William Carleton
Major John Dunbar (1708)	Edward Whitney	Lewis Folliot
Lord Leslie	William Humphreys	James Hill
Knox	Jacob Warne	Pemberton
Henry Smith	Gustavus Hamilton	Christopher Adams

Table 141. Rank and File[8]

Age at Battle	Number
22	1
23	2
36	1
41	1
47	1

---

7 *London Gazette*, 5353, 6–8 August 1715.
8 TNA: WO116/1-3, Chelsea Out Pensions.

THE BRITISH ARMY

Table 142. Rank and File

Years of Experience	Number
0	3
7	1
21	1
26	1

Philip Honywood's Dragoons
Raised in July 1715.

Table 143. Officers[9]

Captain	Lieutenant	Cornet
Colonel Philip Honywood	John Maitland	John Campbell
Lieut. Colonel Alexander Hamilton (1691)	William Lemmon	William Robert Adair
Major Humphrey Bland (1709)	James Mawle	Charles Wheeler
John Suckling	Milkin	John Burroughs
Benjamin Hussum	Charles Stewart	William Gardner
William Robinson	John Mitchell	Watts

Rank and File
Of the men, one was from Darlington, one from Saffron Walden, one from East Lothian and another from Londonderry. Two men had prior experience in other regiments.

Table 144. Rank and File[10]

Age at Battle	Number
23	1
27	2
29	1
30	1
32	1
33	1
36	1
38	1
41	1
42	1

---

9 *London Gazette*, 5353, 6–8 August 1715.
10 TNA: WO116/1–3, Chelsea Out Pensions.

THE SECOND BATTLE OF PRESTON, 1715

Age at Battle	Number
44	2
45	1
47	1
48	2

Table 145. Rank and File

Years of Experience	Number
0	3
4	1
5	2
6	1
7	1
8	1
9	2
10	1
12	1
13	3
19	1
27	2

One of the rank and file was Donald McBane, aged 51. He had served in the army since about 1687 and had been at the battle of Killiecrankie in the following year, as well as serving in Flanders in the subsequent two decades. He was well known as being an expert swordsman. He was a sergeant in this regiment.[11]

At the beginning of September, a newspaper noted that a sergeant and nine men from this regiment were accused of sedition and were escorted from Chelmsford to London.[12]

Thomas Pitt's Horse

This was Wills' only veteran cavalry regiment, founded as it was in 1685 in the wake of the threat caused by the Monmouth rebellion, and had fought in the recent war, in Spain. In 1715 it was on the Irish establishment.

Table 146. Officers[13]

Rank	Name	Remarks
Colonel	Thomas Pitt	
Lieutenant Colonel	James Otway	First commissioned in 1692

---

11 Donald McBane, *Expert Swordsman's Companion* (Fallen Book Publishing, 2015), p.151.
12 *Flying Post*, 3694, 6–8 September 1715.
13 Dalton, *Army of George I*, I, p.326.

Rank	Name	Remarks
Major	Richard Whitworth	First commissioned in 1702
Captain	William Crosby	
Captain	James Dambon	
Captain	Thomas Ligoe	
Captain	Francis Naizon	
Captain	George Walker	
Captain	Peter Naizon	
Lieutenant	William Bland	
Lieutenant	Nicholas Hutchinson	First commissioned in 1714
Lieutenant	Andrew Rankine	
Cornet	William Boyle	First commissioned in 1714
Quartermaster	Nicholas French	First commissioned in 1714
Quartermaster	Nicholas Lawless	First commissioned in 1714

Rank and File

Very few of these soldiers' records mention much about the individuals, but one is recorded as being born in Lisburn, Antrim, one was from Cork and another being born in Ireland, too. Given the regiment was on the Irish establishment this is not surprising.

Table 147. Rank and File[14]

Age at Battle	Number
24	3
31	2
32	3
34	1
35	2
36	3
37	1
38	1
41	1
42	1
44	1
45	3
46	2
47	1
48	2

---

14 TNA: WO116/1–3, Chelsea Out Pensions.

THE SECOND BATTLE OF PRESTON, 1715

Age at Battle	Number
51	2
52	2
54	1
55	1
57	1
65	1

Table 148. Rank and File

Years of Experience	Number
2	1
4	1
7	1
8	3
9	2
10	2
11	2
12	1
13	2
15	1
16	1
17	3
18	2
20	1
21	3
23	2
24	1
25	2
26	1
27	1
32	1
38	1

George Preston's Foot

This was another veteran battalion, founded in Scotland in 1689 by Lord Angus, during the need to raise troops to combat the first Jacobite rising under Viscount Dundee. It served with distinction at Dunkeld in August of that year, holding off superior numbers of Jacobite forces there. During the recent war it had formed part of Marlborough's Flanders army and had taken part in his four major victories: Blenheim, Ramillies, Oudernade and Malplaquet. The colonel's son was one of the captains in his father's battalion.

Table 149. Officers[15]

Rank	Name	Remarks
Colonel (absentee)	George Preston	Commissioned in 1706
Lieutenant Colonel	Lord Forrester	First commissioned in 1691
Major	James Lawson	
Captain	Alexander Ogilvie	Commissioned in 1711
Captain	Robert Preston	
Captain	William Spragge	Commissioned in 1704
Captain	William St. Clair	Commissioned in 1711
Lieutenant	Robert Barclay	
Lieutenant	John Blair	
Lieutenant	Alexander	
Lieutenant	John Colville	
Lieutenant	William Dunston	Commissioned in 1706
Lieutenant	William Dyer	
Lieutenant	William Ferguson	Commissioned in 1713
Lieutenant	James Gordon	
Lieutenant	Francis Gordon	Commissioned in 1706
Lieutenant	Robert Pringle	Commissioned in 1707
Ensign	George Browne	
Ensign	Charles Colville	Commissioned in 1710
Ensign	William Elphinstone	
Ensign	William Russell	
Ensign	Francis Scott	Commissioned in 1708
Chaplain	Samuel Holliday	First commissioned in 1708
Adjutant	John Gilchrist	First commissioned in 1715

One of the officers from this battalion, Ensign Erskine, deserted to the Jacobites at the onset of the campaign.[16]

Rank and File

Very little else is known about these men, in terms of former occupations and origins, but one man had been a husbandman and was from Edinburgh and one was a fellow Scot from Ayr. Another was a Londoner, from St Giles in the Fields.

---

15 Dalton, *Army of George I*, I, p.351.
16 Hibbert-Ware, 'Memorials', p.177.

Table 150. Rank and File[17]

Age at Battle	Number
20	2
23	1
26	1
27	1
29	1
31	2
32	2
33	1
34	1
35	3
36	2
37	2
38	3
39	1
40	3
41	2
42	3
43	2
44	1
45	4
46	3
47	4
49	3
50	4
51	3
52	1
53	1
55	1
56	1
57	3
63	1
69	1

---

17 TNA: WO116/1–3, Chelsea Out Pensions.

Table 151. Rank and File

Years of Experience	Number
0	1
1	2
3	2
4	2
5	2
7	3
8	2
9	1
10	2
11	4
12	3
13	7
14	6
15	1
18	4
19	3
20	3
21	4
22	3
23	2
24	1
25	4
26	2

Lieutenant General George Carpenter's Dragoons

Richard Molesworth's Dragoons
Raised in July 1715.

Table 152. Officers[18]

Captain	Lieutenant	Cornet
Colonel Richard Molesworth	Hardaman	Benjamin Harris
Lieutenant Colonel R. Dansey	Richard Thompson	Vernon
Major Edward Ridley	George Malcolm	James Cresset

---

18 *London Gazette*, 5353, 6–8 August 1715.

THE SECOND BATTLE OF PRESTON, 1715

Captain	Lieutenant	Cornet
William Bellandine	John Arrowsmith	Bernard Fitzpatrick
Anthony La Melloniere	Alexander Knapton	Sir Talbot Clarke
Lord Henry Pawlett	John Strawbridge	George Abell

Table 153. Rank and File[19]

Years of Experience	Number
10	1
16	1
23	1

Table 154. Rank and File

Years of Experience	Number
10	1
16	1
23	1

Charles Churchill's Dragoons

Raised in July 1715.

Table 155. Officers[20]

Captain	Lieutenant	Cornet
Colonel Charles Churchill	Thomas Drysdale	John Girling
Lieutenant Colonel G. Bates	Thomas Brudenald	Richard Robinson
Major H. Drysdale	John Ball	Thomas Merridan
Richard Thomas	Andrew Ross	Olfield
Richard Roberts	Paul George	Robert Kerr
James Ballentine	Stephen Otway	Francis Raineford

Lord Cobham's Dragoons

A veteran regiment raised in 1683 and which had fought in Spain in the recent war.

---

19 TNA: WO116/1–3, Chelsea Out Pensions.
20 *London Gazette*, 5353, 6–8 August 1715.

Table 156. Officers[21]

Rank	Name	Remarks
Colonel	Lord Richard Cobham	
Lieutenant Colonel	Edward Montague	
Major	George Benson	Commissioned in 1706
Captain	John Wyvell	
Captain	Thomas Rogers	
Captain	Peter Rennouard	Commissioned in 1712
Lieutenant	Ernest Shackman	
Lieutenant	Samuel Southouse	Commissioned in 1712
Lieutenant	William Kitson	Commissioned in 1706
Lieutenant	Paul Mallide	Commissioned in 1710
Lieutenant	Thomas Friend	Commissioned in 1707
Lieutenant	Francis Best	Commissioned in 1703
Lieutenant	Andrew Parcier	Commissioned in 1705
Cornet	William Brooke	Commissioned in 1715
Cornet	Henry Carlisle	
Cornet	Charles Dilks	Commissioned in 1712
Cornet	George Benson	Commissioned in 1710
Cornet	William Wentworth	Commissioned in 1702
Cornet	John Memuille	Commissioned in 1715
Adjutant	Thomas Stevens	Commissioned in 1710
Chaplain	Francis Duret	Commissioned in 1708

Some of these officers had been involved in the popular disturbances earlier in the year. Parcier had confronted a Jacobite crowd in Leeds on 10 June 1715. Wyvill had helped keep the peace in Manchester at the end of June. One officer, Cornet Sadler and one man were noted as having Jacobite sympathies, by their use of 'seditious language' when in Manchester in June 1715, though there is no evidence that this was widespread among the regiment.[22]

Rank and File[23]

One man was from Barrington, another from London and one from Cork. One had been a smith, another was an apprentice to a hosier and another an apprentice to a tallow chandler.

---

21 Dalton, *Army of George I*, I, p.106.
22 TNA: SP44/116, p.346, Townshend to Pulteney, 30 July 1715; *Flying Post*, 3680, 18–20 June 1715.
23 TNA: WO116/1–3, Chelsea Out Pensions.

Table 157. Rank and File

Age at Battle	Number
27	1
29	1
30	1
35	1
36	1
43	1

Table 158. Rank and File

Years of Experience	Number
0	1
1	1
4	1
8	1
9	1
12	1

The Battlefield Today

The battle has been scandalously neglected by Preston's modern civic authorities. There is no plaque or marker or monument to the fact that a decisive and bloody battle took place within their jurisdiction; they have preferred expenditure to commemorate the deaths of four rioters in a nineteenth century industrial dispute. The only reference in public to the battle is an erroneous one outside a Wetherspoon's pub on Church Street. The only other public acknowledgement is the fact that a number of streets near to the place of execution are named after Jacobites present at Preston: Derwentwater, Kenmure, Muncaster, Shuttleworth and Arkwright; all of whom suffered death for the cause.

None of the buildings now standing in the town date from the time of the battle. The parish church was rebuilt in the nineteenth century and Hoghton's house is long gone. The Harris Museum (which contains a few relevant relics) is on the site of the Sign of the Mitre and The White Bull has been rebuilt and is now called The Bull and Royal. However, the main streets, Church Street (formerly Churchgate), Fishergate and Friargate still exist and walking around the town and near the Ribble one can appreciate the hill that Wills' men had to traipse up. A number of small side streets run off Church Street and were doubtless used as access points during the attacks.

Local interest in the battle was stimulated during the tercentenary in 2015, resulting in a number of commemorative events taking place then and afterwards. These were well documented and can be viewed at Lancashire Record Office.

Bibliography

Primary Sources

Manuscripts

Berwick Record Office
Berwick upon Tweed Guild Corporation Minute Book, 1697–1716, BA/G/2/1/16.

Blair Atholl Castle
Atholl Papers, Box 45, 12/97, account of the Jacobite southern army to Preston, 1715.

British Library
Additional Mss. 30,381. Anti-Jacobite songs and ballads, 19th century.
Additional Mss. 33,954. Letters, papers and tracts relating to the Royal Family of Stuart, 1688–1788.
Additional Mss. 37,721. Extracts from rate books etc. for Westmorland, 1598–1722.
Additional Mss. 47,028. Egmont Papers, 1st Lord Egmont, Letter Books, CVIII, 1697–1731.
Additional Mss. 63,093. Blakeney Collection, Vol. XV, Miscellaneous Letters and state papers, 1685–1827.
Stowe Mss. 748. Miscellaneous Original Letters on historical subjects, 1703–1759.
Stowe Mss 750. Original Letters addressed to Lord Parker, 1704–1739.

Edinburgh University Library
Laing Mss III, 257. Journal of the Rebellion of 1715 by Peter Clarke.

Hertfordshire Record Office
D/EP F95. Panshanger Collection. Cotesworth to Liddell, 11 October 1715.

Lancashire Record Office
DDHU/53/42. Letter of deputy lieutenants to Derby, 1715.
DDX 194/1r Plan of Preston, with names of householders, 1684.
DDX 2244/1. Partial account of trials of Jacobite prisoners at Liverpool, c.1716.
DDX 1788/1 Plan and account of the Battle of Preston, 1715.
PR 1435 St John's Preston burial registers.
PR 3360/4/1/1 Formby Churchwardens' Accounts, 1703–1733.
PR 2724/15 Halewood Constables' Accounts, 1714–1715.
QJ1/2/10 Lancashire Quarter Sessions.
QSP 1091/2 Quarter Sessions Petitions, 1715–1716.

THE SECOND BATTLE OF PRESTON, 1715

Liverpool Record Office
283, PET1/1 St Peter's, Liverpool, Burial Registers.

The National Archives
FEC1/10, Forfeited Estates Commission, Alder, George: His depositions, 1716.
FEC 1/246, Forfeited Estates Commission, Preston: Original claims for losses, 1–50, 1718.
FEC 1/247, Forfeited Estates Commission, Preston: Original claims for losses, 51–100, 1718.
FEC1/248, Forfeited Estates Commission, Preston: Original claims for losses, 101–150, 1718.
FEC1/249, Forfeited Estates Commission, Preston: Original claims for losses, 151–200, 1718.
FEC1/250, Forfeited Estates Commission, Preston: Original claims for losses, 201–226, 1718.
FEC1/340, Forfeited Estates Commission, Proceedings of communications from Thomas Rishton, 1715–1716.
FEC 1/827, Forfeited Estates Commission, Northumberland depositions, 1716.
FEC1/1585, Forfeited Estates Commission: Towneley and Tildesley, informations, 1715–1716.
FEC 2/94, Forfeited Estates Commission: List of the peers and other persons attainted, 1715–1716.
KB33/1/5 Court of King's Bench: Crown Side, Precedents and Miscellanea,1715–1716.
KB8/66 Court of King's Bench: Crown Side, Baga de Secretis, 1715–1717.
PC2/85 Privy Council Registers, 1714–1716.
PL28/1 Palatinate of Lancashire, Minute Book, 1715.
SP35/5, 7 State Papers Domestic: George I, 1716.
SP44/79a Secretaries of State, State Papers: Entry Books, Criminal Correspondence and Warrants, 1713–1721.
SP44/116, Secretary of State State Papers Entry Book, 1714–1715.
SP44/117, Secretary of State State Papers Entry Book, 1714–1716.
SP44/118, Secretary of State State Papers Entry Book, 1715–1716.
SP44/120, Secretary of State State Papers Entry Books, 1716–1721.
SP44/147, Secretaries of State: State Papers: Entry Books. Domestic. Under Secrertaries' Letter Books, 1714–1724.
SP54/9, Secretaries of State State Papers Scotland, October 1715.
SP54/10, Secretaries of State State Papers Scotland, November 1715.
SP54/26, Secretaries of State State Papers Scotland, October–November 1745.
SP54/30, Secretaries of State State Papers Scotland, April–May 1746.
SP78/160 Secretaries of State State Papers Foreign, France, 1715.
SP94/84 Secretaries of State, State Papers Foreign, Spain, 1715.
TS23/34 Treasury Solicitor's Miscellanea, 1715–1723.
WO4/17 War Office Secretary at War Out Letters, 1714–1715.
WO4/18 War Office Secretary at War Out Letters, 1716.
WO5/20 Secretary at War Marching and Militia Orders, 1714–1716.
WO24/79 War Office Papers concerning establishments, 1715–1716.
WO26/14 War Office Entry Books of warrants, regulations and precedents, 1712–1717.
WO116/1 Royal Hospital Chelsea: Disability and Royal Artillery Out Pensions Admission Book, Infantry and Cavalry, 1715–1727.
WO116/2 Royal Hospital Chelsea: Disability and Royal Artillery Out Pensions Admission Book, Infantry and Cavalry, 1727–1733.
WO116/3 Royal Hospital Chelsea: Disability and Royal Artillery Out Pensions Admission Book, Infantry and Cavalry, 1734–1746.

BIBLIOGRAPHY

National Library of Scotland
ADV MS 13.1.8.43.Advocates' Manuscripts.

National Records of Scotland
GD1/811/9. Miscellaneous Jacobitism. Receipt for levies on Kelso, 1715.
GD220/5/601. Montrose Papers. Letter of Lord Forrester, 1715.

Royal Archives
RCIN 726092. Map of the Battle of Preston, 1715.

Tyne and Wear Archives
CM2/331. Carr to Ellison Manuscripts. Letter of William Cotesworth, 1715.
CP3/22 Cotesworth Manuscripts, Letter of Robert Cotesworth to William Cotesworth, 1716.
QS/NC/1/3. Newcastle Quarter Sessions Order Book, 1700–1719.

University of Leeds Library Special Collections
Townshend–Argyle official despatches, 1715–1716.

West Yorkshire Archive Service (Wakefield)
QS10/13 West Riding Quarter Session Order Book, 1712–1720.

Published
Addy, John and McNiven, Peter (eds), 'The Diary of Henry Prescott, L.L.B., Deputy Registrar of Chester Diocese', II, *Record Society of Lancashire and Cheshire*, 132 (1994).
Anon., *A List of the most Considerable of the Scots and English Nobles and Gentlemen* (Edinburgh: John Moncur, 1715).
Anon., *The Annals of King George the second Year* (London: A. Bell, 1717).
Anon., *A Compleat History of the Late Rebellion* (London: Hinchliffe, 1716).
Anon., *A History of the Affairs of Europe from the Peace of Utrecht to the Quadruple Alliance* (London: Publisher Unknown, 1725).
Anon., *Life of General Carpenter* (London: E. Curll, 1736).
Anon., *A Faithful Register of the Late Rebellion* (London: T. Warner, 1718).
Anon., *A Letter of the Occurrences from and at Preston* (Edinburgh: Publisher Unknown, 1718).
Anon., *Secret History of the Rebels in Newgate* (London: J. Roberts, 1718).
Anon., *History of all the Mobs and insurrections Great Britain, from William the Conqueror to the Present Time* (London: Publisher Unknown, 1715).
Murray, John (ed.), *Chronicles of the Atholl and Tullibardine Families* (Edinburgh, 1908).
Berwick, James, Duke of, *Memoirs of the Marshal Duke of Berwick*, II (London: T. Cadell, 1779),
Bell, Robert (ed.), 'Memorials of John Murray of Broughton, 1740–1747', *Scottish History Society*, series 1, 27 (1898).
Blaikie, Walter Biggar (ed.), 'Origins of the '45', *Scottish History Society*, 2nd series, 2 (1916).
Bridge, J.C. (ed.), 'Diary of Nehemiah Griffiths', *Journal of the Chester and North Wales Archaeological and History Society* (1909).
Buchannan-Brown, John (ed.), *The Remains of Thomas Hearne* (London: Centaur Press Ltd, 1966).
Calendar of State Papers, Colonial America and the West Indies, 1716–1717, 29 (London 1930).
Cowper, Spencer (ed.), *Diary of Mary, Countess Cowper* (London: John Murray, 1864).
Coxe, William (ed.), *Memoirs of an Administration: Walpole, I* (London: T. Cadell and Sons, 1798).

Daily Courant, 1714–1716.

Dickson, William Kirk (ed.), 'Warrender Letters: Correspondence of Sir George Warrender, Bt., Lord Provost of Edinburgh, and Member of Parliament for the City, with Relative Papers, 1715', *Scottish History Society*, 3rd series, 21 (1935).

Doddridge, Phillip, *Some Remarkable Passages in the life of the Hon. Colonel James Gardiner* (Hedley: Thomas Cornish, 1812).

Ellis, Joyce (ed.), 'Liddell-Cotesworth correspondence' (Durham: *Surtees Society*, 118, 1985).

Flying Post, 1715.

Gillow, John (ed.), *The Tyldesley Diary, the personal record of Thomas Tyldesley during the years 1712, 1713 and 1714* (Preston, 1873).

Glasgow Courant, 1715.

Grey, J.M. (ed.), 'The Memoirs of Sir John Clerk of Pencuik, Baronet', *Scottish History Society*, series 1, 13 (1892).

Hibbert-Ware, Samuel (ed.), 'Memorials of the Rebellion of 1715', *Chetham Society*, 5 (1845).

Hillman, Anne (ed.), *The Rake's Diary: The Journal of George Hilton* (Kendal: Curwen Archives Trust, 1994).

Historical Manuscripts Commission
 Calendar of the Stuart Papers held at Windsor, I, II, V, VII (London, HMSO, 1902–1920).
 Manuscripts of the Earl of Carlisle (London, HMSO: 1897).
 Manuscripts of the Marquess of Townshend (London: HMSO, 1887).
 14th Report, Appendix III (London: HMSO, 1894).
 Manuscripts in Various Collections, II (London: HMSO, 1903).
 Report on the Manuscripts of the Earls of Mar and Kellie (London: HMSO, 1904).

Hodgat, Matthew, *Horace Walpole: Memoirs and Portraits* (London: Batsford 1963).

Horner, Craig (ed.), *Diary of Edmund Harrold, wigmaker of Manchester, 1712–1715* (Farnham: Ashgate, 2008).

Hughes, Edward (ed.), 'Some Clavering Correspondence', *Archaeologia Aeliana*, 3rd series, XXXIV (1956).

Jarvis, Rupert (ed.), *The Jacobite Risings of 1715 and 1745* (Carlisle: Cumberland County Council, 1954).

Keith, James, *A Fragment of a Memoir of Field Marshal James Keith, 1714–1734* (Edinburgh: Spalding Club, 1843).

Newton, Lady (ed.), *Lyme Letters, 1660–1760* (London: William Heinemann, Ltd, 1936).

London Gazette, 1715.

Lumby, J. (ed.), 'Calendar of the deeds and papers in the possession of Sir James de Hoghton', *Record Society of Lancashire and Cheshire*, 88 (1936).

McBane, Donald, *The Expert Sword-Man's Companion* (Fallen Book Publishing, 2015).

MacKnight, James (ed.), *Memoirs of Lochiel* (Glasgow: Maitland Club, 1842).

Macky, John, *A Journey through England*, II (London: J. Pemberton, 1722).

Macky, John, *A Journey through Scotland* (London: J. Pemberton, 1729).

Markham, Sarah (ed.), *John Loveday, 1711–1789* (London: Michael Russell, 1984).

Marshall, J.D. (ed.), 'The Autobiography of William Stout, 1665–1752', *Chetham Society*, 3rd series, 15 (1967).

Matthews, William (ed.), *Diary of Dudley Ryder, 1715–1716* (London: Methuen & Co., 1939).

Morris, Christopher (ed.), *The Journeys of Celia Fiennes* (New York: Chanticleer Press, 1949).

Oates, Jonathan (ed.), 'The Memorandum Book of John Lucas, 1712–1750', *Thoresby Society*, 2nd series, 16 (2006).

Oates, Jonathan and Navickas, Katherine (eds), 'Jacobites and Jacobins: Two eighteenth century perspectives', *Record Society of Lancashire and Cheshire* 142 (2006).

Oldmixion, John, *The History of England during the reigns of William and Mary, Anne and George I* (London: Publisher Unknown, 1730).

Original Weekly Journal, 1715.

Patten, Robert, *History of the Rebellion* (London: J Baker & T. Warner, 1745).

Paton, Henry (ed.), 'Journal of several Occurrences from 2nd November 1715', *Scottish History Society Miscellany*, I, series 1, 15 (1894).

Penny London Post, 1745.

Pittock, M.G.H. (ed.), *The Jacobite Relics of Scotland collected by James Hogg* (Edinburgh: Edinburgh University, 2003).

Political State of Great Britain, IX (1715)–XIII (1717).

Postman, 1715.

Penrice, Gerald, *Genuine and Impartial Memoirs of Charles Radcliffe* (London, 1747).

Rae, Peter, *History of the Late Rebellion* (London, 1746).

Raine, James, *History and Antiquities of North Durham* (London: John Bowyer Nichols and Son, 1852).

Rannie, D.W. (ed.), 'Hearne's Collections, VI, 1717–1719', *Oxford History Society*, 43 (1902).

Robson, J.O. (ed.), 'Military Memoirs of Major General the Hon. Charles Colville', *Journal of the Society for Army History Research*, XXV (1947).

Rogers, Pat (ed.), Daniel Defoe, *Tour of the Whole Island* (Harmondsworth: Penguin, 1971).

Scott, Walter (ed.), *Memoirs of the Insurrection in Scotland in 1715* (Edinburgh: Abbotsford Club, 1845).

St. James' Evening Post, 1715.

Shaw, William, and Slingsby, F.H. (eds), *Calendar of Treasury Books*, XXIX, Part 2, 1714–1715 (London: HMSO, 1957).

Ibid, XXX, 1716 (London: HMSO, 1958).

Smith, David (ed.), *Letter Books of Joseph Symson, 1711–1719* (Oxford: Oxford University Press, 2003).

Smith, John Thomas, *Nollekens and his Times*, II (London: Henry Colburn, 1829).

Thoresby, Ralph, *Letters of Eminent Men*, II (London: Coburn, 1832).

Frank Tyrer (ed.), 'The Great Diurnall of Nicholas Blundell, 1712–1718', *Record Society of Lancashire and Cheshire* (1970).

Weekly Journal, 1716.

Secondary Sources

Books

Ainsworth, William Harrison, *Preston Fight* (London: Tinsley Brothers, 1875).

Arnold, Ralph, *Northern Lights: The Story of the Earl of Derwentwater* (London: Constable, 1959).

Barthorp, Michael, *Marlborough's Army, 1702–1711* (London: Osprey Publishing, 1980).

Barthorp, Michael, *The Jacobite Risings, 1689–1745* (London: Osprey Publishing, 1982).

Baynes, John, *The Jacobite Rising of 1715* (London: Cassell, 1970).

Bull, Stephen and Seed, Michael, *Bloody Preston, The Battle of Preston, 1648* (Lancaster: Carnegie Publishing, 1998).

Cormack, Andrew, 'Some Remarks on the provision of cavalry swords', *JSAHR*, 93 (2015).

Cormack, Andrew, 'These Meritorious Objects of the Royal Bounty', The Chelsea Out-Pensioners in the early eighteenth century (Privately published 2017).

Cruickshanks, Eveline, Handley, Stuart, and Hayton, David, *The House of Commons, 1690–1715*, IV (Cambridge University Press, 2002).

Dalton, Charles, *Army of George I, I* (London: Eyre and Spottiswoode, 1930).

Dalton, Charles, *English Army Lists and Commission Registers, VI, 1707–1714* (London: Eyre and Spottiswoode, 1904).

Fishwick, Henry, *History of the Parish of Preston* (Rochdale: James Clegg, 1900).

Gooch, Leo, *The Desperate Faction? The Jacobites of North East England, 1689–1746* (Hull University Press).

Hardwick, Charles, *History of the Borough of Preston* (Preston: Worthington and Company, 1857).

Holmes, Geoffrey and Szechi, Daniel, *Making of a Great Power: Britain 1660–1722* (London: Longman, 1993).

Lenman, Bruce, *The Jacobite Risings in Britain and Europe, 1688–1746* (London: Methuen, 1980).

Lole, Peter, 'A Digest of the Jacobite Clubs', *Royal Stuart Society Papers* (2002).

Lyndon, Barry, 'Military dress and Uniformity, 1680–1720', *JSAHR*, 54 (1976).

Monod, Paul, *Jacobitism and the English People, 1688–1788* (Cambridge: Cambridge University Press, 1989).

Oates, Jonathan, *The Last Battle on English Soil: Preston, 1715* (Farnham: Ashgate, 2015).

Oates, 'The Jacobite Prisoners of the Fifteen', *Record Society of Lancashire and Cheshire* (forthcoming).

Oxford Dictionary of National Biography (Oxford, 2004).

Reid, Stuart, *Sheriffmuir, 1715: The Jacobite War in Scotland* (London: Frontline Books, 2014).

Sankey, Margaret, *Jacobite Prisoners of 1715: Preventing and Punishing Rebellion in Early Hanoverian England* (Farnham: Ashgate, 2005).

Scott, Jenn, *I am minded to rise: The clothing, weapons and accoutrements of the Jacobites in Scotland, 1689–1719* (Solihull: Helion, 2020).

Sedgwick, Romney, *History of Parliament: The Commons*, II (London: HMSO, 1970).

Szechi, Daniel, *1715: The Great Jacobite Rising* (New Haven, CT: Yale University Press, 2005).

Tayler, Alastair and Henrietta, *1715: The Story of the Rising* (London: Thomas Nelson & Sons, 1936).

VCH Cumberland, II (London: Archibald Constable and Co. Ltd, 1905).

VCH Lancashire VII (London: Constable and Co, 1914).

Worton, Jonathan, *The Battle of Glenshiel* (Solihull: Helion, 2018).

Articles

Blackwood, B.G., 'Lancashire Catholics, Protestants and Jacobites during the Rebellion of 1715', *Recusant History* 22/1 (1994).

Oates, Jonathan, 'The Armies operating in the north of England in 1715', *Journal of the Society of Army History Research*, 90/362 (2012).